D0073615

SHAKESPEARE'S *TROILUS AND CRESSIDA* AND THE INNS OF COURT REVELS

To

Angus Fletcher

S. F. Johnson

John M. Steadman

Shakespeare's *Troilus and Cressida* and the Inns of Court Revels

W.R. Elton

Ashgate

Aldershot • Brookfield USA • Singapore • Sydney

Published by
Ashgate Publishing Limited
Gower House
Croft Road
Aldershot
Hants GU11 3HR
England

Ashgate Publishing Company
Old Post Road
Brookfield
Vermont 05036–9704
USA

Ashgate website: http://www.ashgate.com

British Library Cataloguing-in-Publication data

Elton, W.R. (William R.)
  Shakespeare's *Troilus and Cressida* and the Inns of Court revels
  1. Shakespeare, William, 1564–1616. *Troilus and Cressida*
  I. Title
  822.3'3

Library of Congress Cataloging-in-Publication data

Elton, William R.
    Shakespeare's *Troilus and Cressida* and the Inns of Court revels /
  W.R. Elton.
  1. Shakespeare, William, 1564–1616. *Troilus and Cressida*.
  2. Theatre audiences—England—London—History—17th century.
  3. Law students—England—London—History—17th century. 4. Troilus
  (Legendary character) in literature. 5. Law and literature—
  History—17th century. 6. Trojan War—Literature and the war.
  7. Troy (Extinct city)—In literature. 8. Cressida (Fictitious
  character) 9. Inns of court. I. Title.
  PR2836.E48   1999
  822.3'3—dc21   98–11687
                     CIP

ISBN 1 85928 214 8

Typeset in Sabon by Bournemouth Colour Press, Parkstone, Poole, Dorset and printed and bound in Great Britain by MPG Books Ltd, Bodmin, Cornwall

Fabula, qua Paridis propter narratur amorem
Graecia Barbariae lento collisa duello,
stultorum regum et populorum continet aestus.

Horace, Epistles

… toute l'Asie se perdit et se consomma
en guerres pour le maquerelage de Paris.
L'envie d'un seul homme, un despit, un
plaisir, une jalousie domestique, causes qui
ne devroient pas esmouvoir deux harangeres à
s'esgratigner, c'est l'ame et le mouvement de
tout ce grand trouble.

Montaigne, Essais

Contents

Acknowledgements

While expressing my debt to scholars in general, I should thank in particular Philip J. Finkelpearl, G.K. Hunter, John M. Steadman, and Eugene M. Waith for reading earlier drafts of this study; and Gerald M. Pinciss and Wilfrid R. Prest for reading the present version. I am indebted as well to S.F. Johnson for years of scholarly debate on Shakespeare's *Troilus and Cressida*.

For editing this study, I am grateful to Rachel Lynch and Ellen Keeling; and for help in preparing the manuscript to Patricia Belikis and Robert Greer. To my sister, Mildred Boyd, I am throughout indebted. For the opportunity to test my views at New College, Oxford University, thanks are due to Barbara Everett and Emrys Jones; and for similar opportunities at the Ecole Normale Supérieure and the Sorbonne, to Richard Marienstras.

Grants supporting this work have included those from the American Council of Learned Societies, the National Endowment for the Humanities, the Folger Shakespeare Library, and the Huntington Library; and I am pleased to acknowledge research support as first Visiting Mellon Professor at the Institute for Advanced Study, Princeton.

Texts cited

Editions of Shakespeare

Troilus and Cressida is cited from the New Shakespeare edition by Alice Walker (Cambridge University Press, 1957, 1982). Where my reading of the text differs from hers, I have indicated this by inserting 'Q' or 'F', or both. I have also used other editions of *Troilus*, by Kenneth Palmer (1982) and Kenneth Muir (Oxford, 1982). NVS = New Variorum Shakespeare, *Troilus and Cressida*, ed. H.N. Hillebrand and T.W. Baldwin (Philadelphia, Pennsylvania, 1953). Other Shakespearean works are cited from *The Riverside Shakespeare*, textual editor G. Blakemore Evans (Boston, 1974).

Revels

Inns of Court revels are cited from *Gesta Grayorum* (published by William Canning, 1688), ed. D.S. Bland (Liverpool, England, 1968), abbreviated as *Gesta*. The *Prince d'Amour*, from *Le Prince d'Amour, Or the Prince of Love* (London, 1660), is abbreviated as *Prince*. Other revels are cited from D.S. Bland, ed., *Three Revels from the Inns of Court* (Amersham, England, 1984). Unless otherwise noted, place of book-publication is London.

Abbreviations

AC	*Antony and Cleopatra*
AWEW	*All's Well That Ends Well*
AYLI	*As You Like It*
CE	*The Comedy of Errors*
CYM	*Cymbeline*
H	*Hamlet*
1H4	*King Henry IV, Part 1*
2H4	*King Henry IV, Part 2*
H5	*King Henry V*
1H6	*King Henry VI, Part 1*
JC	*Julius Caesar*
KJ	*King John*
KL	*King Lear*
LLL	*Love's Labour's Lost*
M	*Macbeth*
MAAN	*Much Ado About Nothing*
MM	*Measure for Measure*
MND	*A Midsummer Night's Dream*
MV	*The Merchant of Venice*
MWW	*The Merry Wives of Windsor*
O	*Othello*
R2	*King Richard II*
R3	*King Richard III*
RJ	*Romeo and Juliet*
RL	*The Rape of Lucrece*
Son	*Sonnets*
T	*The Tempest*
TA	*Timon of Athens*
Tit.A	*Titus Andronicus*
TC	*Troilus and Cressida*
TGV	*The Two Gentlemen of Verona*
TN	*Twelfth Night*
TS	*The Taming of the Shrew*
VA	*Venus and Adonis*
WT	*The Winter's Tale*

1. Wit — vs what is it?
2. Problem plays — or Inns of Ct. Xmas revels (?md) 1
   Problem play — ?mystery of "category" — 2-3 - vague, shifting — biog., etc. 3
3. Inns revels — Sh. knew of them — Expense of small audience w/ Pander types 4
   Blood + honor (clear) basis, emphasis — also in T&C. 5
   Debate topic women's inconstancy reports. + in T&C 6
   T&C reflects feature of Inns of Ct. traditions —?
   Tradition of crit + bawdy que of theme — 8-9
   Inns of Ct. $$, ability to stage a one-off play — 12   Greene connection 13
   Flattering style of prologue at end — 21-22
   Trol rejects siege of war for siege of love — w/ Pander. 22
        Kitchen metaphors — 22   Ajax jokes — 24
   Mock epic — Cressida comments on honor 25
   Hector, Ajax both introduced unheroically — anger idea —
   Boar (Thersites) + buffoon (Pander) — stock figures of degradation — 26
   Ajax-boar; Ulysses (ironic) also Aristotelian stock figures — 26
   lack of civility — Ajax, Thersity vs Paris overdone speech — 26-27
   Mock adulation of Ajax by Achilles, etc. 28   Greek/small comparisons
   Folly as a constructive element — mirrors held up 28.; Mockeries in both directions
        [Does Ulysses undermine our argument?] 30
   Mockery in trumpets when Cr. is leaving — 30
   Attention to postures — 31   Ajax + male glorasses — 31
   The boregs — ½ insulting ½ comparison greetings 31-32
   Nestor's similes overdone — 31 ; People inspect each other — 33
   Antidramatic content — mock agon — 34   Exchanges — 34
   Thersites sources of pleasure — which displease others — 35
   Troilus double dishonor — Diomedes also gets horse — 36
   Scope of Troilus vow of savage — on tents — 37
   Trojan fall will be small compared to Hector/Troy's — 37
   Dryden's comments + changes — 38 vs Sh's few deaths — 38
   Troilus ll Menelaus — cuckolded — women stolen — 46
   Misrule elements 47 — Patrocles miming; Pander role — 46-7
   Rhetoric also has misrule — inversion, redundancy, 48
   ? Why Aeneas doesn't know Ag. after 7 years? 44   A-R; 1-0
   comparison in I,1 & I,2 — followed by "degree" I,3   50
   "Degree" speech lacks rhetorical order — 52   Nestor's praise? 53
x Identity, order, evaluation — central — 55   self-knowledge 55
   Folly — pride — 55-56; inversion of hierarchy — 57 chain of fools 58
   People don't recognize others, or their degrees — 58
        Parody of theme of degree — in IV — c. 1600
     Notes — on rhetoric — figures speaking it

#of study related words, exercises — "decline", etc. 68-9; antitheses 70
     Mock tutorial deliberation 71 ; ? of what "is". 71
   Rhetorical forms — 76 — excesses, fustian, opposite to intent 77
   kings open councils, — confusedly — 78-79   Argument there — 82
   Cressida as book to be read — 82-83 ; calling witnesses — 83   x 84

Introduction

The problem

Whether or not *Troilus and Cressida* is 'the chief problem in Shakespeare',[1] the play is, scholars agree, among his most puzzling works. In addition to the obscurity of many passages, its very tone and genre are still in question. In views often diametrically opposed,[2] the play is claimed to be a tragedy (cf. F1 1623); a history (cf. *Stationers' Register*, 28 January 1609); a comedy (cf. Epistle, Q 1609); a satire; or a combination of these. Coleridge considered 'no one of Shakespeare's plays harder to characterize'.[3] Yet its earliest account (Epistle, Q 1609) ranks it among his comedies as wittiest: 'So much and such savoured salt of witte is in his Commedies, that they seeme (for their height of pleasure) to be borne in that sea that brought forth Venus. Amongst all there is none more witty then this'.

Troilus and Cressida's controversial status is reflected in a present interpretative division. On the one hand, commentators, following F.S. Boas (1896),[4] customarily group it, along with *Measure for Measure* and *All's Well That Ends Well*, as a 'problem play' – bitter, dark, unpleasant, pessimistic and decadent. On the other hand, more recent scholars, following Peter Alexander (1928–9), concur that it was intended for private performance as at an Inns of Court festivity.[5]

At the Inns of Court law-student revels, we know of two Shakespearean comedies that were presented: *Comedy of Errors* at Gray's Inn revels, 28 December 1594;[6] and *Twelfth Night* at Middle Temple revels, 2 February 1602.[7] We learn of the former performance through an account (*Gesta Grayorum*) of these Gray's Inn revels. We learn of the latter by chance of its mention in John Manningham's Middle Temple 1602–03 diary, fol. 12b (p. 48), for Candlemas Feast 1601/02.[8]

Such Inns of Court revels included, during some two months' well-financed Christmastide celebrations, diverse entertainments. These could have comprised, in addition to dancing and banquets: fustian- and mock-orations; misrule and mock-government; mock-trials, arraignments and sentencings; mock-counsellings; courts of love; processions and progresses; challenges, barriers, trials-by-combat, jousts and mock-duels; mock-proclamations and edicts; mock-prognostications; pageants, masques and plays. Such plays were a regular (if unrecorded) feature of revels celebrations.[9]

Within these festivities, in addition to the revels-produced comedies

1

noted above, other plays by Shakespeare (an Inns of Court favourite) could have been included. Of these, may be investigated the still puzzling *Troilus and Cressida* (*c.* 1601–02), as among plays of potential interest to a law-revel audience.

'Problem play'

Troilus and Cressida has been generally ascribed to a 'problem play' category, itself launched as late as 1896. These plays, their categorizer F.S. Boas claims,

> introduce us into highly artificial societies, whose civilization is ripe unto rottenness ... abnormal conditions of brain and of emotion are generated, and intricate cases of conscience demand a solution by unprecedented methods ... we move along dim untrodden paths, and at the close our feeling is neither of simple joy nor pain; we are excited, fascinated, perplexed, for the issues raised preclude a completely satisfactory outcome ... In *Troilus and Cressida* ... we are left to interpret ... enigmas as best we may.

Hence, he concludes,

> Dramas so singular in theme and temper cannot be strictly called comedies or tragedies. We may therefore borrow a convenient phrase from the theatre of to-day and class them together as Shakspere's problem-plays.[10]

Lacking early performance allusions, Boas reflects the suppositions of Edward Dowden, popular Victorian Shakespeare biographer. Dowden asserts: 'Shakespeare's nearest approach to what we call pessimism is not in Lear, nor even in Timon; it is in ... *Troilus and Cressida* ...'. Accounting for this alleged pessimism, Dowden professes intimate knowledge of Shakespeare's private life. That about 1600 Shakespeare passed through a moral crisis, he claims, is certain:

> he had given away his affections to a friend who had wronged him ... He had yielded to the fascination of an unworthy love, and was betrayed by her who had played with all her art upon his passions, as a musician might play upon the strings of a lute; his pleasure ... turned in the end to bitterness.[11]

Following such intimate revelations, A.C. Bradley (1904) claims that a 'spirit of bitterness and contempt seems to pervade *Troilus*'. In his influential *Britannica* Shakespeare article, similarly, E.K. Chambers (1911) describes the problem plays as unpleasant, noting 'the three bitter and cynical pseudo-comedies'. Later attempts to identify such a group include W.W. Lawrence (1931): 'The essential characteristic of a problem play ... is that a perplexing and distressing complication in human life is presented in a spirit of high seriousness'. Apocalyptically, Una Ellis-Fermor (1945) proclaims that in *Troilus* 'The dark night of the soul comes down upon the unilluminated wreckage of the universe of vision'. For *Troilus*, she laments, is 'the profoundest catastrophe in man's experience ... [with its] idea of chaos, of disjunction, of ultimate formlessness and negation ...'. As though 'problem play' were an established Renaissance genre – instead of an *ad hoc* 'convenient phrase' borrowed by Boas from 'the [Victorian] theatre of to-day' – Ernest Schanzer (1963) disposes of other critics' problem-play candidates while insisting on his own: *Julius Caesar, Measure for Measure* and *Antony and Cleopatra*.[12]

Through a Victorian glass darkly, the so-called problem plays were discerned from the viewpoint of Shakespeare's 'mythical sorrows',[13] as well as from an anachronistic, puritanical perspective regarding sex. What critics, following Boas, perceive as a pigeon-hole in quest of appropriate pigeons turns out to be a questionable pigeon-hole with a changing flock of dubious pigeons. Indeed, such vague and generalized 'problem play' descriptions, rather than sharply delineating a recognizable genre, could apply to a wide range of Shakespearean drama. Each 'problem play' critic offers criteria for the alleged Shakespearean genre which do not always comprise the same plays; which are categorically ill-defined and vague; and which are not fully consistent with those of other 'problem play' critics. Yet genre 'dwells not in particular will' (*TC* II.ii.53). What, we may ask, if the Victorian-designated problem plays were, upon closer inspection, to lack the essential family traits so confidently yet superficially ascribed? Such, it will be suggested, may be the case with *Troilus*.

Inns of Court revels

> You kept such revell with your carelesse pen,
> As made me thinke you of the Innes of Court:
> For they use Revels more then any men.
> W.I., *The Whipping of the Satyre* (1601)

Itaque hospitia Leguleiorum suos habent, quos vocant Dominos ... [Now the Inns of Court have their Lords, as they call them ...]
John Milton, *Prolusiones VI*[14]

While an academic-revels tradition stretches back into the Middle Ages, two detailed accounts of Inns of Court revels describe law festivities within about a half-dozen years of *Troilus*:

1 *Gesta Grayorum* (1594–95), Gray's Inn revels (*Gesta Grayorum or the History of Henry the Prince of Purpoole, who lived and died AD 1594*); and

2 *Prince d'Amour* (1597–98), Middle Temple revels (*Noctes Templariae: or, A briefe Chronicle of the Dark Reigne of the Bright Prince of Burning Love*).

The former festivity would have been familiar to Shakespeare through that Gray's Inn revel's presentation of his *Comedy of Errors*.[15] The second cited revel could have been known to him as performed (1597–98) in the Middle Temple, an Inn of Court frequented by his fellow Warwickshiremen,[16] as well as the place of presentation of his own *Twelfth Night*.[17]

Both the accounts of revels cited above suggest clues for identifying such entertainments: for example the tone of revels and such audience expectations as misrule or world-upside-down burlesque and mock-chivalry, and legalistic double entendres. During seasonal festivities, each of the four Inns of Court ('brotherhoods in cities', I.iii.104) – Lincoln's, Gray's, Inner Temple, Middle Temple – had its own revel ruler: whereas, for example, Gray's Inn had the reign of the Prince of Purpoole, the Middle Temple had that of the Prince d'Amour. Such festive occasions, at Christmastide, established a mock-Prince or ruler of a mock-kingdom. Dressed in a little brief authority, reigning some two months under an aspect of temporary inversion, the mock-ruler parodied government as mis-government, order as disorder, with law, rhetoric and logic, along with rule itself, made to stand on their heads.

In contrast to the larger popular theatre audience, Inns of Court festivities comprised an invited audience of a few hundred law students (including those of other Inns of Court and of chancery), teachers, jurists, and other guests. Such spectators' specialized knowledge and tastes could be anticipated by the dramatist. While revels need not have excluded rowdier guests, participants included benchers, resident and visiting aristocrats, and members of the legal hierarchy.

If directed to an audience of would-be worldly law students, Shakespeare's *Troilus* would have engaged their special concerns as well as their interest and supposed expertise in the love-game comedy. (The Inns of Court student, notes F. Lenton's *Characterismi* (1631), sig. [F4 v], 'holds it a greater disgrace to be Nonsuit with a Lady, than Nonplus in the Law'.) Hence, what might have discomposed Boas' Victorian audience – for example the persistent Pandar – could have been a familiar figure of fun to young students in the London Inns of Court milieu.

Indeed, the Inns of Court man, notes F[rancis] L[enton] in *The Young Gallants Whirligigg* (1629), sig. B2–B2 v, was surrounded by urban temptations: '… *London* doth invent / Millions of vices, that are incident / To his aspiring minde'. Recalling youthful Troilus and his to-be-dismissed 'broker-lackey' (V.x.33), Pandar, are complaints against young Inns of Court gentlemen fallen into the hands of London brokers. Recurrent warning was issued against letting sons loose at the Inns without the care of a tutor.[18]

Their Christmastide revels provided a release for the law students: Ben Jonson dedicated his *Every Man Out of His Humour* to the 'Noblest

Nourceries of Humanity, and Liberty, in the Kingdom; the Inns of Court'. He would 'command it lie not in the way of your more noble and useful studies to the public'. Rather, he would it were enjoyed 'when the gowne and cap is off, and the Lord of Liberty [revels Lord of Misrule] raigns'. Such release was celebrated in the students' own mock-chivalric expression related to revels:

> We have by his Princely access to this Empire, exchanged our heavy Studies, that long besotted our inward sences, into an happy practise of disporting pleasures, yielding every minute renewing Joy to our vital spirits.
> Whereas before we were controulable at the nod of every doting Bencher, oppressed with the yoke of quarrelsome Cases ... we are now become subjects and servants to this famous Prince ... we are prest Soldiers[19] under the sweet Banner of Love, where we receive every hour new encouragements in all our enterprises: We are apparrelled in Ladies Colours, that still breathes life to our reputation ...
>
> *Prince*, p. 54

Further, the Inns of Court revels were intended to help fashion the law students in social manners.[20] Inns of Court students, drawn mainly from the gentry and above, were socially conscious and exclusive. 'Whosoever studieth the lawes of the realme ... shall be taken for a gentleman'.[21] Beneficiaries of 'primogeniture' attended law schools to learn how to manage their 'due of birth' (I.iii.106).[22]

Like the concupiscible 'Lord' Pandar, the irascible bastard Thersites (V.iv and V.vii.16–20) suggests class implications. As Waterhouse on Fortescue (1663) remarks: 'Littleton's rule, A Bastard is *quasi nullius filius*, and therefore can lay claim to no bloud ...' (p. 473). Waterhouse remarks this concerning a law-degree that 'conveys an Addition of Gentility importing Name and Bloud' (p. 547). Such emphasis on 'blood and honour' (V.iv.26) – recognitions and misrecognitions in the play are tied to class or status perceptions – seems ironically echoed in Thersites' confession: to Hector's 'What art thou, Greek? Art thou for Hector's match? / Art thou of blood and honour?' the self-avowed bastardly Thersites hastens to admit, 'No, no; I am a rascal; a scurvy knave; a very filthy rogue'. Hector, who elsewhere slays on less provocation, comically relents: 'I do believe thee. Live' (V.iv.25–9). Later (V.vii.14–22), when Margarelon, King Priam's bastard son, confronts Thersites, the demotic rogue with comic presumption claims privilege on grounds of shared bastardy.[23]

Into the revels was poured academic learning such as an educated gentleman might be expected to recognize. Revels elicited many talents, as was observed by George Buc of Middle Temple: 'The Art of Revels ... requireth knowledge in Grammar, Rhetorike, Logicke, Philosophie, Historie, Musick, Mathematikes, and in other Arts ...'[24] Helping to account for the academic content of law-revels entertainments, Inns of Court students were in large proportion from the universities (cf.

Justice Shallow (*2H4*, III.ii.10–13) on 'my cousin William': 'He is at Oxford still, is he not? 'A must then to the Inns a' Court shortly').[25]

In addition to urban distractions, London offered law students lively intellectual opportunities. The Inns of Court (known also as a book-buying centre) could draw on aristocratic and professional talents and ideas, and a wide variety of learning. Despite the Inns of Court's pleasure-seeking reputation, lawyers comprised also the diligent, as indicated by Spenser, familiar with the Temple area: ('those bricky towers ... / Where now the studious Lawyers have their bowers', 'Prothalamium', ll. 132–4), and by records of contemporary lawyers' book-collections, both private and institutional. These covered not only law, but also a broad range of other disciplines. Sir Thomas Elyot,[26] among others, favoured a broad, humanistic education at the universities as preliminary to legal studies.[27]

Law revels' festivities tended to formulaic repetitions, corresponding to spectator expectations. Among conventional revel components was the paradox, tending to sharpen law students' acuity.[28] Such paradoxes included 'A Defence of Women's Inconstancy'. Where that expected mock-encomiastic paradox was lacking (cf. *Prince*, p. 85), an ironical explanation is present: 'This night one had like to have commended women for their inconstancy, but he was disappointed; therefore now let them never look to be praised for that quality'. In the Middle Templar Marston's *Fawn* (1605), a play with Inns of Court revels affinities, is a set piece on women's inconstancy.[29] From another Middle Temple revel (c. 1610), Edward Pudsey remarks on that paradox in his commonplace book: 'the defence of womens inconstancye ...'.[30] The repetition of such treatments of women's inconstancy, notes a recent editor of Donne's *Paradoxes*, suggests that the topic of women's inconstancy, centrally reflected in *Troilus*, was a convention of Inns of Court revels.[31]

As paradox was known to be a favourite Inns of Court device, *Troilus* may glance at other paradoxical expressions. Indeed, Ulysses attributes such a propensity to Achilles and Patroclus: these mock 'what is or is not, [that] serves / As stuff for these two to make paradoxes' (I.iii.183–4).[32] Among paradoxes we may compare the Middle Temple's John Ford, in his *Honour Triumphant* (1606), with its paradoxical 'Perfect lovers are onely wise' (contradicting Cressid on the inability simultaneously 'to be wise and love', III.ii.155)' and Ford's praise of bastards as more ingenious than legitimates – the case in this play of the clever, surviving Thersites (cf. V.iv.27–9).[33]

From the evidence cited above, *Troilus and Cressida* may be seen to share a number of concerns with Inns of Court revels. The following section correlates features in the revels accounts noted above, relatively close to *Troilus*' date, and suggests similarities in the play.

Revels criteria

Based on law-revels summaries and Inns of Court traditions, such revels may be recognized as follows:

1   A pattern of *misrule* prevails – political as well as personal, parodies of authority in mock-courts and governments, and world-upside-down. Linguistic misrule, including double entendres, scatology, and scurrility, also recurs, along with paradox and mock-encomia.[34]

2   *Mock-rhetoric* or fustian, reflected in *Gesta* and *Prince*, is heard, as in speeches of Agamemnon, Nestor, Hector, Troilus, and Pandarus, as well as of Ulysses.

3   As rhetorical order seems inverted, forms of reason are stood on their head, while *illogic* and fallacies abound in a mock-disputation (cf. II.ii).

4   Mock-trials or arraignments include (as in III.ii) a *Court of Love*. There, Cressid, before her love-night, indicts men (III.ii.176–7) for their failure of promise in performance.

5   *Mock-chivalry* recurs, for example in Hector's reported challenge (I.iii.260–83) and Nestor's senile love-vaunt (I.iii.291–301). (Cf. *Gesta*, p. 14.) Inns of Court members (for example Middle and Inner Templars) traditionally figured as 'knights' – compare Knights Templars.[35]

6   *Social manners* are reflected parodically, for example in Pandarus, as well as through a series of comical social blunders.

7   *Advice* on life's courses (e.g. in III.iii) emerges in revels and play.

8   *Academic emphases* recur on such topics as learning, mind, instruction, stupidity, folly, degrees in schools, books, knowledge.

9   *Law references*, as well as mock-legalisms, recur. Technical legalisms appear, along with legal maxims, and parodic or mocked diction.

10 Among other *revels topoi* are ambassadorial references (recalling revels' mock-emissaries among Inns of Court); ship-of-fools echoes;[36] and dancing (cf. IV.iv.86; instructed at the Inns of Court).[37]

Such features as those cited above can be shown to be reflected in *Troilus and Cressida*.

Homeric burlesque

Acquaintance with Homer, Aristotle (cf. II.ii.166–7) and Chaucer among *Troilus and Cressida*'s audience is implied. Throughout the play, there appears burlesque of schoolroom epic heroes, with less than reverential treatment of Homer (cf. the recognition that 'Quandoque bonus dormitat Homerus', sometimes good Homer nods, as Horace (*Ars Poetica*, l. 359) concedes). Indeed, from antiquity, Homeric heroes were parodied in comedy and satyr drama.[38]

Traditionally, Homer was used in education – students were 'Instructed by the antiquary times' (II.iii.248). As early lawgiver, Homer was utilized in medieval and Renaissance law: 'As truth's authentic author to be cited' (III.ii.180). Opposition in law was, however, expressed to lawyers' traditional dependence on the authority of Homer. Insofar as Homer had been controversially utilized in law, lawyers could have been responsive to Homeric burlesque.[39]

Sixteenth-century detractors of Homer, preferring Virgil to him, and finding indecorous elements in the Grecian works, prepared the way for further Homeric burlesque. In his *De Tradendis Disciplinis* (1531), Juan Luis Vives reviews Jerome Vida's 1527 critique of Homer: Vida censures, for instance, Homeric comparisons, such as that of Ajax to an ass, as well as repetitions of character epithets.[40]

Burlesque treatments of ancient characters form part of a mock-Homeric topos, as also in the farcical interlude *Thersites* (1537), and in Rabelais' *Pantagruel*:[41]

> Achilles was a scald-pated maker of hay-bundles.
> Agamemnon, a lick-box …
> Hector, a Snap-sauce Scullion.
> Paris, a poor beggar …
> Helen, a broker for Chamber maids

Rabelais' antecedents here include Lucian's *Menippus seu Necyomantia*.

Shakespeare himself in *The Rape of Lucrece* (1594), lines 1366ff., on the Troy tapestry, recalls Homer's *Iliad*. In his edition of Aristotle's *Poetics* (1594), Fifth Book, Julius-Caesar Scaliger, favouring Virgil, notably censures Homer as ignorant and lying, while he holds his work to be vulgar, illogical and puerile.[42] Rather than a sage, Homer's Nestor is, remarks Scaliger, a senile buffoon. In midst of battle, moreover, Diomede resembles a lion in a stable. Hector lacks wise military behaviour, and Achilles, even while asleep, is called fleet-footed. Indeed, Achilles is a mere chatterer, and his own horses talk. After slaying Patroclus, Hector witlessly delays removing his spoils, thus allowing an encounter with Greeks arriving to protect the slain man's arms.[43]

In 1599, the year following Chapman's Homer-exalting *Seaven bookes of the Iliades*, appeared, translated from the French,[44] *A Womans Woorth, defended against all the men in the world*. Dedicated by Anthony Gibson to Elizabeth Countess of Southampton, it censures 'Curious Antiquity' which 'Made Homere a deitie'. Burlesque suggestions regarding Homer emerge within the same work's ridicule: in the *Iliades* 'a contempt of royalty, duty and obeysance, in the person of *Achillis* (a meere brothell hunter) who preferred a brutish kinde of affection, before the love of his Countrey, and his owne peculiar hate before the general welfare of his followers'. Homer 'makes a dog of *Agamemnon*; a kitching fellow of *Patrocles*; a mad man of *Hector* ... scarce honestly: as ... in his comparison of *Aiax* to an Asse ...' (fol. 16–17v).

Against Homer and the ancients, moreover, are ranged Renaissance admirers of Tasso – see Tasso's *Discorsi del poema eroica* (1595)[45] and Paolo Beni's *Comparatio de Homero, Virgilio & Torquato* (1607). Tasso views the *Iliad*'s characters as flatterers and deceivers. Reflected in Italian epic-burlesque traditions, parodic treatments of Homer recur also in the Spanish: as, based partly on the *Iliad*, in a burlesque epic poem by Lope de Vega (1562–1635) under the pseudonym of Tomé de Burgillos, the *Gatomaquia*.[46]

Irreverence towards Homer in the Renaissance is further confirmed in the attitudes of Alessandro Tassoni. Shakespeare's near-contemporary (born 1565), he was author of the mock-heroic epic, *La Secchia Rapita* (*The Rape of the Bucket*), begun in the sixteenth century and published in 1622. In that derisive burlesque, and in numerous critical opinions – for example his *Considerazioni sopra le rime del Petrarca* (Modena, 1609) – Tassoni repeated his anti-Homeric ridicule and his opposition to veneration of the ancients and their rules, at the expense of the moderns and pleasurable response.[47] As Tassoni exhibits both burlesque of Homeric epic and an emphasis on the moderns, he, too, in the question of response, recommends 'do as your pleasures are' (*TC*, Prologue, l. 30).

To summarize, abundant evidence exists to confirm a Renaissance climate of Homeric burlesque. Within this climate, unlike Chapman's solemn moralizing of Homer, *Troilus* tends to a burlesque- or parodic-Homeric view, such as is reflected, among other works, in the above-cited *A Womans Woorth* (1599). Like this book (dedicated to a kin of Shakespeare's patron), Shakespeare's *Troilus* in its burlesque treatment appears to relativize and subvert the cult of veneration of Homeric antiquity.

The argument

Shakespeare's problematic *Troilus and Cressida* has elicited two leading interpretative hypotheses: on the one hand, the Victorian-conceived 'dark', 'unpleasant', 'decadent', 'pessimistic', and 'bitter' 'problem play'; and on the other, the festive Elizabethan law revel. While F.S. Boas' Victorian 'problem play' categorization is still widely accepted, other more recent commentators entertain Peter Alexander's private-performance or legal-festivity view. Evaluating such views against an extensive historical–textual scrutiny of the play is the next step that suggests itself.

This study undertakes that next step of testing Shakespeare's *Troilus and*

Cressida against criteria, not only of the alleged problem-play genre, but also of an Elizabethan law-revels tradition. It is hoped that, along with close examination of the play's text, the study will provide a general guide to this difficult and still enigmatic work.[48]

Notes

1. As argued by J.S.P. Tatlock, 'The Chief Problem in Shakespeare', *Sewanee Review*, 24 (1916), 129–47.
2. See NVS, pp. 382–5.
3. *Coleridge's Literary Criticism*, ed. J.W. Mackail (1908), pp. 221–3.
4. Boas, *Shakspere and His Predecessors* (1896; NY, 1968), 'The Problem-Plays', pp. 344–408. (Boas includes *Hamlet* in his category.) See Kenneth Muir and Stanley Wells, eds, *Aspects of Shakespeare's 'Problem Plays'* (Cambridge, 1982). Michael Jamieson, 'The Problem Plays, 1920–1970', *Shakespeare Survey* 35 (1972), 1–10.

    Questioning the problem-play category, however, see also A.H. Scouten, 'An Historical Approach to *Measure for Measure*', *Philological Quarterly*, 54 (1975), 69:

    > (1) Every critic who applies this [problem play] term to Shakespeare's plays gives a definition which is modified or contradicted by other 'problem play' critics and includes a list or grouping which differs from the other lists; (2) most critics who apply this term generally find major flaws, as a result of their attempting to force a Shakespearean play into the school of Ibsen; (3) these critics pile one anachronism on top of another.

    Others questioning the problem-play category include Leo Salingar, *Shakespeare and the Traditions of Comedy* (Cambridge, 1974), p. 321; and G.K. Hunter, *English Drama, 1586–1542* (Oxford, 1997), p. 357 n.
5. Scholars besides Alexander entertaining the Inns-of-Court *Troilus* hypothesis include: W.W. Greg, *The Editorial Problem in Shakespeare* (Oxford, 1942), pp. 111–14. Greg, *Shakespeare's First Folio* (New York, 1955), p. 338. O.J. Campbell, *Comical Satyre* (1938), summary in NVS, p. 353. Leslie Hotson, *Shakespeare's Sonnets Dated* (1949). Arthur Sewell, 'Notes on the Integrity of *Troilus and Cressida*', *Review of English Studies*, 19 (1943), 120–7. Philip Williams, NVS, p. 347. See also NVS, 353, 355–6, 383–4. Alice Walker, ed., *Troilus*, pp. xxiv–xxvi. J.K. Walton, *The Quarto Copy for the First Folio of Shakespeare* (Dublin, 1971), p. 249. Kenneth Palmer, ed. TC, Arden (1982), pp. 307–10. Kenneth Muir, ed., *TC* (Oxford, 1982).

    See Peter Alexander, '*Troilus and Cressida*, 1609', *The Library*, 4 ser., 9 (1928–9):

    > there is much scurrility and the audience are at times addressed directly and familiarly by the most scurril character in the most scurril terms; and the play concludes with an epilogue which prevents disapproval by implying that there will be no hissing except from bawds or panders or their unfortunate customers ...
    >
    > Shakespeare ... may have written the play for some festivity at the Inns of Court ... the subject and its treatment point to such an audience; the deliberate flouting of tradition as established by Homer and Chaucer would

have been intelligible only to instructed spectators ... it is excellent fooling for clerks.

(pp. 278–9)

See Alexander, *Shakespeare's Life and Art* (1939), pp. 193–7:

> Much of this [Homeric and Chaucerian influence] would be lost on an audience who were ignorant of their Chaucer and Homer. But if it was written for a group of worldly-wise young clerks [at the Inns of Court] ... then the cynicism of the piece need not be taken at its face value, but rather as a device to startle these simple worldlings out of their complacency.

See also Alexander, *Shakespeare* (1964), pp. 246–8: 'Internal evidence supports the conclusion that the play was written for private performance, not, however, at the Court, for the epilogue spoken by Pandarus suggests that there may be in the audience some with venereal disease ...'. See Bertrand Evans (*Shakespeare's Comedies*, Oxford, 1960, pp. 167–85) on this play's difference from plays written for usual production; in these latter, Shakespeare prepares his audience for every step in the argument, while in *Troilus* knowledge of the plot is assumed.

6. W.W. Greg, ed., *Gesta Grayorum* (William Canning, 1688; Malone Society, Oxford, 1914), p. vi, suggests 27 December 1594. See Sidney Thomas, 'The Date of the *Comedy of Errors*', *Shakespeare Quarterly*, 7 (1956), 377–84.

7. Both these Inns-of-Court produced comedies have in common twins, of legal interest regarding the problem of precedence in inheritance. See Marie Axton, 'Heirs and Twinned Persons', ch. 6, *The Queen's Two Bodies* (1977). See W.N. Knight, 'Comic Twins at the Inns of Court', *Publications of the Missouri Philological Association*, 4 (1979), 74–81. Manningham himself links the two Inns-of-Court produced plays: see his diary entry Febr. 1601 [1602] (Sorlien ed., p. 48): 'At our feast wee had a play called 'Twelve night, or what you will much like the commedy of errores ...'. Those Inns-of-Court presented comedies share with *Troilus* recurrent misrecognitions, including contradictory identity (cf. *TN*, V.i.222–4) 'One face, one voice, one habit and two persons, / A natural perspective, that is and is not!' and Troilus' 'Bifold authority! ... This is, and is not, Cressid!' (V.ii.144–6). As they question recognition and identity these plays also concern – 'a large proportion of barristers being eldest sons' (E.W. Ives, *Shakespeare Survey*, 17, 1965, 90) – 'The primogenitive and due of birth' (I.iii.106).

8. Cf. H.K. Gras, 'Direct Evidence and Audience Response to *Twelfth Night*: The Case of John Manningham of the Middle Temple', *Shakespeare Studies*, 21 (1993), 109–54.

9. See J. Bruce Williamson, *The History of the Temple* (1924), pp. 313, 500. He notes that a play was usually provided in hall following dinner on Grand Days (All Saints or All Hallows, 1 November, and Candlemas Day, 2 February). Among honoured guests were judges, serjeants and former Inns of Court members. In addition to the twice-yearly readers' dinners, were such occasions celebrating newly made serjeants, which brought the Inns and the court together, and were memorable feasts. For other evidence of dramatic performances at the Inns of Court, see Finkelpearl, *John Marston*, 49–51. See Wilfrid R. Prest, *The Inns of Court under Elizabeth I and the Early Stuarts* (1972), p. 226. For a comprehensive treatment of ceremonies marking the creation of serjeants, see J.H. Baker, *The Order of Serjeants at Law* (Selden Society, 1984). See D.S. Bland, 'A Checklist of Drama at the Inns of Court',

Opportunities in Renaissance Drama, 9, 1996, 46–61; also ibid., 12, 1969, 57–9; 21, 1978, 49–51.

10.   Boas, *Shakspere and his Predecessors*, p. 345.
11.   *Introduction to Shakespeare* (1893), pp. 24, 73–4.
12.   A.C. Bradley, *Shakespearean Tragedy* (1964), p. 275; W.W. Lawrence, *Shakespeare's Problem Comedies* (New York, 1931, p. 4); Una Ellis-Fermor, *Frontiers of Drama* (1945), p. 72; Ernest Schanzer, *The Problem Plays of Shakespeare* (New York, 1963).
13.   Cf. C.J. Sisson, *The Mythical Sorrows of Shakespeare* (1934).
14.   Cf. Leslie Hotson, 'A Shadow King', *Mr. W.H.* (New York, 1964), pp. 42–64.
15.   Cf. D.S. Bland, '"The Night of Errors" at Gray's Inn, 1594', *Notes and Queries*, n.s. 13 (1966), 127–8. Shakespeare alludes to Gray's Inn in *2H4*, III.ii.33. In addition to his patron the Earl of Southampton's connection with Gray's Inn, see the recently discovered Gray's Inn play, *Tom a Lincoln*: M.C. Bradbrook, 'A New Jacobean Play for the Inns of Court', *Shakespearean Research and Opportunities*, 7–8 (1972–74), 1–5. See *Tom A Lincoln*, ed. G.R. Proudfoot (Malone Society Reprint, 1992). See D.S. Bland, *A Bibliography of the Inns of Court and Chancery* (1965).
16.   On Shakespeare's links with the Middle Temple, see (in addition to Hotson, *Shakespeare's Sonnets*) Christopher Whitfield, 'Some of Shakespeare's Contemporaries at the Middle Temple', *Notes and Queries*, n.s. 13 (1966), I.122–5; II.283–7; III.363–9; IV.443–8.
17.   Regarding *Troilus*, Harbage's contention that Shakespeare, for financial reasons, would never have composed a play for individual performance, may be questioned.
        Countering such contentions, cf. the Inns of Court's lavish and well-financed festivities, including their sumptuous masques, themselves intended for individual private performance. Like their masques, Inns of Court plays (e.g. *Gorboduc*) comprised such occasional productions. (Suggesting evidence of 'commissioned plays', see C.J. Sisson, *Lost Plays of Shakespeare's Age* (Cambridge, 1936), indicating, in addition to commissioned court and Inns of Court masques, private individual performance.) The initial contention above may be further countered by recalling Shakespeare's legal friendships and other Inns of Court connections. These, along with sufficient remuneration, could have persuaded him to such a venture. Such Inns of Court bases for questioning the above-noted contention emerge further from the following considerations:
        Troilus' Prologue (F text), which starts the play 'in the middle' (l. 28), points also to the presence of 'massie Staples' (l. 18). If, in the play's familiar punning style, the Prologue thereby glances at place of performance (the Middle Temple was the setting of *Twelfth Night* in 1602), and at portions of the audience (Staple Inn was an inn of chancery linked with Gray's, sponsor of *Comedy of Errors*), it is notable that, like John Marston, Shakespeare had both Staple Inn and Middle Temple connections. (Cf. mock-references to Stapulia in *Gesta*, title page; pp. 14, 27, 19, 21, 38, 71.)
        Such Middle Temple–Staple Inn links converge in Thomas Greene of Warwickshire (called Shakespeare's 'cousin'), who entered Middle Temple on 20 November 1595 from Staple Inn. Greene's sureties were John Marston, bencher, of Coventry in Warwickshire (who had been Stratford counsel in 1590), and his son, the dramatist, John Marston. (*Register of Admissions to the Middle Temple ...*, compiled by H.F. Macgeagh and H.A.C. Sturgess (1949, I.69.)
        Between Shakespeare's two known performances at the Inns of Court,

Thomas Greene provides an arguable link:

1. *Comedy of Errors*, performed at Gray's Inn (28 December 1594), when Greene was probably a student at Staple Inn, Gray's associated inn of chancery, to which Gray's furnished readers.
2. *Twelfth Night*, performed at Middle Temple (2 February 1602), where Thomas Greene studied after Staple Inn. At Middle Temple, he was called to the bar on 20 October 1602 (*Middle Temple Records*, ed. C.H. Hopwood, *The Minutes of the Parliament of the Middle Temple*, ed. C.T. Martin (1904), I. 426).

Thomas Greene was Shakespeare's only known kinsman to have been continuously connected both with him and with Middle Temple; one of the few Stratford men known to have visited Shakespeare in London; and the only known person to have shared his Stratford house, New Place, with him and his family (cf. Christopher Whitfield, *Notes and Queries*, 211 (1966), 446). In Stratford, Greene was solicitor in 1601, and Steward (later Town Clerk) from August, 1603, until March, 1617. In addition, Greene was to share with Shakespeare an interest and investment in tithes: cf. the play's use of 'tithe-soul' (II.ii.19), and a technically legal term for tithes, 'dismes' (II.ii.19). Close to the time of *Troilus* (c. 1601–02), and possibly related to its festivities, was Thomas Greene's call to a law degree in Middle Temple, 1602. (Cf. Hopwood, *Middle Temple Records*, I. 426: 'At a Parliament holden 29 Oct., 44 Eliz. [1602]: "The Calls of Messrs. Thomas Triste and Thomas Grene to the degree of the Utter Bar ... are confirmed"'.) Greene's call to a Middle Temple degree (1602) – cf. 'degrees in schools and brotherhoods in cities', I.iii.104 – could link him to the contemporaneous *Troilus* as well as to the Middle Temple-produced *Twelfth Night* (acted in Middle Temple, 1602). Thomas Greene thus connects Gray's with the Middle Temple, Shakespeare's own law-school associations; while Greene's date of call to the bar (1602) coincides with dates ascribed to *Troilus* and *Twelfth Night*. Greene thus suggests an occasional or facilitating link with Shakespearean productions at Gray's Inn and Middle Temple.

See Rupert Taylor, 'Shakespeare's Cousin, Thomas Greene, and his Kin ...', *PMLA*, 60 (1945), 81–94; Christopher Whitfield, 'Some of Shakespeare's Contemporaries at the Middle Temple', *Notes and Queries*, 211 (1966), 122–5, 283–7, 363–9, 443–8; Hotson, *Shakespeare's Sonnets*, pp. 44–6; Mark Eccles, *Shakespeare in Warwickshire* (Madison, Wisconsin, 1963), pp. 131–9.

18. So Joseph Hall (*Quo Vadis?*, 1617, in Hall, *Works* (1625), p. 671) charges, 'many brokers of villany' within the 'concourse of a populous citie' 'live upon the spoyles of young hopes, whose very acquaintance is destruction'. Against young Inns of Court students falling under the influence of knavish 'brokers' is Thomas Lodge of Lincoln's Inn: dedicated to the Gentlemen of the Inns of Court is his *An Alarum against Usurers* (1584) (*Complete Works*, Hunterian Club, 1883, especially I.19). Recurrently inveighing against 'broker-lackey[s]' (V.x.33), Lodge quotes (*ibid.*, ll. 20–5) a father of an Inns of Court student warning against such temptations. As Justice Shallow reminisces on his law-school experiences (*2H4*, III.ii.21–4): 'You had not four such swingebucklers in all the Inns a' Court again ... we knew where the bona [robas] were and had the best of them all at commandement'.

19. 'Prest soldiers' as conscripted: cf. Achilles to Thersites (II.i.95–7): 'Your last service ... 'twas not voluntary ... you as under an impress'. Cf. John Donne's

dedication to James I, in *Pseudo-Martyr* (ed. F.J. Sypher, Delmar, New York, 1974, sig. A 2).

20.   Cf. *Troilus* on such social talents, IV.iv.85–6. Sir John Fortescue remarks of revels' dancing and 'such other accomplishments and diversions (which are called *Revels*) ... such as are usually practised at Court'. *De Laudibus Leges Anglie* (Cambridge, 1942), p. 119. See Ulysses' adverse manners-comment: 'The elephant hath joints, but none for courtesy; his legs are legs for necessity, not for flexure' (II.iii.104–5); and Pandar's 'complimental' manners (III.i.40–1, 44–7 and *passim*). Regarding Pandar's 'complimental assault' at the court of Helen and Paris, Queen Helen mockingly admonishes, 'Dear lord, you are full of fair words' (III.i.40–1, 48). On 'compliment', see also Jonson, *Poetaster*, II.ii.209; III.iv.84.

21.   Sir Thomas Smith, *De Republica Anglorum* (1583), Lib. 1, ch. 20; ed. L. Alston (Cambridge, England, 1906), pp. 39–40.

22.   Cf. E.W. Ives, 'The Law and Lawyers', *Shakespeare Survey*, 80: 'Half the barristers ... enjoyed the ... advantage of being eldest sons'. On social class at the Inns of Court, see John Ferne, *The Blazon of Gentrie* (1586); W.C. Richardson, *History of the Inns of Court* (Baton Rouge, Louisiana, 1977).

23.   On legal implications of bastardy, see Thomas Ridley, *A View of the Civile and Ecclesiastical Law* (1607), pp. 199–208. Recalling Thersites' claim to escape on grounds of low status is Lapet in Francis Beaumont and John Fletcher's *The Nice Valour* (1647; IV.i). Cf. similar escape by Castruchio in Beaumont and Fletcher's *Double Marriage* (1647; III.i).

24.   Appendix, in John Stow, *Chronicle of England* (1615), p. 988.

25.   See also Thomas Middleton, *Michaelmas Term*, ed. Richard Levin (Lincoln, Nebraska, 1966): 'He shows you there he was a Cambridge man, sir, but now he's a Templar. Has he not good grace to make a lawyer?' (II.iii.409–10). Cf. L.A. Knafla, 'The Matriculation Revolution and Education at the Inns of Court in Renaissance England', in A.J. Slavin, ed., *Tudor Men and Institutions* (Baton Rouge, Louisiana, 1972), p. 242: university students among entrants to the Inns of Court rose from 42 per cent in 1582 to 49 per cent in 1601. Cf. Knafla, 'The Influence of Continental Humanists and Jurists on English Common Law in the Renaissance', in R.J. Schoeck, ed., *Acta Conventus Neo-Latini Bononiensis 1979* (Binghamton, New York, 1985), p. 66. Similar is Lawrence Stone's conclusion ('The Educational Revolution in England, 1560–1640', *Past and Present*, no. 28 (July 1964), 55): 50 per cent of Inns of Court entrants had previously attended a university. Inns of Court students who had one or two years at a university or college before admission increased to 56 per cent by 1600.

26.   *The Boke Named the Governour* (1531), ed. Foster Watson (1907), p. 64.

27.   Some lawyers were known to possess extensive intellectual interests, as witnessed by their collections. Cf. R.J. Schoeck, 'The Libraries of Common Lawyers in Renaissance England ...', *Manuscripta*, 6 (1962), 155–67. See *A Catalogue of the Library of Sir Edward Coke*, ed. W.O. Hassall (New Haven, Connecticut, 1950). Sir Roger Wilbraham, bencher of Gray's Inn, drew up, *c.* 1600, a broad list of proposed reading, including scientific works. See W.R. Prest, *The Inns of Court under Elizabeth I* (1972); and Prest, 'The Legal Education of the Gentry at the Inns of Court, 1560–1640', *Past and Present*, 38 (1967), 20–39.

Cf. W.R. Prest, *The Rise of the Barristers* (Oxford, 1986), pp. 200–5. See L.A. Knafla, *Law and Politics in Jacobean England* (Cambridge, 1976), pp. 7–8, on the Inns of Court as centres of humanistic studies, beyond purely legal concerns. Cf. K. Charlton, 'Liberal Education and the Inns of Court in the Sixteenth Century', *British Journal of Educational Studies*, 9 (1960–61), 25–38. Visiting the Inns of Court, Paul Hentzner in 1598 observed 'numbers of the young nobility, gentry and others are educated, chiefly in the studies of philosophy, theology and medicine', in addition to the law (W.B. Rye, ed., *England as Seen by Foreigners in the Days of Elizabeth and James the First* (1865), p. 283). See J.H. Baker, *The Third University of England: The Inns of Court and the Common Law Tradition* (Selden Society, 1990).

28. As in Charles Estienne's translation of Ortensio Landi's *Paradossi* (1593): on paradoxes '... to exercise yong wittes'. See *The Defence of Contraries. Paradoxes Against common opinion, debated in forme of Declamations ... only to exercise yong wittes in difficult matters* (1593), sig. A4: 'for him that woulde be a good Lawyer ... he must adventure to defend such as a [paradoxical] cause ... thereby to make himselfe more apt and ready, against common pleaders in ordinarie cause of processe'.

29. *Fawn*, Act II, ll. 362–86.

30. Attributed also to John Donne of Lincoln's Inn. Pudsey: Bodleian MS Eng. Poet. d.3. Cf. William Cornwallis, 'That Inconstancy is more commendable than Constancie': R.E. Bennett, 'Four Paradoxes by Sir William Cornwallis', *Harvard Studies and Notes in Philology and Literature*, 13 (1931), 237.

31. Donne, *Paradoxes and Problems*, ed. Helen Peters (Oxford, 1980), p. xlvi. Concurring, cf. also Finkelpearl, *John Marston*, p. 228: that the same topic as in *TC* ('women's inconstancy') should appear in two law revels, suggests that this was a standard item of such revels.

32. Cf. the bawdy character Paradox in Gray's Inn revels of 1617–18. On paradoxes and Inns of Court interest in them, cf. Finkelpearl, *John Marston*; and Manningham, *Diary*, p. 382. Cf. the Liar's paradox (V.ii.119: 'Shall I not lie in publishing a truth?'). See Rosalie Colie, *Paradoxia Epidemica: The Renaissance Tradition of Paradox* (Princeton, New Jersey, 1966). Cf. Donne, *Paradoxes and Problems*, ed. Helen Peters (Oxford, 1980), pp. xviff.

33. Ford, *Nondramatic*, pp. 25, 48–52.

34. The play's pervasive double-entendre pattern (anticipatable at law-revels festivities) has, for the purposes of the present argument, not been emphasized in this study.

35. Cf. a formulaic chivalric challenge in *Gesta*, p. 14, and such challenge in I.iii.260–90; cf. II.i.120–5; II.ii.127–9. On the Templars and law, see Gregory Wilkin, 'Spenser's Rehabilitation of the Templars', *Spenser Studies*, 11, 1990, 89–100.

36. The ship of fools motif is recurrent in academic *facetiae*. Cf. Marston's *Fawn*, held to be an Inns of Court play, indebted to the Middle Temple's *Prince d'Amour* revels. Its first act contains, like the first act of *Troilus* (I.i.105–6), echoes of the ship of fools. Cf. also *Fawn* (IV.i and *passim*). (See Milton's academic *Prolusion VI*, on the 'illustrious Ship of Fools'.) In *Troilus* there is a suggestion of a ship of fools, as the lover embarks with 'this sailing Pandar, / Our doubtful hope, our convoy and our bark' (I.i.105–6) – parodic Palinurus and appetitive steersman; cf. 'Love my lewd Pilot' (Spenser, *Faerie Queene*, III.iv.8–9). Troy is transformed to an appetitive symbol (as in Renaissance commentators on the *Aeneid*: e.g. Landino – cf. D.C. Allen, *Mysteriously Meant* (Baltimore, Maryland, 1970), p. 150), while the Fall of Troy is parodically foreshadowed in *Troilus* and his 'Pandar's fall' (V.x.47).

37. Inns of Court revels' criteria as reflected in Marston's *Fawn* are argued in Finkelpearl, 'Christmas Revels', pp. 199–209. See also his 'Marston's *Histrio-*

Mastix', pp. 223–34, arguing (p. 233) that this play was written for the Middle Temple's Christmas revels of 1598–99.

38.   Michael West, 'Homer's *Iliad* and the Genesis of Mock-Heroic', *Cithara*, 21 (1991), 3–22. Cf. 'Ulysses and the Discrediting of Homer', in W.B. Stanford, *The Ulysses Theme* (New York, 2nd edition, 1968), pp. 146–58; Ulysses as grandson of Autolycus, pp. 8–24; on Homeric burlesque, cf. pp. ix, 8, 214, 270–1, 318–19; and on Homer and *Troilus*, pp. 164–70, 270–2.

    Homer's work was itself held to contain burlesque or serio-comic elements, for example relating to the gods. Homer was considered to have burlesqued himself: the seventeenth-century Samuel Butler in his *Hudibras* suggests that Homer initiated such mockery, noting '... a Race of Champions, / Of which old Homer first made Lampoons' (I.ii.217–18). Friedrich Wild, *Die Batrachomyomachia in England* (Vienna, 1918), containing, pp. 92–124, William Fowldes' translation of 'The Strange ... Battell betweene Frogs and Mice', 1603 (attributed to Homer).

    On Homer and Horace, see R. Schröter, 'Horazens Satire I, 7 und die antike Eposparodie', *Poetica*, I (1967), 8–23; Vincent Buchheit, 'Homerparodie und Literarkritik in Horazens Satiren I 7 und I 9', *Gymnasium*, 75 (1968), 519–55.

    Cf. Homer and Lucian, *Menippus or the Descent into Hades*, Lucian, IV (1969), pp. 73–109. See R.B. Branham, *Unruly Eloquence*, especially p. 250; and C.A. Mayer, *Lucien de Samosate et la Renaissance Française* (Geneva, 1984), pp. 26, 50. Lucian's burlesque of Homer is pervasive. O. Bouquiaux-Simon, *Les lectures homériques de Lucien*, Académie Royale de Belgique, Classe des Lettres, Mémoires, vol. 59.2 (Brussels, 1968).

39.   Cf. G.C.J.J. Van Den Bergh, '*Auctoritas Poetarum*: the Fortunes of a legal argument', in Alan Watson, ed., *Daube Noster* (Edinburgh, 1974), pp. 27–37. Filippo di Benedetto, 'Leonzio, Omero e le "Pandette"', *Italia medievale e umanistica*, 12 (1969), 53–112, against the authority of Homer as primeval lawgiver. See Van Den Bergh, *Themis en de Muzen* (Haarlem, 1964), pp. 20ff. and *passim* on the *auctoritas poetarum* and the *auctoritas Homeri*. Scipio Gentili, *Parergorum* ... (Francofurti, 1588), Book 2, on topics, including Homer, regarding poets and law. See Hans Erich Troje, 'Die europäische Rechtsliteratur unter dem Einfluss des Humanismus', *Ius commune*, 3 (1970), 55ff.; reprinted in Troje, *Humanistische Jurisprudenz* (Goldbach, Germany, 1993), pp. 45–75.

40.   Vives is quoted at length in Foster Watson, ed., *Vives on Education* (Cambridge, 1913), pp. 146–7; and in Howard Clarke, *Homer's Readers* (Newark, Delaware, 1981), pp. 115–16. Vives' philosophy teacher, Gaspard Lax, called Homer, 'insanus senex nugarum omnium parens' and sophist in R. Radouant, 'L'union de l'éloquence et de la philosophie au temps de Ramus', *Revue d'Histoire Littéraire de la France*, 31 (1924), p. 163. Lax is cited in A.-J. Namèche, *Mémoires sur la vie et les écrits de Jean-Louis Vives* (Bruxelles, 1841), p. 15.

41.   Rabelais, *Works*, ch. 30, I.419–21.

42.   'Ridiculum est. Fatuum est. Homericum est ...', *Poetices Libri Septem* (1594), p. 571. On Scaliger, cf. Howard Clarke, *Homer's Readers* (Newark, Delaware, 1981), pp. 117–18. See S. Shepard, 'Scaliger on Homer and Virgil. A Study of Literary Prejudice', *Emerita* (Madrid), 29 (1961), 313–40, giving reasons for Scaliger's deprecation of Homer: Homer's indecorum in conduct, language and thought; his portrayal of undisciplined behaviour; irrationality of Homeric heroes; deceptiveness of Ulysses; incongruities in heroes'

descriptions; improprieties of the Homeric gods; Homer's liberties in form
and content. Following Chaucer's 'Oon seyd that Omer made lyes' (*Hous of
Fame*, 3.1477), among those who accused Homer of lying, Thomas Nashe
remarks, 'not unlike to *Homer*, who cared not what he fained, so hee might
make his Countrimen famous' (*Works*, I.24.6–7).

See Thomas Bleicher, *Homer in der deutschen Literatur (1450–1740)*
Stuttgart, 1972), pp. 129–45, 250–54; Karlernst Schmidt, *Vorstudien zu einer
Geschichte des komischen Epos*, Halle (Saale), 1953.

43.   See also Noémi Hepp, 'Homère en France au XVIe siècle', *Atti della
Accademia delle Scienze di Torino, Classe di scienze morali, storiche e
filologiche* 96 (1962), 389–508; Hepp, *Homère en France au XVIIe siècle*
(Paris, 1968); Georg Finsler, *Homer in der Neuzeit von Dante bis Goethe*
(1912; reprinted Hildesheim, 1973).

44.   Alexandre de Pont-Aymery, *Paradoxe apologique ou il est fidèllement
demonstré que la Femme est beaucoup plus parfaicte que l'homme* ... (Paris,
1596). Anthony Gibson is described in Franklin B. Williams, *Index of
Dedications* (1962) no. 11831, as Groom of the Chamber.

45.   Tasso, *Discourses on the Heroic Poem*, eds Mariella Cavalchini et al.
(Oxford, 1973).

46.   L.F. de Vega Carpio, *La Gatomaquìa; poema jocoseria*, ed. F. Rodriguez
Marin (Madrid, 1955). Where Lope parodies the *Iliad* as a cat-fight, Henry
Fielding's *Joseph Andrews* parodies it as a dog-fight. Cf. Jonson's mockery of
Iliad, I.528–30, in *Poetaster*, IV.v.114–15; and mockery in that play of Homer
himself, I.ii.79–87.

47.   Alessandro Tassoni, *La Secchia Rapita*, ed. Pietro Puliati (Modena, 1989), cf.
index, s.v. Omero. In Tassoni, *Pensieri*, ed. Pietro Puliati (Modena, 1986), cf.
index, s.v. Omero, pp. 775–802. Cf. Erich Loos, *Alessandro Tassonis 'La
Secchia rapita' und das Problem des heroisch-komischen Epos* (Krefeld,
Germany, 1967). Cf. Giovanni Setti, 'Tassoni Erudito e Critico d'Omero',
Reale Istituto Veneto di Scienze, Lettere ed Arti, 66, Part 2 (1906–07),
219–88. On Italian treatments of Homer, see Bernard Weinberg, *A History of
Literary Criticism in the Italian Renaissance* (Chicago, 1963), 2 vols, *passim*.

48.   Monographs on *Troilus* generally do not focus on this study's question: see,
for example, O.J. Campbell, *Comicall Satyre and Shakespeare's 'Troilus and
Cressida'* (San Marino, California, 1938); Robert K. Presson, *Shakespeare's
'Troilus and Cressida' and the Legends of Troy* (Madison, 1953); Karen
Schmidt di Simoni, *Shakespeare's 'Troilus and Cressida': eine sprachliche-
stilistische Untersuchung* (Heidelberg, 1960); Robert Kimbrough,
Shakespeare's 'Troilus and Cressida' and Its Setting (Cambridge,
Massachusetts, 1964).

Part I   Folly

Part I Folly

1.   Burlesque, mock-epic and folly

> Although the folie of men is great … yet … so great folie to take roote in their hartes, that the wisedom of the Grecians, should not rather caste of as naught, the beautie of Helena: rather then the whole multitude … to stande in perill for the beautie of one …
>
> Richard Rainolde, *The Foundation of Rhetorike* (1563)

This chapter examines the play's burlesque, mock-epic and folly elements, recalling aspects of the law-revels tradition.[1]

'What's past is prologue'

After the Prologue's epic opening, the periods suddenly stop: this grand expedition's purpose is but to retrieve the slumbering queen. Abruptly, four words arrest the forward action: 'and that's the quarrel' (l. 10).

Anticlimactically, as the play deflates the epic–heroic, the Hellenic resonance of 'Dardan, and Timbria, Helias, Chetas, Troien, / And Antenorides' (ll. 16–17) becomes brusquely the local-team trimeter of 'Sperr up the sons of Troy' (l. 19). Grandeur descends further in 'tickling skittish spirits' (l. 20). From polysyllabic epic description, the Prologue flattens to its final ten monosyllables (l. 32): 'Now good or bad, 'tis but the chance of war'.

Act I scene i

Lovesick Troilus: 'gradus amoris'

> Bee thou the Lady *Cresset-light* to mee,
> Sir *Trollelollie* I will prooue to thee.
>> Samuel Rowlands, *The Letting of Humors Blood in the Head-Vaine … with … Seuen Satyres* (1611), sig. [C8]

As the Armed Prologue exits on the shout of 'war', Troilus unmilitarily enters. Following the Armed Prologue's 'suited / In like condition as our argument' (ll. 24–5) emerges a disarming warrior-lover, himself *un*suited and '*not* in confidence' (l. 23). Countering the epic-opening 'Arma virumque cano' is thus Troilus' opening military indecorum. His unheroic aim is to 'unarm again' (I.i.1) – this is to be followed by Cressid's mockery (I.ii.11, 31–2, 51) of heroic anger. From the first, the protagonist's negative self-comparison to the weakness of a woman's tear, sleep's tameness, ignorance's folly, a virgin's lack of nocturnal valour, and an infant's skillessness (I.i.8–12), suggests a questionably heroic posture. As confessedly 'Less valiant than the virgin in the night', Troilus could have provoked derision among his youthful male spectators. Initially, Troilus' encomia of the Greeks in *auxesis* (or mounting degree) are matched (cf. III.iii.11–12) by progressive self-deprecation. Hardly here a *vir fortis*, Troilus seems not like a hero, nor demi-divine. 'What ho! Where's my spaniel, Troilus?' Petruchio summons his dog of the same name (*TS*, IV.i.149–50). As the dominating Petruchio is the antithesis of the lovesick Troilus, Petruchio's spaniel named 'Troilus' marks a submissive and devoted creature.

Indeed, Troilus' recurrent self-derogation and simplicity-avowal, with his later unavenged public love-dishonour, are, for a hero, uncommon. If 'there is no love-broker in the world can more prevail in man's commendation with woman than report of valor' (*TN*, III.ii.36–8), Troilus' contrary confession (*to* a love-broker, I.i.7–12), and disavowal of wooing skills (*to* his beloved, IV.iv.84–8), anticipate loss of such commendation. What may, from the Trojan War setting, foreshadow an epic–heroic conflict, leads anticlimactically to a lover's wooing a procurer to woo for him. Disarming from the siege of war, Troilus solicits Pandar's intervention for the siege of love.

Pandar in his instruction to Troilus that he 'must tarry the bolting' repeats, 'Ay, the bolting' (I.i.19, 21), recalling the Prologue's 'bolts' (l. 18). Since bolts (cf. Chapter 8, and Appendix II) were, like moots, a required legal debate exercise, members of a law-student audience would (like Troilus) themselves have had to 'tarry the bolting'.

Pandar's 'culinary' stages (I.i.14–28) towards gaining the lady contribute a low parodic tone. Such kitchen allusions were a stock-in-trade of Renaissance and later burlesque renditions of Homer, Virgil, Horace and Ovid.

In addition, Pandar's love-recipe recalls the five (sometimes four or six) steps of the medieval and Renaissance 'ladder of lechery', or *gradus amoris*: *visus* (sight), *alloquium* (talk), *contactus* (touch), *osculum* (kiss), *factum* (deed) – 'Cinq Points en amour'.[2]

Troilus in I.i exhibits the *passio* of love deriving from 'sight' (*visus*), the first of the *gradus amoris*. As the lovers' *visus* is implied in Act I, *alloquium*, *contactus* and *osculum* occur in III.ii, with *factum* to follow. Separated from Troilus, Cressid among the Greeks (IV.v.18–52) dispenses *oscula*. Eventually, in Troilus' and others' witness (V.ii), Cressid rehearses the *gradus amoris* with Diomede, the lover's rival, including the first four stages and promising the last. Guide in his pupil's 'maiden battle' (IV.v.87), Pandar here outlines the curriculum: love advances couched in kitchen metaphors.

Struck by Cupid's arrow, Troilus is sick with desire and fastened to a 'tetchy' counsellor (I.i.98). His maladroit invocation of the unsuccessful Apollo 'for thy Daphne's love' (I.i.100) is ironical, as is his appeal (at Diomede's removal of Cressid) by the name of the abductor Pluto (IV.iv.127–9). Such appeals suggest the infelicity of Troilus' supernatural petitions.[3] Incidentally, of Shakespearean 'Troilus' allusions which occur outside this play (*RL, TS, MV, MAAN, AYLI, TN*), most provide a consensus of weakness or ineptitude.[4] Indeed, Troilus, *As You Like It* reminds us, 'had his brains dash'd out with a Grecian club' (IV.i.97).[5]

Citing the mad Cassandra as mind-exemplar – 'I will not dispraise your sister Cassandra's wit, but –' (I.i.48–9), Pandar is interrupted by Troilus' complaint concerning Cressid's traits. These features Pandar pours into the lover's heart (I.i.55–7): 'Her eyes, her hair, her cheek, her gait, her voice / Handlest in thy discourse'.[6]

Pretending to allay youthful fires, Pandar drives Troilus into further love-excitation. To his confusion is added another comic element: the lover's supposition that he requires, for a lady already predisposed, the intervention of her procuring uncle. Committing his fortunes to his parodic Palinurus, the 'tutor and the feeder' of his license, Troilus sails with Pandar and his 'bark' (I.i.105–6). Troilus reveals himself from the first as an incontinent passenger, with Pandar his licentious 'convoy' (I.i.106).[7]

While Pandar is committed to his coupling, Troilus is a dedicated knight-*enfant* in quest of the beauteous *pucelle*. Indeed, Troilus shares with Quixote hyperbolic delusions regarding a beloved, and like Quixote with his *Amadis*, Troilus yearns through idealized, romantic forms – if not through Pandar's mediating 'glass' (I.ii.286). A youthful lover spouting academic or philosophical learning and lacking sophisticated courtly skills, Troilus suggests a recurrent butt of satirists: one of the academically crammed students 'skilless' (I.i.12) in social or practical affairs.

Act I scene ii

'Caveat' *Hector: Ajax*

Recurrently, the name 'Ajax' summons up a familiar Elizabethan pun on a jakes, or privy, a jest popularized in John Harington of Lincoln's Inn's *Metamorphosis of Ajax* (1596). This burlesque work was printed by Richard Field, Shakespeare's Stratford townsman, who had also printed his *Venus and Adonis* and his *Rape of Lucrece*, and was to print Chapman's translation of Homer's *Iliad* (1611). According to Harington, Ajax ('a very man per se', I.ii.15) could have been heard by Elizabethans in terms of *latrina lingua*, as a familiar household instrument *pour faire les nécessités*, a *chaise percée* or commode.[8]

Antithetical to Jonson's self-styled unified 'Horace' persona,[9] Ajax brings to mind the disordered creature described at the start of Horace's *Ars Poetica* (ll. 1–5). To have Cressid react to such confusion as ridiculous, as causing her laughter, is also Horatian. Suggesting his own Horace-persona, Jonson may be ironically glanced at in Ajax's I.ii 'character' as it recalls Horace's *Ars Poetica*.[10] Like Ajax, Horace's familiar opening there conjures up a monstrous creature that (I.ii.19–20) 'hath robbed many beasts of their particular additions'.[11] (So the Prologue's 'Beginning in the middle' (l. 28) suggests the Horatian *in medias res*: cf. Horace's *Ars Poetica*, l. 147.) Further, Horace ends with a question echoed by Cressid, at hearing such a monstrously confused description: 'spectatum admissi risum teneatis, amici'? (Could you, my friends, if allowed a view, refrain from laughter?) Thus, Cressid seems Horatian, as well, regarding 'this man, that makes me smile ...' (I.ii.31–2).[12]

Cressid's mockery

Surveying the Trojan warriors in a mock-*Heldenschau*, or heroes' parade, Cressid brings to mind heroic anger: Wrath, the *Iliad*'s initial *menis*, includes Homer's invocation on the deadly wrath that brought the Greeks innumerable woes. With belittling sarcasm, Cressid sustains the 'angry' joke: 'What, is he [Troilus] angry too?' (I.ii.58). Near the start, Troilus is thus implicitly contrasted with the Achillean epic hero, and witnessed in a mock-epic mode.[13]

If Ajax elicits Cressid's smile, and Ajax is the conqueror of Hector, Hector is, from this view, ridiculous to a girl, and no greater than Ajax. Like Troilus, both Hector and Ajax are introduced unheroically. Relevant here is the value paradox of the instrumentally in-use Ajax, low but mounted high – Ajakes indispensable – vying with the out-of-use great champion, Achilles.

As he turns from the *matière* of Hector to the 'Matter of Ajax', Alexander descends from blank verse to prose.[14] Hector's defeat by Ajax is recollected in the scene's closing assertion (II.iii.260–1): Ajax (as through natural necessity) shall defeat 'knights from east and west' who 'come to cull their flower'. This defeat recalls an earlier punning jest: 'Ajax [as convenience] employed plucks down [divests] Achilles' plumes' (I.iii.385): *Ajakes vincit omnia*. In the encounter with Ajax, Hector has been – unheroically – driven to a regimen of 'fasting and waking' (I.ii.35), capitulating to the domination of Ajakes. Pandar reminds the spectators of Hector's intestinal condition: the champion 'was stirring early' (I.ii.50; cf. III.iii.184). Later, in response to Ajax and his 'colik[e]' (Q, F, IV.v.9), 'No trumpet answers': ''Tis but early days' (IV.v.12). So Spenser's Amoret in a necessary walk – 'Walkt through the wood, for pleasure or for need' (*Faerie Queene*, IV.vii.42) – anticipates that of Ajax, who 'goes up and down the field, asking for himself' (III.iii.244–5).

Paralleling Troilus' initial self-deprecation (I.i.8–12), Hector is thus introduced as shamefully defeated by Ajakes (I.ii.33–5). This intestinal event is suggested also in the initial report that Hector 'today was moved' (I.ii.5), a gag recollected, for example, in Hector's self-description, 'There is no lady of more softer bowels' (II.ii.11). As the Host claims of Dr Caius, 'he gives me the potions and the motions' (*MWW*, III.i.102–3), the 'potion' of Hector's shame gives him the 'motion'.

Personages in this play invertedly perform their traditional roles: Agamemnon is an indecorous King–General; Ulysses a dubious adviser; Helen a commonplace queen. So the decrepit Nestor incongruously intimates mutual excitation: 'the thing of courage, / As roused with rage, with rage doth sympathize' (I.iii.51–2). 'The thing of courage' (or erotic desire; cf. Williams, *Dictionary*, s.v. courage) confronts its opposite, recalling other such confrontations, as in 'eye to eye opposed' and 'Salutes each other with each other's form' (III.iii.107–8). Such encounters suggest complementary arousals[15] or matching excitations. Having been aroused, Nestor's 'thing of courage' (I.iii.51) shrinks back – 'retires' (Q/F; i.e. withdraws; I.iii.53–4).[16]

Act II scene i

Thersites versus Ajax

Thersites and Pandar recall Aristotle on the old comedies' scurrilous diction producing laughter (Aristotle, *Works*, 1128 a 22–4). (Cf. Aristotle, *Nicomachean Ethics*, 2.7 and 4.14.) If Pandar suggests the laughter-provoking buffoon, Thersites recalls Aristotle's notion of the boor, 'one ... useless for ... social purposes; he contributes nothing, and takes offence at everything'.[17] The boor (*agroikos*) and the buffoon (*bomolochos*) – defect versus excess – are both distant from the mean of wit and truthfulness. Like the comic mask cited in Aristotle's *Poetics*,[18] Thersites' physical appearance is an example (as in Aristophanes or Molière) of the ugly and ludicrous lacking the suggestion of pain. In sum, *Troilus* comprises a cast of comic characters familiar from Aristotle: the *alazon* or the boaster (Ajax); the *eiron* (ironic man) (Ulysses);[19] the boor (Thersites); and the buffoon (Pandarus) – comprising stock figures of laughable degradation.

As II.i recalls Renaissance comic theory, it summons up Aristotle's definition of comedy and the ridiculous (*Poetics*, 1448 b 32–7): 'comedy ... an imitation of men worse than the average ... as regards ... the ridiculous, which is a species of the ugly'. The ignorant Ajax, for example, parallels Thersites' physical and mental deformity by his own repugnance of the mind.[20]

Hence, II.i mirrors confrontingly two modes of rudeness – brutish stupidity (Ajax) versus deformed 'wit' (Thersites). As 'porpentine' (II.i.25), the latter is a symbol of discourtesy. These personages' exchange of insults reflects a failure of *comitas* or civility (II.i.52): 'do, rudeness; do'. The demotic boor and his brutish pounder could provide, like the play itself, festive relief to the 'fair beholders' (Prologue, l. 26) from the constraints of hierarchical and social amenity.

Act II scene ii

Language upside down: parodied terms

Troilus contains Elizabethan locutions already singled out in a revels account as mocked or 'perfumed' words to be avoided: 'that in no case he [the Knight] use any perfumed terms, as spirit; apprehension, resolution, accommodate, humors, complement, possessed, respective, &c' (*Prince*, p. 43). Noted in this Middle Temple revel (the *Prince d'Amour*, 1597–98), such mocked terms recur also in *Troilus*. Their contexts are construable as burlesque – that is, exaggerated, verbose, high-flown, or mock-heroic – in rhetorical and dictional mockery. So Paris' speeches display in close sequence (along with 'I protest', II.ii.138) such terms as 'propension', 'stand the push', 'propugnation' (II.ii.133, 136–7). Pedantic polysyllables contribute to fustian or burlesque periphrasis (II.ii.136): 'What propugnation is in one man's valour'. Such is Hector to Achilles (IV.v.249–51): 'Think'st thou to catch my life so pleasantly / As to prenominate in nice conjecture / Where thou wilt hit me dead'?

While exploiting the language of music and love, III.i bandies currently parodied words. Of three terms singled out by the foolish Aguecheek for admiration – '"Odors", "pregnant", and "vouchsafed"; I'll get 'em all three ready' (TN, III.i.90–1) – two are used in Troilus. (Cf. Aguecheek's 'vouchsafed' and Pandar's 'My lord, will you vouchsafe me a word?', III.i.60.) As in Aguecheek's 'pregnant', the lover confesses to Cressid his deficiency in the courtly graces 'To which the Grecians are most prompt and pregnant' (IV.iv.88).[21]

Act II scene iii

Mock-encomia: eminence of Ajax

'portable and commodious Aiaxes'
Tommaso Garzoni, The Hospitall of Incurable Fools (translated 1600, sig. [B4]).

As Hector bids 'Let me embrace thee, Ajax' (IV.v.135), Hector swears, 'By him that thunders [Jupiter Altitonans], thou hast lusty arms' (l. 136). Clasping the thunder-evoking Ajakes and his appendages, the Trojan champion proclaims, 'Hector would have them fall upon him thus' (IV.v.137).

Mock-encomia of Ajax recall Ajax's genealogy as a comic topos in Harington's Metamorphosis (e.g. p. 71). Subverting such 'encomia' are simultaneous manifestations of the same faults in Ajax, an eager receptacle of praise: 'He's not yet through warm. Force him with praises. Pour in, pour in' (II.iii.220–1).

When he threatens to go to Achilles and beat him, his fellows hold back their Ajax. ''Tis said he [Achilles] holds you [Ajakes] well'; and (as by the persuasions of nature) 'will be led, / At your request, a little from himself' (II.iii.178–9). Should the demands of nature prevail, Achilles will go to Ajax.

Ulysses, in dubious compliment, claims: were Nestor as young as Ajax, 'Nestor should not have the eminence of him' – not be over Ajax: Nestor should 'be as Ajax' (II.iii.253). At this tender moment, Ajax begs to enroll himself as Nestor's son: 'Shall I call you Father?' (II.iii.254). Suggestion of the brutish Ajax as a nursing baby, 'Praise ... she that gave thee suck' (II.iii.238), culminates in the large Ajax's adoption by the doddering Nestor as 'my good son' (II.iii.254). Ajax – in use – will 'physic the [out-of-use] great Myrmidon' (I.iii.377), or administer a purge to the grandiose, combat-withdrawn Achilles.

Praising the 'humourous'-ly discomposed Ajax (I.ii.19–30), Ulysses thanks 'the heavens, lord, thou art of sweet composure' (II.iii.237). 'Composure' has its other use in the play in a context of folly: 'it was a strong composure a fool could disunite' (II.iii.98–9). Following encomiastic convention, Ulysses lauds Ajax's temperament; his parents; his tutor; his learning; his military skill; his vigour; his wisdom (II.iii.237–47). So the brutal, pounding Ajax is mock-adulated: 'no less noble, much more gentle, and [anticlimactically] altogether more tractable' (II.iii.148–9). The tractability (or portability) of Ajax contrasts with Achilles' military intractability – 'an engine / Not portable' (II.iii.133–4).[22]

Grecian embassy to Achilles

Rebuffing the minion Patroclus, the Greek King–General, seeking Achilles, refuses such intermediaries: 'In second voice [cf. vice] we'll not be satisfied' (II.iii.139). Such unsatisfying 'second voice' recalls the ancient Nestor's garbling of Ulysses: 'And in the imitation of these twain, / Who as Ulysses says, opinion crowns / With an imperial voice' (I.iii.185–7). In context, the 'second voice' confusedly recalls the 'imperial voice [vice]' with which 'opinion crowns' (I.iii.186–187) 'these' loving 'twain', Achilles and Patroclus.[23]

Inverting protocol, King–General Agamemnon and court visit Achilles. 'Let him be told so', the King, concerning his visit, instructs Patroclus, 'lest perchance he think / We dare not move the question of our place', or (cf. Dogberry), 'know not what we are' (II.iii.80–2). His King–General bids Achilles' lover instruct the hero that 'A stirring dwarf we do allowance give / Before a sleeping giant' (II.iii.136–7). Size has already figured in the General's 'we come short' (I.iii.11), and in Nestor's 'small pricks / To their subsequent volumes' and 'baby figure of the giant mass / Of things to come at large' (I.iii.343–6). Recollections recur of the topos, to compare great things with small,[24] for example, equivocally, 'The one as infinite as *all*, / The other blank as *nothing*' (IV.v.80–1). As rhetorical comparisons of 'great things and small' recur in Homer, they re-emerge here to parodic effect.

Having Ajax go *to* Achilles would be 'to enlard' the latter's 'seam' or 'fat-already pride' (II.iii.183, 193). Agamemnon bids Ajax 'go ... greet ... [Achilles] in his tent', so Achilles 'will be led, / At your [Ajax's] request, a little from himself' (II.iii.177–9): the great Greek hero is to answer the call of Ajax.

'Privileged' folly: Thersites

Thersites, his own confessed fool (II.iii.63), is a licensed fool, himself as 'privileged' (II.iii.57) recalling Erasmus' Folly: 'I speak like a fool' because it 'was the prerogative of fools to speak what they like ...'. Thersites is 'privileged' fool within a larger context of licensed folly (*TN*, I.v.94–5): 'an allow'd fool' who does 'nothing but rail'.

Folly is in the play, like degree, a relational element: reverse mirrors correlate I.iii and II.iii – degree of folly versus folly of degree. If Achilles is a fool to serve Agamemnon, Thersites would be a fool to serve Achilles. The rogue's service of folly thus recalls the folly of service, or, parodically, degree itself. In terms of folly, Patroclus 'is a fool positive' (II.iii.65), definitely or absolutely a fool. (This use of 'positive' is, like 'Derive', II.iii.60, or 'decline', II.iii.52, also grammatical: 'positive', the first degree of comparison, is opposed to 'relative', or relational.) If relation is folly (cf. Pandarus[25]), non-relation (for example Thersites', or Ajax's in 'standing alone'), is also folly: 'Fools on both sides!' (I.i.92).

Act III scene iii

Potent reasons

Act III scene iii reverses the Ulyssean report-relays of I.iii. Whereas in I.iii Ulysses transmitted Achilles' and Patroclus' mockery *to* their victims (Agamemnon and Nestor, I.iii.142–84), in III.iii Ulysses directs such victims in a mockery of their mocker, Achilles. The Grecian parade now changes direction, *to* the unparticipating Achilles, to disdain and degrade him.

'Cas[ing] his reputation in his tent', Achilles tells Ulysses, is a matter of 'privacy' for which the retiring warrior has 'strong reasons' (III.iii.191). Yet (cf. I.iii.138) Ulysses opposes other 'potency' against Achilles. Exploiting the equivoque of 'potent' 'reasons' (cf. 'raisings'), Ulysses argues 'But 'gainst your privacy / The reasons are more potent and heroical' (III.iii.191–2).

Towards Achilles (who in II.iii denied parley to his king), Ulysses in III.iii stage-manages a pageant of contempt. The Greek leaders pass by Achilles who (equivocally) 'stands in th' entrance of his tent' (Q) (III.iii.38). Agamemnon accepts direction of Ulysses, and instructs 'each lord' to 'shake him [Achilles]' (III.iii.52–3) – shake his 'standing'. Achilles bids Patroclus (III.iii.234–7) approach Thersites in a ceremonious invitation to Ajax to invite Hector to Achilles' tent.

Since Ulysses speaks of the transience of glory-recognition, including 'desert in service' (III.iii.172) – 'subject all / To envious and calumniating Time' (III.iii.173–4) – his persuasions to Achilles are self-subversive: If

Achilles does return to combat, his deeds will shortly be forgotten. If he does not, they will, in any case, be forgotten. Relativistically, Ulysses here, as elsewhere, undermines his own arguments.

Act IV scenes ii and iv

Troilus, Cressid and Ulysses

Behind Troilus' solicitude for Cressid's sleep, and her uncle's teasing, is the wakeful night-of-love joke. After his love-night, Troilus unceremoniously leaves Cressid (IV.ii.8–11), whom he had shortly before (III.ii.35–9) addressed in terms of vassalage to majesty. Told she is to be taken from him, he responds (e.g. in IV.ii.69) unlike the furiously vengeful, love-lorn Achilles. Night's brevity Troilus assails, with incongruous alliteration: 'Beshrew the *w*itch! with *v*enomous *w*ights she stays / As tediously as hell' (IV.ii.12–13), anticipating his ultimate plosive splutter: 'You vile abominable tents, / Thus *p*roudly *p*ight upon our *P*hrygian *p*lains' (V.x.23–4). Dictional and syntactical aberrations affect the 'plain and simple' Troilus (IV.iv.108). With burlesque circumstance, he swears 'there's no maculation in thy heart' (IV.iv.64).

Troilus, in a series of equivoques, exclaims, 'Some say the Genius so, / Cries, "Come!" to him that instantly must die' (IV.iv.50–1). As Genius in Gower is both orthodox priest and priest of Venus, commissioned to inform Amans about love, Pandar brings to mind such traditional functions: as in I.i, tutor in love; in III.ii, marital 'priest' of love. So Troilus' evocation of Genius recalls Pandar's own love-ministering roles.[26]

From Troilus, Cressid's departure with Diomedes is punctuated by Hector's trumpet-mockery, a sound which underlines Troilus' final vaunt to Diomedes. The trumpet-sound recurs in Agamemnon's request to the 'dreadful Ajax', to 'Give with thy trumpet a loud note to Troy' (IV.v.3–4). Such noises mock (as in charivari) the removal by his rival of Troilus' beloved. Subsequent reference recurs in the equivocal response to Cressid: '*All*. The Trojan'*s t*rumpet' (IV.v.64).

Cressid's 'When shall we see again?' (IV.iv.57) has the soft omission of the verbal object. Her question ironically anticipates V.ii, when Troilus will indeed 'see' Cressid 'again'. Here, to Troilus' obsessive 'be thou but true of heart –' (IV.iv.58), she retorts, 'I true! how now!' adding, with burlesque archaism, 'what wicked deem is this?' (IV.iv.59).[27] When Troilus tactlessly insists, 'But be not tempted', Cressid's 'Do you think I will?' (IV.iv.91–2) forces him defensively to keep apologizing.

Act IV scene v

Burlesque postures

In the play, remarkable postures recur: for example, 'set your seat [Q] on the attentive bent' (I.iii.252); 'bending angels' (I.iii.235–6). Marveling, Paris demands, 'Can it be / That so degenerate a strain as this / Should once set footing in your generous bosoms?' (II.ii.153–5). Paris here recalls Ulysses' wandering foot; as in Ulysses' repeated steps (I.iii.128, 132: 'pace': I.iii.130, 131: 'step'), and Ulysses' diagnosis of the 'fever that keeps Troy on foot' (I.iii.135). 'Troy in our weakness stands' (I.iii.137).

Along with foot allusions, knee postures recur: Cressid's Pandar-appeal, 'on my knees I beseech you ...' (IV.ii.88–9). 'Pursue we him on knees', Andromache begs Hector's sister (V.iii.10). 'Not Priamus and Hecuba on knees', cries Troilus (V.iii.54). Ulysses concludes: 'for supple knees / Feed arrogance and are the proud man's fees'.[28]

Postures are also suggestive regarding Cressid. If she 'wide unclasp[s] the tables of ... [her] thoughts / To every tickling reader' (IV.v.60–1), she is, in Ulysses's description, a *livre d'occasion* – an acquiescent spoil of opportunity (IV.v.62).[29] Ulysses's Cressid-derogation counters, feature by feature, her earlier positive blasons (I.i.42–61). Her 'eye, her cheek, her lip', even her foot, have expressively functions of utterance: 'her foot speaks' (IV.v.56). Her least motion is suggestive: 'every joint and motive of her body' (IV.v.57).

Wearing 'his tongue in's arms' (III.iii.269), Ajax scorns utterances: 'Speaking is for beggars' (III.iii.268). The *miles gloriosus* too self-exalted merely to speak must express himself by pounding – as Thersites (in II.i) had it impressed upon him. Recalling the unlinguistic Ajax and Nestor's 'experienced tongue' (I.iii.68) is Troilus, 'Speaking in deeds and deedless in his tongue' (IV.v.98). If Ajax 'wears his tongue in's arms', Troilus wears his 'heart upon' his 'sleeve' (cf. *O*, I.i.64). In Kyd's much-parodied *Spanish Tragedy*, a lover swears against a rival, 'either [to] lose my life, or win my love' (II.i.133). So, in mock-epic bravado, Troilus vows against his rival: 'I come to lose my arm, or win my sleeve' (V.iii.96).

In his oratorical posture, King Agamemnon composes indecorous analogies: 'every action that hath gone before / Whereof we have record, trial did draw / Bias and thwart, not answering the aim' (I.iii.13–15); compare Pandar's 'rub on, and kiss the mistress' (III.ii.49). (Cf. *TS*, IV.v.24–5.) Legal echoes mingle with bowling allusions (as in trial, action, record, answer, bias): direction of the twisted and crosswise bowling ball does not, in trial, correspond to the aim.

Just before IV.v.184–6, however, there is characteristic self-tripping courtesy, with a clumsy attempt at rectification. King Agamemnon's curious greeting-insult to the Trojan champion, Hector, 'as welcome as to one / That would be rid of such an enemy –' is retrieved by 'But that's no welcome' (IV.v.163–5). If 'th' appurtenance of welcome is fashion and ceremony' (*H*, II.ii.371–2), the King's maladroit ceremonial confuses gracious greeting of a foe with gratifyingly ridding oneself of him.

Nestor

In Nestor's Hector-encomium, with his repetitive 'I have seen' (IV.v.183, 185–6, 192, 194), is a formulaic opening for elaborate Homeric simile. The stock phrase is parodically recalled in Henry Fielding's *Tragedy of Tragedies*: 'So have I seen the Bees ...'. If, in the *Iliad*, Nestor is noted for similes, it is he, in *Troilus*, who carries them to absurdity: for example in IV.v.183–200, as well as in I.iii.31–54, where the *senex* applies Agamemnon's twisted clichés. In burlesque-Homeric terms, Nestor repeats his Hector-encomium, employing the epic formula 'I have seen':

> *I have*, thou gallant Trojan, *seen thee* oft ...
> ... and *I have seen thee*,
> As hot as Perseus, spur thy Phrygian steed,
> And *seen thee* scorning forfeits and subduements ...
> And *I have seen thee* pause and take thy breath ...
> ... This *have I seen*,
> But this thy countenance, still locked in steel,
> *I never saw* till now
>
> IV.v.183–96 (italics added)

Such profusion of 'seeings' anticipates Fielding's burlesque of elaborate Homeric simile-introductions: his King, replying to the Ghost's repeatedly used 'So have I seen' (*Tom Thumb*, III.ii), explodes, 'D—n all thou'st seen!'[30]

Burlesque building imagery

> build there, carpenter
> III.ii.50

Burlesque elements include building imagery. Recalling Cressid's 'strong base and building' is Ulysses' hendiadys in praise of Hector: Troy's 'base and pillar' (IV.v.212).[31]

Among such edifice references is Ulysses' 'ram that batters down the wall' (I.iii.206). Before Achilles and Ajax succeed in toppling the walls, notes Thersites (II.iii.9), they will stand till they fall of themselves – or in Ulysses' bizarre terms, 'kiss their own feet' (IV.v.221). Hector politely declines the prophecy: 'There they stand yet; and modestly I think / The fall of every Phrygian stone will cost / A drop of Grecian blood' (IV.v.222–4). To

Ulysses' top-and-toe kissing metaphor, Hector, with a flourish of 'modestly', replies, mingling less modest bodily parts. Each 'Phrygian stone' (paradoxically, Phrygian, as effeminate, or 'stone'-less) sustains the building imagery: pillar, base, basis, foot, wall, tower, stone. Troy's failure to be down 'upon his basis' (I.iii.75) is caused, Ulysses explains, by the Grecians' 'fever' that 'keeps Troy on foot' (I.iii.135). In would-be courteous counter-claim to Ulysses' falling towers, Hector's 'I must not believe you' (IV.v.221) gives the lie indirect to Ulysses' contortional foot-kissing image.

Hector's 'way': Hector and Achilles

Troy's imminent catastrophic epic Fall is juxtaposed to mundane young-love disappointment. These disparate events stand in antithetical terms: in the rhetorical topic of 'large and small', as 'in the extremity of great and little' (IV.v.78). Greeks and Trojans pursuing each other 'to the edge of all extremity' (IV.v.68) are set alternatively against division by 'voice' (I.iii.187). Reinforcing the mode of Grecian 'voice' (cf. vice), Agamemnon asks, 'Which way would Hector have it?' (IV.v.71). In the event, Hector is to 'have it' Achilles' 'empaling' way.[32] Achilles' is 'An appetite that I am sick withal, / To see great Hector ... to my full of view' (III.iii.238–41), and in his body parts to consummate destruction. 'In which part of his body', demands Achilles, 'Shall I destroy him? – whether there, or there, or there?' (IV.v.242–3).

Following the body parts' 'reflection' (III.iii.102–11), Achilles and Hector engage each other in a mock-epic boasting contest (IV.v.231–71). Hector (who will fail to recognize the evidently low Thersites, V.iv.25–6) inquires of the celebrated Greek hero, 'Is this Achilles'? Proudly, the latter retorts: 'I am Achilles' (IV.v.233–4). Achilles having inspected Hector 'joint by joint', Hector, in turn, examines Achilles' proud 'standing' (IV.v.235). At Hector's looking-over, Achilles (III.iii.74–92) complains of being too soon overlooked. Since Hector seems himself so cursory, Achilles now offers to reinspect Hector's 'pride'.

With a flourish, Hector demands of Achilles, 'proud man ... Stand again'. Hector adds, 'Think'st thou to catch my life so pleasantly ...' (IV.v.247–9). Theatrically, as Achilles and Hector inspect each other, each demands (as actor from spectator) greater applause. Hector will pick Achilles out by his rival's well-known 'proud' attribute, as well as 'by his large and portly size' (IV.v.162). Hector recalls the proudly expansive Achilles: 'Things small as nothing, for request's sake only, / He makes important' (II.iii.167–8).

Hector's and Achilles' heroic brags suggest a mock-Homeric gab or flyting, with threats to run through the other's body. Hector tops Achilles' threat to wound him 'there, or there, or there?' (IV.v.243), with his own burlesque hyperbole: 'I'll not kill thee there, nor there, nor there ... /

But ... everywhere'. Unsatisfied with this lethal ubiquity, he will repeat the process, 'yea, o'er and o'er' (IV.v.254–6). Hector, in burlesque terms recalling Pistol, loftily demands of the underwhelmed Achilles: 'Think'st thou to catch my life so pleasantly / As to prenominate in nice conjecture / Where thou wilt hit me dead?' (IV.v.249–51).

Act IV nears its end as it begins: with temporary reconciliation of boastful foes. As Hector encounters Achilles, the two warriors engage in emulative scanning of each other's 'pride'.

Mock-agon: Hector versus Ajax

Ajax, part Trojan and part Greek, is recalled in Hector: 'half Hector stays at home', alliteratively observes Aeneas, 'Half heart, half hand, half Hector comes to seek / This blended knight, half Trojan and half Greek' (IV.v.84–6). Hector being kin to Ajax, the King–General sibilantly notes, 'Half stints their strife before their strokes begin' (IV.v.93). The burlesque duel between the champions Hector and Ajax is itself subject to *aposiopesis* – abruption. While IV.v's Greek and Trojan exchanges occupy over two hundred lines, the champions' duel having been anticipated, anticlimactically within four lines (IV.v.113–16) their contest is over, on account of nearness of blood. One touch of nature makes both foes kin.

Paralleling the Helen–Cressid plot-exchanges, including Cressid's proposal for Antenor, and Cressid's Diomedes–Troilus exchange, is Ajax's exchange for Achilles. As the battle commences between Trojan and Greek champions, Hector and Ajax, the bystanders cheer them on. When later, Ajax, 'Roaring for Troilus', 'foams at mouth' (V.v.36–7), Nestor admonishes the heroic receptacle both to fight and to contain himself: 'Now, Ajax, hold thine own!' (IV.v.114).

To the combat, terms such as 'uttermost' (IV.v.91) lend a mock-chivalric tone. Recalling a burlesque Tournament of Tottenham, Diomedes for the Greeks and Aeneas for the Trojans are to determine the order of battle: either finally *à outrance*, or else to a 'breath'. In the event, the duel is aborted: instead of *à outrance*, it is *à plaisance*. Cressid's 'touch of consanguinity' (IV.ii.97) is recalled here in the 'consanguinity' of Ajax. The champions' abortive duel parallels the eponymous lovers and their love affair's abruption: 'the issue is embracement' (IV.v.148) – Ajax is embraced by Hector, his relative; and Cressid by Diomedes, Troilus' rival. In parody of ordeal or trial-by-combat, the long-awaited contest between Greek and Trojan champions is called off because of the mingled contents of Ajax.

As Grecian champion against Hector, Ajax is saluted by King–General Agamemnon. 'Here art thou in appointment fresh and fair, / Anticipating time ...' (IV.v.1–2). 'Ajax is ready' (III.iii.35) – fairly prepared, before need.

Appalling the air, Ajax is (IV.v.3–6) to 'pierce' Hector's 'head' and 'hale him hither'. In response to this 'colick'-y salute, Ulysses remarks, 'No trumpet answers'. Such absence of trumpet-noise Achilles explains by the early hour. As ''Tis but early days' (IV.v.12), participants are not yet 'stirring'.

Troilus re-enters, announcing Ajax's capture of Aeneas: Ajax shall not carry Aeneas – 'I'll be ta'en too, / Or', Troilus equivocally insists, 'bring him off' (V.vi.24–5; cf. I.iii.334: 'That can from Hector bring his honour off'). Here, Ajax himself seems intractable, despite his mock-encomium as 'altogether more tractable' (II.iii.149). The jest comprises also a reversal: instead of a man carrying Ajakes (cf. 'not portable', II.iii.134), Ajakes carries a man. Ajax has taken Aeneas; V.vi thus recalls the gag in II.iii: the mock-epic issue, whether a man go to Ajakes, or Ajakes to a man.

Act V scene i

Thersites versus Achilles and Patroclus

In parody (cf. II.i, IV.v) of the larger conflict, a contest of slighter personages takes place. Patroclus exchanges a series of diminutive slurs with Thersites: 'core', 'botch', 'box', 'butt', 'gall', and 'finch-egg' (V.i.4–35).

As Thersites' 'preposterous' denounces Patroclus (V.i.23), the railer's 'wear ... on both sides' (III.iii.264) transforms preposterously (i.e. back-frontward), as he sees the world; or downward, as he metamorphoses mankind to beast. Thersites' 'Hold thy whore, Grecian! Now for thy whore, Trojan!' (V.iii.23–4) and his 'The cuckold and the cuckold-maker are at it. Now, bull! now, dog!' (V.vii.9–10) have the levelling effect 'on both sides' (I.i.92). Thersites' disempathy stems also from *Schadenfreude*: 'those things do best please me', gloats Puck, 'That befall prepost'rously' (*MND*, III.ii.120–1). What displeases others pleases the adversity figure best (V.ii.123–4).

Act V scene vi

Ajax, Diomedes and Troilus

As from one side Ajax, and from the other Diomedes, pursue Troilus, the Grecians converge and clash. An emulous privy and an opportunist womanizer competing for a dishonoured lover compose a burlesque triangle.

A further touch of *corrector morum* occurs in Ajax's competition with Diomedes. When Diomedes claims, 'I would correct him', Ajax proposes: 'Were I the general, thou shouldst have my office [or house of office] / Ere that correction' (V.vi.4–5) – correlating the General and Ajax (cf. Ajax on

Thersites as General, III.iii.260–2). Were Ajax the General, he would bestow upon Diomedes the 'office' of Ajax.

Defeated and robbed (by Diomede, cf. V.vi.7) of his horse, Troilus is, like Falstaff, 'colted' (cheated) and 'uncolted' (unhorsed).[33] In his next encounter with Diomedes, Troilus seeks revenge, not for his stolen love, but for his purloined 'horse' (V.vi.6–7). As Troilus charges Diomedes to 'pay the life thou ow'st me for my horse [cf. whore's]' (V.vi.7), the Trojan ironically recalls Hector's 'Nature craves / All dues be rendered to their owners' (II.ii.173–4). Prince Troilus is a multiple 'dues' loser: his honour, his brother, his beloved – and his horse. If the knight deprived of a horse emblematizes chivalric dishonour, loss of his horse to a rival who has also removed his lady multiplies the dishonour. What 'carries' Troilus 'away', ultimately, is not Cressid – not even, as with Hotspur, his 'horse' (*1H4*, II.iv.378–9) – but his *lack* of a horse.

Parodic 'Hamlet'

Troilus (c. 1601–02) ends on a note upon which *Hamlet* (c. 1600–01) commences: a young princely protagonist's revenge-haunting of a relative's murderer – 'like a wicked conscience still' (V.x.28). Indeed, *Troilus'* conclusion suggests a burlesque revenge-play: the protagonist's vengeance sought not for the loss of a father (as in *Hamlet*), or for a son (as in Kyd's *Spanish Tragedy*), but (along with a brother) for a horse (V.vi). *Troilus'* end thus suggests a revenge plot gone astray: with parallels to Quixote and Rosinante, its mock-chivalry links a Knight of the Burning Cresset (or Cressid) to the quest for a *cheval*.

As Paris and Menelaus exit fighting, a bastard son of King Priam enters. Addressing Thersites as 'slave' (V.vii.13), the Bastard, unlike Hector (V.iv.25–6), recognizes the rogue's low status. Paradoxically, it is now the base-born Thersites who demands rank: 'What art thou?' (V.vii.14). Thersites claims affinities with an illegitimate 'king's son' (cf. *1H4*, II.iv.378–9) – one touch of bastardy makes the whole world kin. If pander and bastard are (like cuckold and cuckolder) symbiotic, interrelated, too, are Pandar and Thersites, the concupiscible and the irascible, complementary aspects of the appetitive soul.

Act V scene x

Double note: '*seria-ludicra*'

> What dire offence from am'rous Causes springs,
> What mighty contests rise from trivial things
> Alexander Pope, *The Rape of the Lock*

Malvolio 115

As Troilus, lovesick, enters (I.i.1) like a concupiscible, yearning Orsino, he exits (V.x.23–4) like an irascible, deprived Malvolio. Like the disappointed would-be lover Malvolio, threatening revenge 'on the whole pack of you' (*TN*, V.i.378), the disappointed lover Troilus threatens revenge on the whole pack of 'You vile abominable tents ...' (V.x.23–6). Among potential dramatic effects are, depending on perspective, pity or laughter, or both: If Pandar, a solicitor soliciting pity, evokes bathos or ridicule (V.x.45–9), Troilus, on another level, may elicit both pity and laughter.

tears

tear overflow

Combining *seria* and *ludicra*, Troilus' own tearful excess is multiplied in Cassandra's 'lend me ten thousand eyes, / And I will fill them with prophetic tears' (II.ii.101–2). Excessive tear-gushing (as in Kyd's *Spanish Tragedy*, 'O eyes no eyes, but fountains ...') was at Troilus' Elizabethan period burlesqued.[34] Such excesses are echoed in Pandar's 'Hecuba laughed, that her eyes ran o'er', and Cressid's 'more temperate fire under the pot of' Cassandra's 'eyes' (I.ii.144–8). Hyperbolic to the end, Troilus predicts 'maids and wives' will, at word of Hector's death, liquefy into tearful wells (V.x.19).

Further, Troilus' outburst against a 'great-sized coward' (V.x.26) recalls 'the great bulk Achilles' (IV.iv.128). His brother's body 'dragged' in 'beastly sort' (V.x.5), Troilus directs his frenzy upward: 'Frown on, you heavens' (V.x.6). Recalling Thersites' 'same scurvy doting foolish young knave's sleeve of Troy ...' (V.iv.3–4) are Troilus' complex genitives, 'at the murderer's horse's tail' (V.x.4). As the work stops short of the 'hideous crash' (*H*, II.ii.498) of Ilium's fall, there are lesser elements which here survive – a dallying girl, a displaced lover and a bathetic pander. After the climax of Achilles' Myrmidons' mass assault on Hector (V.viii), Troilus' final scene has the effect of whimpering anticlimax. Against the epic fall of Troy (and its doomsday symbolism) is set the fall of Troilus and his Pandar. Troilus' name thus anticipates (like Pandar's humble-bee, V.x.41) a mock-catastrophic fall.

Against Troy's grand-scale debacle, moreover, the fickleness of a young girl seems less than earth-shaking: *perjuria ridet amantium Iuppiter*, Jove laughs at lovers' perjuries. Blamed finally for Troilus' love-debacle, and recalling Helen's 'this love will undo us all. O Cupid, Cupid, Cupid!' (III.i.110–11), Pandar is as Cupid–Pandar by love undone. As, at the close of Jonson's *Cynthia's Revels* (1600–01), Cupid is banished, Troilus' irate dismissal of Pandar is itself a *Hue and Cry after Cupid*. Here, a panderly scapegoat speaks the epilogue, an expression not shared by such other scapegoats as Falstaff, Shylock, Malvolio or Parolles. *Narrenfreiheit* is in its own terms self-limiting and brief – 'a slave to limit' (III.ii.82): the work's last word is that of a *sot compère* of this play of foolish war and love. Characters are introduced and depart unheroically, as does the spluttering Troilus dismissing his panderly love-guide; and as does Pandar in his own leave-taking complaint with a whimper.

Poetic injustice

> Swich fyn hath, lo, this Troilus for love!
> Swich fyn hath al his grete worthynesse!
> Swich fyn hath his estat real above,
> Swich fyn his lust, swich fyn hath his noblesse!
> Swich fyn hath false worldes brotelnesse!
> Chaucer, *Troilus and Criseyde*

Poetic justice is inverted in burlesque works such as Gay's *Beggar's Opera*, which display such 'justice' favouring pimps and bawds. Asserting poetic justice is, however, Dryden's preface (1679, 1695) to his *Troilus*. His poetically just adaptation of the play contains a double suicide, with Cressid's repentant recognition of loss of innocence, 'too late'. Concerning Shakespeare's *Troilus*, Dryden complains of the end of the 'tragedy': 'The latter part of the tragedy is nothing but a confusion of drums and trumpets, excursions and alarms. The chief persons, who give names to the tragedy, are left alive; Cressid is false, and not punished.'[35]

Despite the play's 'winnowing' motif (e.g. I.iii.26–30; III.ii.166; cf. I.ii.242–3), 'distinction' does not survive. On the other hand, neither Achilles, nor Cressid, nor Diomedes, nor Helen, nor Paris, within Shakespeare's play, receives retribution. The named figures who are punished on stage are not the knaves (e.g. Thersites, Diomede), but the victims of love, Troilus; of chivalry, Hector; of reciprocal trust, both these brothers; and of coupling devotion, Pandar. Ironically, the voice of poetic justice, Thersites, is the play's most repellent personage.

Troilus, of all the play's characters, swears most oaths of revenge. While reportedly effective off stage (V.v.37–42), on stage Troilus threatens profusely, yet visibly slays no one. This disparity is sharpened when set against estimated figures of slaughter in the *Iliad*, where Homer's heroic warriors kill a number of named opponents each. For all the Prologue's 'cruel war' (l. 5) and the *Iliad*'s sacrifice of countless dead, among a cast of almost thirty in this Trojan War play, only two named figures (Patroclus and Hector) perish – and only one on stage. Troilus' last speech is an unfulfilled spluttering threat to 'through and through' these 'vile abominable tents ... proudly *p*ight upon our *Ph*rygian *p*lains' (V.x.23–4). His brother's death unavenged, Prince Troilus is left deprived and dishonoured, *sans* beloved, *sans* brother, *sans* revenge – and *sans* horse. Diomede, who has stolen Troilus' 'fair steed', bids it be presented to 'my Lady Cressid'. The Grecian claims now to be 'her knight by proof' (V.v.2–5).

In bathetic self-pity, Pandar's *casus* or fall is his own 'litel myn tragedye' (Chaucer, *Troilus and Criseyde*, V.1786).[36] Chaucer's Knight interrupts the Monk's lists of falls: 'I seye for me, it is a greet *disese*, / Whereas men han been in greet welthe and *ese*, / To heeren of hire sodeyn fal, allas!'[37] Aptly, the dramatic coupler's final utterance at his own downfall couples (like Chaucer above on the 'sodeyn fal') *eases* and *diseases* (V.x.54–5). As Troilus remarks 'The bonds of heaven' (V.ii.154, 156), Pandar arraigns the 'world' (V.x.36), while both figures generalize from an instance of personal displacement. Pandar's is a self-pitying mock-sermon on earthly injustice, including a 'verse for it' (V.x.39–40), a proof-text on the bee. In a work whose opening suggests '*Dis*-arming and the man' and whose female lead subverts heroic anger, mock-epic culminates in the misfortunes of a bee.[38] Rather than falling from 'heigh degree', Pandar's is the descent of a procurer with not far to fall.[39]

His formerly merry humble-bee is at last 'subdued in arméd tail' (V.x.43), reflecting the play, itself 'an arméd tale': Pandar's 'dying love' does not 'live still' (III.i.124). As it early intimates mock-epic, the work's reduction of great to small recurs anticlimactically at its close. There, recalling an epitaph for the Virgil-attributed *Culex*, or *Gnat*, is Pandar's mock-epitaph (V.x.41–4) for the humble-bee. As his plot exposes its own play-within-the-play, Pandar's mock-tragic insect-fall completes the series *de casibus*: Troilus', Hector's, Pandar's – and the bee's.

Sharing the play's last moments – like its first – are a lachrymose lover and his self-pitying Pandar. Opening with an Armed Prologue in military array, and a complaining lover and pander, the play closes with a complaining lover and pander in disarray. Culminating the pitiful tale anticipating Troy's Fall ('O lamentable fall of famous towne', *Faerie Queene*, III.ix.39), Pandar's epilogic self-pity embraces 'all pitiful goers-between' (III.ii.199–200). Unlike the ending of Jonson's *Cynthia's Revels*, 'Now each one drie his weeping eyes ... purged of your maladies', Pandar fears a failure of 'eyes, half out' to perform their lachrymose purgation (V.x.47). Instead of Chaucerian Troilus-apotheosis and *contemptus mundi*, Pandar's end laments *his* worldly sorrows and the unjust fate of benevolent flesh-purveyors. Seeming to intend *pathopoeia*, in a vain appeal to spectators for sympathy, he achieves not pity and fear, but bathos: his *lugete* bathetically invites 'Good traders in the flesh' (V.x.45) to participate in a *planctus lenonis*, a pander's lament at worldly ingratitude.

To summarize, this chapter has examined the play's recurrent burlesque elements, including mock-epic and folly, as well as expressions of mock-heroic, mock-encomia, and parody. As such burlesque transforms epic characters (for example Agamemnon, Nestor, Ajax, Achilles, Hector), the effect is mock-epic inversion suited to the world-upside-down occasion of a revel.

Notes

1.   On burlesque, see François Bar, *Le Genre Burlesque en France au XVIIe siècle* (Paris, 1960). See, on the diction of burlesque, A.H. King, *The Language of Satirized Characters in 'Poetaster'* (Lund, Sweden, 1941). For burlesque in relation to Inns of Court students, see Eccles' Beaumont article. Cf. burlesque and the sonnet cycle *Zepheria* (1594). See Richmond P. Bond, *English Burlesque Poetry, 1700–1750* (New York, 1964).

On burlesque and food, see Silvia Longhi, 'La cucina di Parnaso', *Lusus: Il Capitolo Burlesco nel Cinquecento* (Padova, 1983), pp. 57–94. On food references, see Curtius, *European Literature*, 'Alimentary Metaphors', pp. 134–5; 'Kitchen Humor and Other *Ridicula*', pp. 431–5. See Madeleine Lazard, 'Images Culinaires dans la Comédie de la Renaissance', in Andrew Lascombes, ed., *Spectacle and Image in Renaissance Europe* (Leiden, The Netherlands, 1993), pp. 94–108; and Werner Mezger, *Narrenidee und Fastnachtsbrauch* (Konstanz, Germany, 1991). Jean-Claude Margolin and Robert Sauzet, eds, *Pratiques et Discours Alimentaires à la Renaissance* (Paris, 1982). Michel Jeanneret, *A Feast of Words* (Oxford, 1991). John R. Fryar, 'Some Social Customs of the Old English Christmas', *Ecclesiastical Review*, 39 (1908), 601–17.

Pandar's Troilus-instruction, combining the erotic and the culinary (I.i.13–28), could, for law students, recall the Inns of Court's fleshly environs. Among these was the notorious Ram Alley. The 'Ram' ran into the Temple's wall – cf. 'the ram that batters down the wall' (I.iii.206). See L. Barry's *Ram Alley*; and Sugden, *Dictionary*, s.v.

2.   Through medieval and Renaissance Latin traditions, the *gradus amoris* or ladder of lechery was transmitted. The first scene's steps are transformed in the last act's 'lechery, five-finger-tied' (V.ii.157). On the *quinque lineae amoris*, see Curtius, *European Literature*, pp. 512ff; Peter Dronke, *Medieval Latin and the Rise of European Love-Lyric* (Oxford, 1961), I.49, 62, 258; II.488–9 (and references there given); Dronke, in *Classica et medievalia*, 20 (1959), 167ff. Cf. Baldwin, *Small Latine* II.163–64; Alfred Adler, 'The Topos *Quinque lineae sunt amoris* ...', *Bibliothèque d'Humanisme et Renaissance*, 15 (1953), 220–5; L.J. Friedman, 'Gradus Amoris', *Romance Philology*, 19 (1965), 167–77. Cf. W.C. Waterhouse, 'A Classical Echo in "Come Again"', *Notes and Queries*, n.s. 30 (1992), 357, recalling the *quinque lineae* in Donatus' commentary on Terence.

3.   Troilus' self-subversive invocation of Apollo (patron-deity of law) 'for thy Daphne's love' (I.i.100) suggests tactless recollection of the god's love failure. See Ovid's *Metamorphoses* (Loeb, 1960, II.452–600) on Apollo as divine and comical. Mary E. Barnard, *The Myth of Apollo and Daphne from Ovid to Quevedo* (Durham, N. Carolina, 1987); Barnard, 'Myth in Quevedo: The Serious and the Burlesque in the Apollo and Daphne Poems', *Hispanic Review*, 52 (1984), 499–522; Wolfgang Stechow, *Apollo und Daphne* (Berlin, 1932); Y.F.-A. Giraud, 'Traitements Burlesques du Mythe', *La Fable de Daphne* (Paris, 1968), pp. 301–24.

Cf. a questioning 'dishonour of honour' climate and chivalric burlesque: not only its expression in Spain with *Don Quixote*, or in England with the *Knight of the Burning Pestle*, but also in Italy, with Berni, Pulci, Boiardo and Ariosto. Cf. G.A. Borghese, 'The Dishonor of Honor', *Romanic Review*, 32 (1941), 44–55.

4.   Exceptions include *Merchant of Venice*, which sets Troilus' name, however, among betrayed women (V.i.4); and *Rape of Lucrece* (l. 1486).

5.   The lover's hyperbolic conceits blason Cressid's hand, 'to whose soft seizure / The cygnet's down is harsh, and spirit of sense / Hard as the palm of ploughman!' (I.i.59–61). 'To whose soft seizure' suggests equivocally that, compared to, or upon, her hand's 'soft seizure', the 'spirit of sense' is 'hard'. So, hyperbolically, all whites confess that they are black ink in comparison to Cressid's white hand, inscribing their own deficiency. Regarding a lady's whiter-than-white skin, the burlesque blason is echoed in Pope, *Sinking in Poetry*, p. 51.

6.   Cf. the Middle Templar Hoskyns' advice to a Templar student, c. 1600, concerning 'her face, her eyes, her haire, her voice, her bodie, her handes, her gate …' ('Direccions For Speech and Style', in Hoskyns, *Life*, p. 137). On the equivocal 'Handlest', cf. *H5*, II.iii.37; *MM*, V.i.272, 275. *Troilus*' (I.i.55–7) face, eyes, etc., blason echoes the Inns of Court Hoskins, with equivoques on gait (gate) and voice (vice). (Note variant spellings: Hoskyns, Hoskins.)

7.   Through motives not mercenary, but eleemosynary, serving for pleasure not reward, Pandar is the pander *avant la lettre*. Pandarus combines *compère* and *commère*, *mezzano* or *vetula*, his diseases and comical self-pity recurrent among Renaissance dramatized bawds.
     Pandar here reflects secondary characters of Roman comedy, not only the *leno* – in Italian comedy, the *maquerello* – and the *parasitus* (the *parassito*), but also, in his food-preparation metaphors, the *cocus* (I.i). Pandar as *praeceptor amoris* (I.i.14–28) parallels Cressid (I.ii.287–96) in a convention related to the love-instructing 'lenae' of New Comedy, and Ovid's *Ars Amatoria*: that of eratodidaxis.

8.   Evidence for pronouncing Ajax as Ajakes is suggested in Harington's *Metamorphosis*: one 'somewhat costive [who] … complained, I tell you age akes, age akes. I feele it, age akes … [he] … termed the place age akes: which agrees fully in pronunciation, though … since, some ill orthographers have mis-written it … now it passeth currant to be spoken and written A Jax' (p. 78). If Ajax is privily unheroic, he surpasses Hector, himself coped by Ajax (I.ii.33–5). Ajax in Harington's sense recurs in Tommaso Garzoni, *The Hospitall of Incurable Fooles* (translated 1600, sig. B3–B3v): '… *Stercutio* … Protector of *Ajax*'. Cf. sig. [B4] on '… portable and commodious Aiaxes'.

9.   Linking Jonson further with Ajakes is also Jonson's previous profession of bricklayer and his bricklaying work at Lincoln's Inn, celebrated for building a jakes. See Harington's *Metamorphosis*, pp. 3, 164–5, congratulating Lincoln's Inn (where Harington had been a student) on its famous convenience – on what Marston (*What You Will*, III.i) called 'the glorious *Ajax* of *Lincolnes Inne*'.

10. Cf. Robert B. Pierce, 'Ben Jonson's Horace and Horace's Ben Jonson', *Studies in Philology*, 78 (1981), 20–31; Elton, 'Portrait of Ajax'; James P. Bednarz 'Shakespeare's Purge of Jonson: The Literary Context of *Troilus and Cressida*', *Shakespeare Studies*, 21 (1993), 175–212. See Jonson on law and lawyers, as well as actors, in his Apologetical Dialogue to *Poetaster*, 11. 68–70: 'they say you taxed / The law and lawyers, captains, and the players / By their particular names'.

11. 'Humano capiti cervicum pictor equinam / iungere si velit, et varias inducere plumas / undique collatis membris, ut turpiter atrum / desinat in piscem mulier formosa superne'. ('If a painter wished to join a human head to the neck of a horse, and to spread over limbs various feathers picked up everywhere, so that what at the top is a beautiful woman ends below in a foully hideous fish …'.

12. Horace, *Ars Poetica*, ed. C.O. Brink (Cambridge, 1985), II.55.
13. Recalling Homer and Virgil, a parodic-epic question is posed: 'What was his cause of anger?' (I.ii.11). *Troilus* recalls a literary convention including Lucian: comic derogation of epic heroism (cf. Branham, *Unruly Eloquence*, p. 117).
14. Cressid's 'man', Alexander, who characterizes Ajax (I.ii.19–30), is, as 'Alexander', linked with Ajax [Ajakes] in *Love's Labour's Lost*: 'you have overthrown Alisander the conqueror! You will be scrap'd out of the painted cloth [cf. *TC*, V.x.45] for this. Your lion that holds his poll-axe sitting on a close-stool, will be given to Ajax; he will be the ninth Worthy' (V.ii.573–8). See Horst Schroeder, *Der Topos der Nine Worthies in Literatur und bildender Kunst* (Göttingen, Germany, 1971).
     Alexander's portrait of the humorous, discordant and ill-assembled Ajax contrasts with Jonson's *Cynthia's Revels* (1600) in its self-congratulatory portrait of Crites (Jonson) – cf. Mercury's description of Crites as a foil to Ajax, 'A creature of a most perfect and divine temper. One, in whom 'the *humours* and *elements* are peaceably met, without *emulation* of precedencie ...'.
     As Alexander, reporting on Hector's defeat by Ajax, joins Ajax with Hector, Cressid's exchange with her 'man' Alexander links Hector's epic wrath with Ajax (I.ii.33–4; cf. I.ii.4–5; III.iii.181–2).
15. As in Pope's 'Parts answ'ring parts shall slide into a whole', Epistle IV, to Richard Boyle, Earl of Burlington, *Works*, ed. John Butt (1966), p. 316, l. 66.
16. Cf. Nestor in relation to the comic convention of the 'old man': Hans G. Oeri, *Der Typ der komischen Alten in der griechischen Komödie* (Basel, 1948). Cf. 'Fooles doe Nestorize', in John Davies of Hereford, *Complete Works*, ed. A.B. Grosart (New York, 1967), II.89.
     Nestor's allusion to his King's 'godlike seat' (I.iii.31) recalls the revels' misrule Prince and his elevated seat on a throne under a cloth of state. Cf. *Gesta*, p. 29: 'the Prince, then sitting in his Chair of State in the Hall'; cf. p. 35: 'the Prince ... ascended his Throne at the high End of the Hall, under His Highness's Arms'; p. 58: 'And when the Prince was ascended to his Chair of State ...'; p. 37: 'the Prince came down from his Chair of State ...'.
17. See M.A. Grant, *Ancient Rhetorical Theories of the Laughable* ..., University of Wisconsin Publications in Language and Literature, no. 21 (Madison, Wisconsin, 1924). Ernestus Arndt, 'De ridiculi doctrina rhetorica' (dissertation, Bonn, 1904).
     Thersites suggests the correlation of blaming and biting, and the relation of the canine and the Cynics with poetry of blame. See R.B. Branham, *Unruly Eloquence*, pp. 266–7. Cf. Lucian's *Demonax*, 61, on Thersites as a Cynic diatribist.
18. Aristotle, *Poetics*; Aristotle, *Eudemian Ethics*, 3.2; *Nicomachean Ethics*, 4. 7–9 on Old Comedy buffoons.
19. Cf. Zoja Pavlovskis, 'Aristotle, Horace, and the Ironic Man', *Classical Philology*, 63 (1968), 22–41.
20. Cf. Lane Cooper, *An Aristotelian Theory of Comedy* (Oxford, 1924), pp. 107–11, 121; Richard Janko, *Aristotle on Comedy* (Berkeley, 1984). Cf. Marvin T. Herrick, *Comic Theory in the Sixteenth Century* (Urbana, Illinois, 1950), on comic character types.
21. On Pandar's 'complimental assault' (III.i.40–1), cf. the Middle Templar Hoskyns' advice to a Temple student on 'compliment' as 'performance of affected ceremonies in words, looks, or gesture' (Hoskyns, *Speech and Style*,

fol. 89, p. 13). Cf. Manningham, *Diary*, fol. 39, April, 1602, p. 88: on 'a very complementall gentle[man]. A Barrester but noe lawyer'. 'Compliment' is a type of fustian in Marston's *Jack Drum's Entertainment* (III.209). Cf. 'complimental assault' (III.i.40–1), in *Troilus*' complimental-strewn scene and the Prince d'Amour's (1635–36) 'Edict against Retayling of Complements'. See also Hotson, *Shakespeare's Sonnets*, p. 242.

If *Troilus*' Armed Prologue includes a response to Jonson's *Poetaster*, the same Prologue's use of 'confidence / Of author's pen' (ll. 23–4) recalls 'confidence' in Jonson's own Armed Prologue to *Poetaster* (pp. 74–5).

Cf. 'elements' (*TC*, I.iii.41) also as a mocked word in Jonson, *Poetaster*, I.ii.35–6. As the Clown agrees, 'I might say "element", but the word is overworn' (*TN*, III.i.56–7). Malvolio remarks, 'I am not of your element' (*TN*, III.iv.123). Cf. Dekker's *Satiromastix*, 'out of my Element' (I.ii.187–8; cf. I.ii.134; V.ii.326), considered a Jonsonian verbal mannerism. As Jonson's Tucca (*Poetaster*) advises, 'Let the element alone, 'tis out a' thy reach'. On 'element' (*TC*, I.iii.41) as mocked term, cf. also A.H. Marckwardt, 'A Fashionable Expression: Its Status in *Poetaster* and *Satiromastix*', *Modern Language Notes*, 44 (1929), 93–6.

'Remuneration' is also among the mocked words. As Ulysses warns against seeking 'Remuneration for the thing it was' (III.iii.170), Nestor recalls the thing it was: cf. Erasmus' *senilis stultitia*, or 'dotage'.

Cf. Paris' 'propugnation' (II.ii.136) and W. Percy, *Cuckqueanes* (1601; ed. 1824, p. 13), indicative of burlesque: 'Propugnest thou mee? I will oppugne thee …'.

Cf. 'prenominate', IV.v.250, and 'nominate', *Poetaster*, V.iii.270; p. 238n.

Cf. *Troilus*' 'expostulation' (IV.iv.60) and Polonius' 'expostulate' with *Prince*'s (pp. 37–40) fustian tobacco-speech 'Expostulation'. Cf. *Hamlet* (II.ii.86); Polonius' pretentious 'expostulate' turns up in Troilus' love-*consolatio* (IV.iv.60): 'Nay,' he soothes Cressid, 'we must use expostulation kindly'.

Conscious of the peculiar status of certain words, and echoing the *Prince d'Amour*, the Middle Temple Hoskyns, c. 1600, stylistically advises a Temple student (*Speech and Style*, p. 7; cf. p. 60); 'You are not to cast a ring for the perfumed terms of the time, as *apprehensiveness, compliments, spirits, accommodate*, etc. …' As if to stress the burlesque nature of their uses, most of Hoskyns's 'perfumed terms' recur in *Troilus* (see Appendix I).

22. On the ironic encomium, cf. Adolf Hauffen, 'Zur Literatur der ironischen Enkomien', *Viertel Jahrschrift für Litt. geschichte*, 6 (1893); 161. Henry Knight Miller, 'The Paradoxical Encomium', *Modern Philology*, 53 (1956), 145–78, with a chronological list of paradoxical encomia; A.H. Tomarken, *The Smile of Truth: The French Satirical Elegy and its Antecedents* (Princeton, New Jersey, 1990).

23 Traditionally, the 'imperial vice' was ascribed to such as Julius Caesar; cf. Dante, *Purgatorio*, XXVI.76–8. Cressid threatens her own attribute with: 'Crack my clear [also *clarus*, famous] voice' (IV.ii.108). The 'voice-vice' equivoque recurs in Troilus' complaint on 'handling' Cressid (I.i.55–6).

24. Cf. J.S. Coolidge, 'Great Things and Small: The Virgilian Progression', *Comparative Literature*, 17 (1965), 1–23. Cf. Werner von Koppenfels, '*Parva componere magnis*: Vergil und die "mockheroische" Perspektive des Klassizismus in England', in Viktor Pöschl, ed., *2000 Jahre Vergil. Ein Symposion* (Wiesbaden, 1983), pp. 153–73.

25. While Troilus is said to be the pandar's first employer (*MAAN*, V.ii.31) – and

'baptizer' (cf. V.x.33–4) – the audience was aware that Pandar's name was already a common-noun byword, that name, even more than in Chaucer's time, recalling the flesh-trading profession. Hence, Pandar's professional impulses here peep through his degree-inflated 'lordship' (III.i.11–12). At the moment of love-declaration in III.ii, much of the audience already (cf. Shakespearean Troilus-allusions) knows Troilus' love-fate. So Pandar's name is comically recognizable in Shakespearean drama: for example 'Shall I Sir Pandarus of Troy become ...' (*MWW*, I.iii.75); 'I would play Lord Pandarus ...' (*TN*, III.i.51).

26. On Genius, cf. Donald Schuller, 'Gower's Characterization of Genius in *Confessio Amantis*', *Modern Language Quarterly*, 33 (1972), 240–56; D.N. Baker, 'The Priesthood of Genius: A Study of the Medieval Tradition', *Speculum*, 51 (1976), 277–91; E.C. Knowlton, 'Genius as an Allegorical Figure', *Modern Language Notes*, 39 (1924), 90.

27. *OED* marks this noun 'deem' usage obsolete, citing as pre-1629 only this passage. Dictionally, Cressid's archaic 'deem' (IV.iv.59) anticipates Ulysses' 'ken' (IV.v.14), as well as Troilus' 'wights' (IV.ii.12) and 'pight' (V.x.24).

28. *Troilus*' use of 'knees' (III.iii.48–9) and the 'proud man's fees' echoes Dekker's War of the Theatre's *Satiromastix* (*Stationers' Register* 11 November 1601; V.ii.38–40): '*Ter*. All pleasures guard my King, I heere present, / My oath vpon the knee of duety: knees / Are made for Kings, they are the subiects Fees'. The man in 'pride' thus took his 'fees'. The 'proud man's fees' suggests payment by gratification; cf. *Tit.A*., II.iii.179–80: 'So should I rob my sweet sons of their fee. / No, let them satisfice their lust on thee'.

29. Manningham's Middle Temple diary (fol. 70b, November 1602) recalls this 'wide-unclasping' woman-as-book image: 'One told him [a wenching gentleman] that his booke was a fayre volume, but it had but twoe leaves ... to open ...'.

30. Henry Fielding, *Tom Thumb and the Tragedy of Tragedies*, ed. L.J. Morrissey (Edinburgh, 1970), pp. 86, 119. There, in III.ii.46–53, the Ghost recites a familiar form for elaborate Homeric comparison:

> So have I seen the Bees in Clusters swarm,
> So have I seen the Stars in frosty Nights,
> So have I seen the Sand in windy Days,
> So have I seen the Ghosts on *Pluto's* Shore,
> So have I seen the Flowers in Spring arise,
> So have I seen the Fruits in Summer smile,
> So have I seen the Snow in Winter frown.

On burlesque simile, cf. G. Monaco, *Paragoni burleschi degli antichi* (Palermo, 1963); on comic uses of simile, cf. Quintilian 6.3.57–65; Aristotle, *Rhetoric*, 1406 b 20–1407 a 17.

31. Conventionally connecting 'pillar' and the law, cf. *MV*, IV.i.239, '... by the law, / Whereof you are a well-deserved pillar'; and the Middle Temple's Sharpham, *Cupids Whirligig*, II.i: 'the Lawyers are the pillars of the Realme'. Cf. Dekker, *Satiromastix*, IV.iii.186: 'law is one of the pillers ath land'. Like Cressid's 'strong base and building' (IV.ii.104) of her Troilus-love, Hector's 'base and pillar' as support of Troy proves defective.

32. Hector himself may, 'a little proudly', misprize the Achillean 'pride' of his partner in the encounter. 'In the extremity of great and little / Valour and pride excel themselves in Hector' (IV.v.78–9). Cf. Hector versus Achilles as an academic topos, a contrast between the Trojan and Greek heroes. Cf.

Aphthonius, *Progymnasmata* (Cambridge, 1631), pp. 244–5. Cf. *WT*, IV.iv.667.

33.   *1H4*, II.ii.41. See Harry Levin, 'Falstaff Uncolted', *Shakespeare and the Revolution of the Times* (New York, 1976), pp. 121–30.

34.   Cf. *H*, IV.vii.185–6. On the 'seria-ludicra', in addition to Curtius, *European Literature* (pp. 417–35), cf. Branham, *Unruly Eloquence*, on the *spoudogeloios*, pp. 26–8, 234 n. 79; and the serio-comic style, 26–8, 47–51, 56–7, 234 n. 79.

35.   NVS, p. 489. Cf. Wolfgang Zach, *Poetic Justice. Theorie und Geschichte ... Komödienkonzeption* (Tübingen, Germany, 1986).

36.   Troilus' cursing rejection of Pandar recalls a classical topos of invective against a procurer. Cf. Archibald A. Day, *The Origins of Latin Love-Elegy* (Hildesheim, Germany, 1972), pp. 124–5.

37.   Prologue of *The Nun's Preest's Tale*, ll. 3961–63. Cf. Milton, *UC*, 2.21: '*Ease* was his chief *disease*'. Cf. Thomas Kyd's *Spanish Tragedy*, ed. Philip Edwards (Cambridge, Massachusetts, 1959): 'O eyes no eyes, but fountains fraught with tears' (III.ii.i).

38.   Cf. D.C. Allen, *Image and Meaning* (Baltimore, Maryland, 1968), pp. 20–41. Cf. Pandar's bee 'subdued in arméd tail' (V.x.43) and the pun in *Gesta*, p. 17, 'in *Cauda*'.

39.   Cf. the Chaucerian aim to 'biwaille, in manere of tragedie, / The harm of hem that stoode in heigh degree, / And fillen so that ther nas no remedie / To brynge him out of hir adversitee ...' (*The Monk's Tale*, ll. 1991–4).

2.   Misrule, *mundus inversus* and degree

> ... about Christmas ... the King of Misrule, whom we invest with that
> title ... but to countenance the bacchanalian riots and preposterous disorders ...
> Thomas Urquhart, *The Jewel* (1652)

> E se tu vuoi che 'l ver non ti sia ascoso,
> tutta al contrario l'istoria converti:
> che i Greci rotti, e che Troia vittrice,
> e che Penelopea fu meretrice.
> Ariosto, *Orlando Furioso*, canto 35

This chapter concerns the play's misrule, 'degree', and world-upside-down
patterns, recalling inversions of the revels tradition.

Act I scene iii

Misrule

The play's King–General, old men, or betrayed husband or lover are (as in
charivari) flouted in their functions. Indeed, the work inverts traditional
notions of Homeric characters, as summarized by Puttenham: 'the
magnanimitie of *Agamemnon*, the prudence of *Menelaus*, the prowess of
Hector, the maiestie of King *Priamus*, the gravitie of *Nestor*, the pollicies
and eloquence of *Ulysses* ...' (*Poesie*, p. 4).

Displaced, the initially cuckold Menelaus-scorning Troilus (I.i.113–14)
ends as the deprived cuckold Menelaus commences. Characters support that
for which they seem least suited: the decrepit Nestor, for example, drops

childbirth images, and proclaims himself as lover (I.iii.291–301). The play treats 'things without honour':[1] a Pandar, bastards, cuckolders and cuckolds, and 'a jakes'. The dénouement, eluding poetic justice, is appropriate to a world-upside-down play, wherein law is stood on its head and injustice survives. For celebration of misrule (or 'preposterous discoveries', V.i.23), law revels' inversions would have provided a suitable occasion.

Misrule is reflected in the play from beginning to end. Following a Prologue which recommends hedonism as a guide to action ('do as your pleasures are', l. 30), the first scene shows a Pandar as a youth's love-counsellor. There, a suitor woos a Pandar for love-intercession. The second scene, moreover, exhibits a Pandar as supposed guardian of a young girl's reputation (cf. I.ii.263–4) – he is, in III.ii, a guarantor of her fidelity.

Act I's third scene opens with the indecorous Grecian King–General errantly orating to his world-upside-down court. Amidst this scene's reflections of Grecian disorder are Ulysses' report to their leaders of Patroclus' mimetic derision. Act II opens with the disorder of the Greeks that Ulysses' degree-speech had in the previous scene reproved. Here, Thersites is pummelled by Ajax, 'mind' beaten by brute body: stupidity misrules 'wit'. II.ii, among the Trojans, displays logic stood on its head, reason cast out, the defender of reason and law Hector qualifying the 'way of truth' (II.ii.189) and joining the party of unreason. II.iii exhibits the mock-exaltation of Ajakes. III.i presents a postlude of the legendary great lovers, Helen and Paris, with a bored Queen Helen seducing an effete Pandar to 'perform'. III.ii preposterously enacts a 'betrothal' officiated, not by a priest, but by a Pandar. V.ii exhibits private misrule: a young woman's displacing a man, with a Trojan prince's public dishonour by a Grecian rival.[2] V.vii and V.viii act out chivalric misrule: massed Myrmidons impaling the solitary Hector, himself (within II.ii) law's champion. In misrule's inversion of body and mind, body takes over, with its functions, appetites, and desires. Where 'reason [panders] will' (*H*, III.iv.88), Pandar is the inverted 'reason' of Troilus' will.

As in V.ii Troilus questions his perspective on 'reality' ('Will 'a swagger himself out on's own eyes?', demands Thersites, V.ii.136), the lover inverts a view of 'truth' – what is, to what is not, what is not, to what is. Love-troth, sworn to last forever, is momentary. Whirl is king – along with ineffectuality, fickleness, folly.

Entering, Troilus is first shown as disordered, calling 'again' for his armour-removal (I.i.1). So also Pandar's name itself suggests the 'disordered' (*OED*, s.v. †2), with the latter term's Renaissance sense of 'morally irregular … unruly, riotous' (*OED*; disordinate, *obs*.). The work moves from disorders of love and misrule to Pandar's final promised bequest of disorders ('And at that time bequeath you my diseases') – his reference to diseases (or disorders) is the play's last word (V.x.55).

As the play revalues value, it instantiates itself as disorderly revels genre, with Lord Pandarus of Licia, among others, as ill-timed Misrule.[3]

Dependencies

> Troy in our weakness stands
> I.iii.137

Priam's 'crutch' (V.iii.60), on which he depends – the *volte-face* Hector (II.ii.end) – suggests 'slippery standers' (III.iii.84) and other shaky dependencies. Such dubious reliances include those upon King–General Agamemnon, or on king's counsellor Ulysses; Troilus' reliance upon Pandar, as surety of Cressid's fidelity, and on Cressid herself; and Hector's dependence on Achilles' supposed reciprocal chivalry (V.viii). As Cressid depends on Lord Pandar (I.ii.263–4), in contrast, 'depending' upon *the* Lord (III.i.5) is the Servant. Because a young girl, after a 'knot' tied by her panderly uncle, is seen dallying with another, Troilus concludes, 'The bonds of heaven are slipped, dissolved and loosed' (V.ii.156).

From a rational viewpoint, if Agamemnon and Nestor (in I.iii) reflect the condition of rule, 'the state totters' (*T*, III.ii.7). In value terms, what happens to a polity when, its basis shakily indecorous, fools in a questionable chain are shown at the top? By a reverse selective process, these could also comprise a chain of the *un*fittest.

Rhetoric of misrule

King–General Agamemnon's 'matter needless, of importless burden' (I.iii.71) sets a self-reflexive, rhetorically burlesque tone. Such also is the monarch's allowance to speak, granted to the 'Prince of Ithaca', Ulysses, by the equivocal 'nerve and bone of Greece' (I.iii.55).[4] This permission exemplifies a royal proclivity to self-tripping compliment (cf. IV.v.163–71, the King's maladroit welcome to Hector). His royal permission to his counsellor confusedly adds: 'and be't of less expect / That matter needless, of importless burden, / Divide thy lips than', his twisted 'compliment' continues, 'we are confident, / When rank Thersites opes his mastic jaws, / We shall hear music, wit and oracle' (I.iii.69–74).

The King–General's opening oration (I.iii.1–30) is defeated by its errant redundancy and by instances contrary to his purpose. Instead of calling his forces to order, he exemplifies by rhetorical 'knots' his own 'tortive' impulse, itself 'bias and thwart, not answering the aim' (I.iii.15). Such 'tortive' misresponse to 'the aim' recurs in Ulysses' speech-opening on degree, in Nestor, as well as elsewhere (e.g. II.ii.8–17) in Hector's initial response.

King Agamemnon inverts traditional patterns of authority, of *regnum* and *sacerdotium*. Recalling 'this dotage of our general's' (*AC*, I.i.1), the King-'general' is, in syllogistic terms, the dubious major premise whence faulty conclusions are drawn. As Jonson's Cynthia observes: 'Princes, that would their people should doe well, / Must at themselues begin, as at the head'. This leads 'men, by their example', to 'patterne out / Their imitations, and regard of lawes'. Yet, if 'A Vertuous Court a world to vertue drawes' (*Cynthia's Revels*, V.vi.169–73), Agamemnon's disposition draws his world to folly. Agamemnon is 'generally' whence error and misrule flow, while the General's state could be said to resemble 'a botchy core' (II.i.6). The Greeks in general censure take corruption from that particular fault – the General, as they 'with one voice / Call Agamemnon head and general' (I.iii.221–2).

In its misrule, the play evokes antimasque, with the latter's 'preposterous discoveries' (V.i.23).[5] As in Jonsonian antimasque,[6] the world of *Troilus* is one of appetites and inverted values.

> 'Do you know a man if you see him?' (I.ii.63)

Peculiar misrecognitions recur; for example, the ambassador Aeneas' inability to recognize the Greek king, after seven years' conflict, in a question which undercuts itself: 'How may / A stranger to those most imperial looks / Know them from eyes of other mortals?' (I.iii.223–5); 'those most imperial looks' should be themselves self-evidently recognizable.

Ironically, just after Ulysses' defence of degree and 'authentic place' (I.iii.108), Aeneas professes his inability to distinguish 'that god in office', the exalted Grecian king (I.iii.223–5, 231–2). In question are thus the identity of the King in his 'office', or the ambassador Aeneas' perception, or both. By similar contradiction, Pandar cannot at first distinguish his idol, Troilus (I.ii.228–9); or discern the 'mortal Venus', Helen (III.i.33). While, in the masque, the ruler was eminently and focally seated among the spectators, his misidentification (I.iii.263–5) here casts doubt on royal authority or identifying spectator, or both. Whereas in the hierarchic code the masque shows the monarch as supreme figure, here King Agamemnon in his 'godlike seat' (I.iii.31) is mock-exemplar, saluted equivocally (I.iii.55), and his 'works' called 'shames' (I.iii.18–19). Antithetical to royal concord,[7] the play's discords include humours and appetites warring against order and degree.[8]

Masks of rank

> 'truthes' complexion, where they all weare maskes'
> Jonson, *Works*, VIII.118

Addressed to the indecorous King Agamemnon and his court, the trickster-*eiron* Ulysses' degree defence suggests a rank encomium within a degree-inverting setting. 'Degree being vizarded, / Th'unworthiest shows as fairly in the mask' (I.iii.83–4).[9] Degree thus suggests a device of visible discrimination, upon which status-recognition depends. Yet, if degree is a perceptible criterion of value, recognition by externals is itself recurrently mistaken.[10] Nestor himself notes the distinction between 'valour's show and valour's worth' (I.iii.46). Further, exteriors of rank may conceal 'a botchy core' (II.i.6): as 'goodly armour' 'so fair without' conceals a 'putrified core' (V.viii.1–2); and as external allure, such as Helen's, is said to conceal a 'contaminated carrion weight' (IV.i.73; cf. *H*, IV.iv.27–9). Within his shining armour, Hector's sumptuously clad Greek 'war-man is dead and rotten' (*LLL*, v.ii.660). Indeed, for the 'bauble' Helen the Trojan War is fought, for a piece of alluring 'show'.

While recognized in Lear's countenance is 'authority' (*KL*, I.iv.30), *Troilus*' misrecognitions subvert authority and 'authentic place' themselves. If 'What have kings that privates have not too, / Save ceremony'? (*H5*, IV.v.238–9), the 'ceremony that to great ones longs' (*MM*, II.ii.59) seems here insufficient for recognition. Theatrically, as in 'show' versus 'that within' (*H*, I.ii.85), *Troilus* probes a dialectic of 'outward' and 'inward'.

Ulysses' degree speech may be heard in the inverted context of misrule, while defending rule – or misgovernance masked as Good Governance. Further, the occasion may be one, as Thersites implies, suggesting its own inverted hierarchy (II.iii.61–4), with the most foolish at the top. Social structure may be critically inspected in either direction: from the bottom up, as in the knavish Thersites' dog's-view, or from the top down, as in Agamemnon's royal-fool's view.

Ulysses' degree defence appears multiple-edged. On the one hand, vizards conceal worth. Yet on the other, such vizards may also mask unworthiness – masking the unworthy from being judged so: 'Th' unworthiest shows as fairly in the mask' (I.iii.84). Ulysses' argument, as it cuts at opponents of 'authentic place', thus cuts as well as at those who depend on vizarded degree to mask unworthiness. If retention of vizards conceals those who may thus be masked fools, all may be, indistinguishably, 'Fools on both sides!' (I.i.92).

Ulysses' speech – in the play's world-upside-down pattern – may intimate also that such 'degree' allows questionable figures to 'stand in authentic place' (I.iii.108), that it props up what may otherwise be shaky. If one 'by degree stand[s] in authentic place' (I.iii.108), what validates such degree and such 'place'? Who, indeed, 'stand[s] in authentic place'? King–General Agamemnon? Nestor? Ajax, who for unflattering privy reasons 'stands alone' (I.ii.16)? Reassurances to Ajax (himself composed of inauthentic borrowings, I.ii.19–29) of his 'authentic place' are subverted not only by mock-encomia (II.iii), but also by his equivocal name: ''tis this naming of him does him harm' (II.iii.225).

The play's opening two scenes exploit comparisons, internally and externally: Troilus vying with Pandar to praise Cressid; Cressid compared with the absent Helen; Troilus compared with Hector, and Pandar inflating

Troilus, while Cressid deflates him. The second scene further concerns relations: Ajax, standing alone, is internally and relationally questionable, his parts borrowed from others and dysfunctional (I.ii.19–30). The third scene brings 'comparative' and 'relational' together in the speech on 'degree', or the social interconnections of value and rank.

Rhetorically, insofar as Ulysses' speech espouses degree-order, an argument about degree could itself 'by degree, stand in authentic place' (I.iii.108). Insofar as it is 'about' itself, its own syntax and order, the degree speech recalls the play's *mise en abyme* or reflexive nest-of-boxes pattern: a series of involuted containers analogous to the 'degrees' or 'grees' of ranged spectators (especially if, as at a law revel, hierarchically seated by degree).[11]

Degree-speech rhetoric: Ulysses and Canterbury

Ulysses in his degree speech recalls other Shakespearean apologists for rank or degree (for example Canterbury, Rosencrantz, Menenius). While ostensibly for the public weal, their rhetoric comprises apologies for 'order', masking power or the *status quo*.[12]

Citing a 'rule in nature' teaching 'The act of order' (*H5*, I.ii.188–9), the Archbishop of Canterbury urges Henry V's decision to take arms against France. Like Canterbury, Ulysses instances cosmic and earthly correspondences as a 'rule in nature' teaching order. Nevertheless, both royal counsellors undermine the absolute principles they proclaim: the Archbishop by self-interested war-advice; Ulysses by degree-subversion (for example at I.iii.366–85) and incitement (for example at III.iii.145–90) to emulation.

While Canterbury's and Ulysses' lengthy orations concerning order are in respects similar, they differ in coherence and construction. Both Canterbury and Ulysses, each not above suspicion, in a crisis address a monarch; each provides 'paraenesis', or counsel;[13] each employs 'bee' analogies (exemplary of social order from Virgil to Elyot); and each aims to advise his royal auditor of a course of action.

Despite these similarities, however, the Canterbury oration (*H5*, I.ii.183–220) moves by relatively smooth transitions and logical progressions: for example, his initial 'Therefore' (l. 183) seems directly functional, in contrast to Ulysses' abrupt 'And therefore' (*TC*, I.iii.89). Canterbury's 'for' (in l. 187) introduces evenly the bees' analogy, followed by descriptions (ll. 187–204) of their social order, with 'Which' (l. 195), 'who' (l. 197), and 'their' (l. 200) lucidly progressing. The Archbishop's conclusion ('Therefore', l. 213), while setting forth alternatives to direct action, emerges clearly from his analogical argument. Contrasting with Canterbury's oration, however, Ulysses' degree-speech opening raises suspicion of a less than perfect coherence.

Rhetoric of disorder

> And not by old gradation, where each second
> Stood heir to th' first ...
>
>   *Othello*, I.i.37–8

In the scholastic tradition of the ranking of creation, order or arrangement was a form of rational value.[14] If, according to Quintilian (I.10.34–49; Loeb ed., I, 1969), order or logical presentation is as requisite to rhetoric as to geometry, Ulysses' opening lacks something of that requirement. Rhetorically, Ulysses' degree speech subverts its own topics: *ordo* or arrangement, *collocatio*, and *dispositio*. Though Ulysses' oration espouses 'proportion', '... in all line of order' (I.iii.87–8), parts of his own speech seem, in contrast, disordered. Deploring chaos, Ulysses yet appears, by imitative form, to reflect it: in the peculiar, disconnected 'order' of his degree-speech opening, as well as elsewhere (e.g. I.iii.357–85) in the questionable effects of his plot. Through such intimations of disorder, Ulysses recalls the digressive orations of his king and the latter's ancient counsellor.[15]

Commencing, Ulysses announces, 'Troy ... [would have been] down / ... / But for these [to be particularized] instances' (I.iii.75–7). Yet Ulysses' own 'ample proposition' may itself 'come short' (I.iii.3, 11); for following these promised and expected *causal* 'instances' for Grecian victory-delay is his diagnosis of neglect of 'specialty of rule' (I.iii.78). That, in turn, is succeeded by the *effects*, or results, not causes: 'And look how many Grecian tents do stand / Hollow upon this plain, so many hollow factions' (I.iii.79–80). The 'hollow' Grecian tents are more a symptomatic *consequence* of neglected 'specialty of rule' than the promised *causal* instance 'But for' which Troy 'had been down'.[16] Following the dangling 'And look ...' is Ulysses' reflection on the General as unlike the hive, with its consequent absence of honey-expectation. Before the listener can absorb the bee-honey relevance, he is rushed into another *sententia*: 'Degree being vizarded' makes the unworthy and the worthy indistinguishable (I.iii.83–4).

In a speech ostensibly espousing order, items of unclear or disordered significance, lacking adequate transitions, are thus rapidly brought up and passed over. As his King–General's oration (I.iii.1–30) seems a disordered call to order, Ulysses' speech affirming order may itself be suspected of something less. Indeed, Ulysses' curiously inconsequential 'And' (I.iii.79), followed from '... but for these instances: / ... / *And* look how many Grecian tents do stand ...' (I.iii.77–9) anticipates Hector's anomalous contradictory 'And': 'Paris and Troilus, you have both said well, / *And* on the cause and question now in hand / Have glozed – but superficially' (II.ii.163–5).

Structurally, Ulysses' order-espousing degree speech alternates between positive and negative elements. Preceding 'stands in authentic place'

Structure of "degree" speech

(I.iii.108) are negative illustrations, as when the planets wander 'In evil mixture' (I.iii.94–5). Before that is a positive statement on the Sun and its medicinable eye, and the analogy of the heavens with regard to order (I.iii.89–94). Preceding such comparison is a negative instance of the disordered hive: the general as unlike the hive, and the tents as hollow factions (I.iii.79–83). Yet this curiously alternating sequence, these inverted or abrupt juxtapositions, form a speech purportedly in praise of order. Insofar as syntax and verbal order are modes of standing 'in authentic place', Ulysses' sequence (following Agamemnon's and Nestor's) suggests that, as the Trojan council (II.ii) inverts logic, the Greek council (I.iii) subverts rhetoric.[17]

The disordered hive

Wandering from his promised citation of victory-delay *causes*, Ulysses' diagnosis elicits from the doting Nestor a dubious endorsement. 'Most wisely hath Ulysses here discovered / The fever whereof all our power is sick' (I.iii.138–9). As encomia from the dotard Nestor seem suspect, his 'most wisely' may also suggest something less.

'When that the general is not like the hive' (I.iii.81)[18] is, moreover, a curiously inverted construction to follow the charge of the army's neglect of 'specialty of rule' (I.iii.78). By Ulysses' earlier diagnosis, the disordered hive would be singled out, rather than the General. Further, the General, to whom Ulysses' speech is on stage directed, is General Agamemnon – to remark pointedly, to his face, on the 'General' as being deviant ('not like the hive') could constitute an indecorous breach. (But the latter would be no worse than that in which Ulysses salutes his monarch as, equivocally, 'nerve and bone of Greece', I.iii.55.) Yet Ulysses' anomalous correlation of General and hive, observed by eighteenth-century editors,[19] itself echoes an inversion-pattern recurrent in the play. That pattern comprises rhetoric and logic, to be discussed in later chapters. Such patterns of inversion would have suited a festive occasion of '*mundus inversus*' misrule.

After brief apiary-allusion (I.iii.81–3), unlike Canterbury's developed bee-analogy (*H5*, I.ii.187–204), Ulysses' hive image is dropped as suddenly as it is introduced. Abandoning both tents and bees, Ulysses (I.iii.83–4) diverges and reverts to a sententia parallel to his earlier (I.iii.78) 'specialty of rule hath been neglected'.[20] Ulysses' *degradatio* continues with wearying explicitness: 'The general's disdained / By him one step below, he by the next, / That next by him beneath ...' (I.iii.129–31). Not satisfied with this downward iteration, the speaker particularizes further: 'so every step, / Exampled by the first pace that is sick / Of his superior ...' (I.iii.131–3).

Contradictorily, moreover, the degree-speech opening, 'Troy, yet upon *his* basis' (I.iii.75), becomes twice at its conclusion '*her*': 'Troy ... *her* own sinews ... *her* strength' (I.iii.136–7). As he closes in such pronominal contradictions to his opening, Ulysses, having in the same speech condemned 'Strength' as 'lord of imbecility' (I.iii.114), concludes (I.iii.136–7) on a strength–weakness recognition.[21]

In sum: Ulysses' degree-speech opening deviates from his initially promised 'instances' (I.iii.77) of *causes* for victory-delay. Instead, he divergently at length catalogues *effects*, symptoms, as well as generalities (I.iii.78–126). Against its usual out-of-context interpretation, the degree speech may more appropriately be grasped in terms of what has been seen, and is to be seen, of such 'degree'. Set within a sequence of rhetorically disordered speeches (as of Agamemnon, Nestor, Priam and Hector), the degree speech's opening and close rehearse the play's upside-down pattern. Like others in the work, Ulysses' utterance subverts its apparent direction: it is 'Tortive and errant from his course of growth ... / Bias and thwart, not answering the aim' (I.iii.9, 15). Ulysses' oration thus suggests grounds to question it as unqualified endorsement of orthodox degree-doctrine.

Ulysses' pattern of rhetorical digression is dramatically evident elsewhere: as in Agamemnon's opening address (I.iii.1–30), with its aberrancies and commonplaces; and in Nestor's deviant response, aiming, with clichéd generalities, to 'apply / Thy latest words' (I.iii.32–3). Analogous is Hector's misresponse to King Priam regarding Helen's return: Hector's initial ten lines (II.ii.8–17) wander from Priam's opening question. So, in reply to his own king's demand concerning the Grecian 'fever' – 'The nature of the sickness found, Ulysses, / What is the remedy'? (I.iii.140–1) – Ulysses diverges at length (I.iii.142–84) from the issue of 'remedy'. Instead, he relays, in extensive detail, to King Agamemnon himself, degree-subversive slanders of his monarch. Hence, rather than supplying a Grecian 'remedy', Ulysses himself contributes to the Grecian 'fever' (I.iii.135). Such instances as those cited above would be appropriate to a world-upside-down occasion of rhetorical and related misrule.

Act II scene iii

Degree of folly

If identity is discernible, it is here part of a chain of folly. Before the fools' Identity Game (II.iii.42–67), Thersites has already dismissed Achilles as an ignorant fool, and Patroclus as a 'gilt counterfeit' (II.iii.24). Responding to Achilles' 'what's Agamemnon'? with 'Thy commander, Achilles', Thersites next addresses Achilles' minion: 'then tell me, Patroclus, what's Achilles?' (II.iii.44). Mocking Agamemnon may be well and good, but the General ranks higher than Achilles, and Achilles is supposed to serve *him*. From your own male-varlet's perspective,

Thersites implies to Patroclus, can you identify Achilles? Achilles' minion responds, 'Thy lord, Thersites' (II.iii.46) – whoever Achilles may be, he is better than, and can command, such a thing as Thersites. In turn, Patroclus questions Thersites: 'then tell me, I pray thee, what's thyself?' (II.iii.46–7). Identity, degree-order and valuation of the evaluator are among the play's central issues here in question, as much as those of the object valued. Thersites' reply is apt: 'Thy knower, Patroclus' (II.iii.48). Whatever his own value-status, the demotic railer exists to put the minion down by knowing his abject lack of value.

In a judgment-by-parody of the 'degree' principle, Thersites surveys the links that bind order: 'Agamemnon is a fool to offer to command Achilles; Achilles is a fool to be commanded of Agamemnon; Thersites is a fool to serve such a fool; and Patroclus is a fool positive' (II.iii.61–4). Rather than unalterably sacred, 'degree' may also be relative to the viewer and the position from which it is viewed.

While Thersites 'knows' the folly of such hierarchy, he is also, in his deformed knavish folly, himself known. As Patroclus' knower, Thersites demands, 'what art thou?' Against Thersites' scorn for the minion's 'preposterous' function (cf. V.i.23), Patroclus challengingly inverts the question: 'Thou mayst tell that knowest' (II.iii.50). At the war-declining Achilles' urging, 'O tell, tell', Thersites, parodically mirroring him, recites, 'I'll decline the whole question' (II.iii.51–2). Using 'decline' also in its grammatical sense, Thersites perversely first 'declines' the whole matter; then runs, mock-academically, in another sense, through a paradigm chain-recital of various noun forms: 'Agamemnon commands Achilles; Achilles is my lord; I am Patroclus' knower and Patroclus is a fool' (II.iii.52–4). In this reductive chain-summary is invertedly implied much of the dramatic fools' probing: relation of rank or degree to value; or relation of knowledge to the object of knowledge. If the inevitable cause of Patroclus' folly is not Thersites, but that of the 'Creator' (F, II.iii.66), the hierarchy of fools exists. Thersites thus intimates an upside-down cosmos, with the power above as arch-progenitor of folly.

Parodically, II.iii revives the identity questions of I.i and I.ii ('to know a man'). 'What Cressid is, what Pandar, and what we?' (I.i.101), demanded of a god (Apollo), becomes in II.iii a question of the identity of the King–General, demanded of a rogue. As both Achilles and Patroclus put such questions to Thersites, to be demanded by an 'idol of idiot-worshippers' (V.i.7) and his 'male varlet' (V.i.15, 16), what replication should be made by the 'son of a whore' (V.vii.21)?

Identity may also be perceptible by degree-position – ironically, in a climbing ladder (cf. I.iii.102, 128–9) of fools. (If 'degree ... is the ladder of all high designs' (I.iii.101–2), such a 'ladder of ... high designs' suggests rather the social-climbing Malvolio than settled 'authentic place' (I.iii.108).) By a mocking decorum, Achilles in this link starts with the

King–General: 'what's Agamemnon?' (II.ii.43). Relationally, Achilles can be identified as commandable by such a one as Achilles' commander (cf. 'thyself upon thyself', II.iii.26). Reversing Ulysses' hierarchy of degree, the lowly Thersites demands, of the one below, the identity of the one above. Invertedly querying the links of the chain, he exposes its perversity: running up and down the chain, he knavishly suggests (with 'privileged' licence) degree-relations as interdependently foolish.

As Ulysses and other Greek leaders praise the unrelationally disposed Ajax (I.ii.16), folly itself eulogizes – indeed, validates – folly. Like folly, '... pride is his own glass' (II.iii.154): the folly of pride is the pride of folly. Hence, when Patroclus and Achilles are reported to make fools of the Greek command (I.iii.142–96), fools (Erasmus- and Jonson-like) comment on other fools – and still another fool reports them to their foolish victims. As Thersites diagnoses a hierarchy of fools, he is ironically himself an arch fool (II.iii.63). In a world of folly and knavery, it is the despised bastardly butt from below who knavishly perceives and foolishly names hierarchy's fools' chain – and paradoxically survives.

Having (in II.i.2–9) slandered the General, Thersites is ironically faced (in III.iii.262) with Ajax having taken *him* for the General. Only 'a very landfish, languageless, a monster' (III.iii.262–3) could commit that offensive mistake: Thersites' insult cuts both ways, at the mistaker and the mistake (what the railer is taken for). Hoist with his defamatory petard, the roguish Thersites is thus made part of his own identification chain.

At a mention of 'fool' (II.iii.65), as if on cue, King–General Agamemnon enters in a pageant of folly. Having depicted the Greek leaders as fools, Thersites turns to point their entrance. Perceiving them, Achilles stalks off stage, bidding Thersites 'Come in with me' (II.iii.68–9). Like Lear (*KL*, I.iv.315–16), he would 'take the Fool with' him.

Glorious Ajax: precedence of folly

Although King–General Agamemnon with his royal 'appertainments' (II.iii.79) indecorously goes *to* Achilles, Ulysses objects that Ajax 'Must not so stale [soil] his palm ... / By going *to* Achilles' (II.iii.189–92). (Regarding 'stale', Harington's *Metamorphosis of Ajax* (1596) was punningly titled *A New Discourse of a Stale Subject*.)

In the same scene occurs a mock-heroic question of precedence (II.iii.200–2): between two 'prides', whether the intractable 'bulk Achilles' (IV.iv.128) – 'an engine / Not portable' (II.iii.133–4) – is to be brought to Ajakes, or the 'tractable' commode Ajakes is to be brought to Achilles. Against his king's 'Let Ajax go to *him* [Achilles]', Ulysses' mock-encomium of Ajax concludes: 'Jupiter forbid, / And say in thunder "Achilles go to him"', that is, Ajax (II.iii.176, 196–7). Aptly, 'By him that thunders' (IV.v.136; cf. l. 137), the necessary convenience Ajax and his appendages

Scutagium!

are praised. Who should go to whom is an issue of degree-status in parodic (academic, legal, social) precedence.

Indeed, Ajax, in his convenience aspect, had near the time of the play's performance been considered as 'idol': Marston's recently built Inns of Court convenience, the 'glorious Ajax of Lincolnes Inn' as adored by the 'Idolatrous vulgar', which, Marston observes, 'worship Images' (*What You Will*, III.i; *Plays*, II.260).

If Ajax will not 'go to' Achilles, Achilles, correlating precedence not with rank, but with natural necessity, must 'go to' Ajax (II.iii.197). As Hector reportedly (I.ii.33–5) succumbed to Ajax, Achilles will thus be led a little from himself at the behest of the necessary Ajax. The play contains not only an indecorous royal visit to Achilles, but also a mock-exercise in ambassadorial manners: 'go[ing] *to*' Ajakes (II.iii.197). The necessary Ajax (and theatrical need of such conveniences) suggest an unsettled audience, among which (III.iii.132–3) 'some men do, while some men leave to do'.

Previously reported (I.iii.142–84), *lèse majesté* or *scandalum magnatum* (offence to king or nobles) is now (with festive impunity) acted out. As Ulysses conveys, to Agamemnon and Nestor, Achilles' and Patroclus' mimicry of them (I.iii.142–84), Patroclus devalues the leaders with Achilles' relayed response – to the King–General and his retinue, the Greek hero is snubbingly not 'at home' (II.iii.106–11). Once again, the play exhibits comically discourteous courtesy. For Achilles' transmitted reply suggests that the King–General and his courtiers have not travelled to a subject but to relax their stomachs (II.iii.109–11). Achilles' irreverent answer thus transforms the monarch's embassy into a trivial purpose: 'how unworthy a thing you make of me!' (*H*, III.iii.354–5). The 'precedence debate' is parodic of degree (for example the mock-epic question whether Achilles is to go to Ajakes, or Ajakes to Achilles (II.iii.133–7). Insofar as the Greek royal court and Achilles are concerned, violating decorum, King–General Agamemnon and retinue go *to* Achilles (II.iii.75–140).

King and rogue: degree as folly's chain

Thersites demands, 'What think you of this man, that takes me for the general?' (III.iii.261–2). The rogue is insulted to be mistaken for the General: as he would not care to be the lowest in creation, 'so I were not Menelaus', the General's cuckold brother (V.i.59–64).

Inversion of hierarchy, anticipated in Thersites' ladder of fools (II.iii.61–4), recalls other confusedly perceived identities (e.g. I.iii.223–5). Mistaken for the exalted Agamemnon by Ajax (III.iii.262–3), Thersites himself parodies the role of Ajax (III.iii.269–98). If the pre-eminent King–General can be mistaken for the low bastard-rogue (III.iii.260–2), where is degree?

'Commands' (II.iii.53) and 'depend' (III.i.4, 5, 6) invertedly rehearse the play's degree articulations. Insofar as they do, they help probe order connections via a fool's 'privilege' (cf. II.iii.57). In Thersites' catechism (II.iii.42–67), Agamemnon is identified relationally, as in parody of essential definition (cf. I.i.101) and degree. The relation of Agamemnon as commander of Achilles is enough to impugn both parties, implying a judgment on both, as well as on degree-order itself. Not only cannot Agamemnon command; Achilles, the recalcitrant, cannot be commanded.

To repeat Thersites' summary another way: Having defined himself as Patroclus' 'knower', Thersites inquires, 'then tell me, Patroclus, what art thou?' (II.ii.48–9). Thersites implies that Patroclus is, in value and status, low – a fool. I am better because I know that he is – while I can know him, he, as fool, lacks self-knowledge: 'Ay, but that fool knows not himself' (II.i.65). In identifying himself as Patroclus' knower, Thersites implies that such a slight task of recognizing folly is sufficient: Patroclus in his insignificance would have 'slipped out of' Thersites' 'contemplation' (II.iii.25–6).

Perceived from below, as by Thersites, in degree-inverted mirrorings, is identity dependence, the chain of fools from Agamemnon down. Displacing the King, traditional source of honours, is Thersites, fountainhead of dishonours. Though the monarch traditionally has the coining monopoly (cf. *KL*, IV.vi.83), here it is Thersites, parodic of royal prerogative, a 'slave whose gall coins slanders like a mint' (I.iii.193).

Facing the visibly demotic Thersites, Prince Hector imperceptively demands, 'Art thou for Hector's match? / Art thou of blood and honour?' (V.iv.25–6). This pattern of comic misrecognition recurs not only in Hector, but also in Aeneas' insulting incapacity to distinguish the high and mighty King–General Agamemnon (I.iii.223–5); and in Aeneas' and Hector's insulting inability to distinguish the Greek hero, Achilles. Thus, '*Aeneas*. If not Achilles, sir, / What is your name? *Achilles*. If not Achilles, nothing'. Whence Aeneas' triumphant parodic-logic deduction: 'Therefore Achilles' (IV.v.75–7). So Hector demands of the celebrated Grecian warrior, 'Is this Achilles?' (IV.v.233). Further, Thersites' identity is confused by one of whom Thersites had himself unmistakenly declared: 'Whosoever you take him to be, he is Ajax' (II.i.62–3).

The fools' chain of identification (II.iii) thus appears ironically analogous to the chain of degree (I.iii). Indeed, it seems its parodic mirror. For, if eminences are known socially by rank, so are fools – considering degree also as a fools' ladder. The permutative links of Agamemnon, Achilles, Patroclus and Thersites, as well as the questioner, the subject of his question, and the person questioned, contribute their relational ironies.

Of note, moreover, is the choice of personages for this configurational inquiry: the commander of the Greeks, indecorously a fool; the hero of the Greeks, the unparticipating Achilles, and his minion; and the snarling deformed intellect who 'knows' them all. (Thersites literally becomes ironically what he is: the anti-fool as Fool – the perspective of deempathized, deformed mind.) If Grecian folly includes dependence on Agamemnon, Troilus among the Trojans is a fool to depend on Pandar and on Cressid, as is Hector to depend on Achilles and his chivalry. Each level (as in Erasmus' *Encomium Moriae*) contributes its share to this 'Fooles play' (Q, F; V.iii.43) of 'preposterous discoveries' (V.i.23).

'Most mighty for' his 'place' (I.iii.60), the King warns lest Achilles think 'We dare not move the question of our place' (II.iii.81). Officiously, the monarch recalls the clownish Dogberry's 'Dost thou not suspect my place?' (*MAAN*, IV.ii.74). The question of 'place' is, indeed, a question of the play (cf. I.iii.108): it is still more ironical as asserted by the King–General, presumed head of 'place'. He adds, with grandiose anticlimax, 'Or know not what we are' (II.iii.82). Such obtuse vanity the King earlier exhibits against the ambassador Aeneas' mis-identification (I.iii.223–56). What the exalted King–General Agamemnon is, the audience may indeed recall – Ulysses' 'nerve and bone of Greece' (I.iii.55), asserting his supreme priority (II.iii.61–4) in a hierarchy of folly.

To summarize, this chapter has traced the play's misrule manifestations, including degree disorders and folly. Such recurrent expressions would have suited such a rank-subversive, world-upside-down occasion as an Inns of Court revel.

Notes

1. Cf. A.S. Pease, 'Things without Honor', *Classical Philology*, 21 (1926), 27–42; Henry Knight Miller, 'The Paradoxical Encomium with Special Reference to its Vogue in England 1600–1800', *Modern Philology*, 53 (1956), 145–78. Theodore C. Burgess, *Epideictic Literature* (Chicago, 1902).

2. On woman's *maistrie* as inversion, see Natalie Z. Davis, *Society*, pp. 124–51, 310–15.

3. Breakdown of 'specialty of rule' (I.iii.78) suggests *misrule* (*OED* 2), 'a state of disorder, anarchy, or rebellion'. On misrule and festivity, see Natalie Z. Davis, 'The Reasons of Misrule', *Society*, pp. 97–123, 296–309. Cf. misrule (*OED* 3), *Lord of Misrule*: 'one chosen to preside over the Christmas game and revels in a great man's house'. As the Master of Misrule presides over a state involving breakdown of 'rule', he recalls (*OED*, s.v.), *Misrule*: 'Disorderly conduct or living; misconduct; ill conducted or irregular life'. Hence, misrule comprises private licence, as well as public disorder and abrogation of 'specialty of rule' (I.iii.78).

    On Misrule as a disorder figure in an academic revel, see, for example, John Mason (of Cambridge), *Princeps Rhetoricus* (1648). Insofar as *Troilus* evokes a 'sermon of Misrule', cf. the tradition of English *sermons joyeux*, or burlesque sermons; Malcolm Jones, 'The Parodic Sermon in Medieval and Early Modern England', *Medium Aevum*, 66 (1997), 92–114. Cf. Affinati D'Acuto, *Il Mondo al roverscio* (Venice, 1602); Giacomo Giuseppe Cocchiara, *Il mondo alla rovescia* (Torino, 1963). Ian Donaldson, *The World Upside-Down. Comedy from Jonson to Fielding* (Oxford, 1970); François Laroque,

'La Notion de "Misrule" à l'époque élisabéthaine ...' in Jean Lafond et al., eds, *L'Image du Monde Renversé* ... (Paris, 1979), pp. 161–70; Christopher Hill, *The World Turned Upside Down* (Harmondsworth, England, 1985); Michael Bristol, *Carnival and Theater* (New York, 1985); Barbara Babcock, ed., *The Reversible World: Symbolic Inversion in Art and Society* (Ithaca, New York, 1978); Peter Burke, *Popular Culture in Early Modern Europe* (1978); Anthony Fletcher and John Stevenson, *Order and Disorder in Early Modern England* (Cambridge, England, 1985); Natalie Z. Davis, 'The Reasons of Misrule: Youth Groups and Charivaris in Sixteenth Century France', *Past and Present*, no. 50 (1971), 41–75; Peter Stallybrass, 'The World Turned Upside Down: Inversion, Gender and the State' in Valerie Wayne, ed., *The Matter of Difference* (New York, 1991), pp. 201–20.

4.   Cf. Ulysses' equivocal 'nerve and bone' (i.e., Agamemnon, I.iii.55); 'sinew' (Achilles, I.iii.143); and 'base and pillar' (Hector, IV.v.212). On pillar, cf. Williams, *Dictionary*, s.v.

5.   See, on the preposterous, Patricia Parker, 'Preposterous Events', *Shakespeare Quarterly*, 43 (1992), 186–213.

6.   Cf. Jonson's *Vision of Delight* (1617); and Jonson's *Hymenaei* (1606), l. 116, in which dancers, drawing swords, 'disturbe the Ceremonies'.

7.   Cf. H.N. Paul, *The Royal Play of 'Macbeth'* (New York, 1950), pp. 354–66.

8.   In *Troilus*, as in the law-revels-produced *Comedy of Errors* and *Twelfth Night*, an appropriate initial question is, 'Who governs here?' (*TN*, I.ii.24). Cf. also *The Comedy of Errors*, which contains its own 'degree' speech (II.i.15–25), and at its close affirms a previously threatened degree. *Twelfth Night* displays degree order challenged, on the one side, by festive misrule (Toby *et al.*) and, on the other, by upstart or repressive misrule (Malvolio). If, as Malvolio claims, the Countess is 'nothing allied to' Toby's revelling 'disorders' (*TN*, II.iii.97), she is nothing allied to her steward's climbing disorder. In *Twelfth Night*, the ducal head of state, Orsino, seems in his love-sickness inverted; as in excessive grief-sickness is the mistress of the great house, Countess Olivia. Both figures suggest 'ruling', yet self-indulgent, humour characters of a world-upside-down or licensed occasion.

9.   'Degree' is 'vizarded' in a mask danced by Anne Boleyn at court in 1522: King Henry VIII as Ardent Desire woos Lady Beauty. (Cf. Sydney Anglo, *Spectacle, Pageantry, and Early Tudor Policy* (Oxford, 1969), pp. 120–1.) In the mask, the King, among his allegorical companions, was 'visored'. In a mask in 1527, Wolsey offers the chair of state to Sir Edward Neville, mistaking him for the King: 'Degree being vizarded, / Th' unworthiest shows as fairly in the mask' (I.iii.83–4). (Cf. Marie Axton, 'The Tudor Mask and Elizabethan Court Drama', in Marie Axton and Raymond Williams, eds, *English Drama* (Cambridge, England, 1977), p. 30.) *Troilus'* motif of Ardent Desire wooing Lady Beauty recurs in the Temple revels (see Marie Axton, 'Robert Dudley and the Inner Temple Revels', *Historical Journal*, 13 (1970), 372–3). On vizards and actors, see also Puttenham, *Poesie*, pp. 32–3. Ulysses on 'vizarded' and 'mask' recalls relations among 'vizardings', 'disguisings' and 'masks', at the Inns of Court. See Axton, 'The Tudor Mask', above.

10.   On valuation through externals, cf. 'degree', and Henry Peacham, *The Compleat Gentleman* (1636; ed. V.B. Heltzel, Ithaca, N.Y., 1962, p. 144): social evaluation is by exteriors – citing Ecclesiasticus, '*By gait, laughter, and apparel, a man is knowne what he is*'. 'For the apparel oft proclaims the man' (*H*, I.iii.72). See also Nigel Llewellyn, 'Claims to Status through Visual Codes ...', in Sydney Anglo, ed., *Chivalry in the Renaissance* (Woodbridge, England, 1990), pp. 145–60.

Ulysses *polytropos* has it more than one way. Conventionally a dissimulator, Ulysses on vizards anticipates the Cartesian *larvatus prodeo* (masked, I go forward). On conventions of Ulysses' character, see W.B. Stanford, *The Ulysses Theme* (2nd edition, New York, 1964); Gérard Defaux, *Le Glorieux, et la sagesse du monde dans la première moitié du XVIe siècle* (Lexington, Kentucky, 1982).

11.   On theatrical use of 'degree' or 'gree', related to tiers of seats, cf. Leslie Hotson, *The First Night of Twelfth Night* (New York, 1954), pp. 15, 69–79. Cf. seating by 'degree': 'You know your own degrees, sit down' (*M*, III.iv.1). Cf. the Inner Temple's Christmas festivities and seating by degree, in W. Dugdale, *Origines Juridiciales* (1680), p. 158:

> The Degrees of Tables in the Hall. (1) The *Benchers Table*. (2) The *Utter-Barristers*. (3) The *Inner-Bar Table*, which consists of two for those of the Masters Commons. And a third short Table, at the lower end of the Hall, called the *Clerks Commons Table*. There was also a Table without the Skreen, for the Benchers Clerks, called the *Yeomans*.

12.   Cf. Ulysses' 'mystery … of state' (III.iii.201–2) and E.H. Kantorowicz, 'Mysteries of State: An Absolutist Concept and its Late Mediaeval Origins', *Harvard Theological Review*, 48, 1955, 65–91, omitting, however, notice of Ulysses' allusion. Kantorowicz (p. 74) declares the 'Mysteries of State … inseparable from the sphere of law …'. See James I on 'my Prerogative or mystery of State', and 'our government or mysteries of state'. See C.H. McIlwain, ed., *Political Works of James I* (Cambridge, Massachusetts, 1918), pp. 332 ff. *Parliamentary History of England* (1806), I. 1326–7. Peter S. Donaldson, *Machiavelli and Mystery of State* (Cambridge, England, 1988), especially Ch. 4, 'Machiavelli and the *Arcana imperii*'. See the Middle Templar John Ford, *The Fancies Chaste and Noble* (1638), p. 252: 'Y'are well read / In misteries of state'. Also in Ford, *Perkin Warbeck* (1634), II.iii.122. Noting that 'The "Mysteries of State" were practically always bound to the legal sphere', Kantorowicz's above-cited article remarks also (p. 76) that 'the king solemnly married his realm' – recalling a Renaissance political topos of 'married states', recurrent in speeches of Elizabeth and James I. (Cf. Ulysses' 'married calm of states', I.iii.100.) This political topos, along with 'mystery … of state', seems legalistically echoed in both Kantorowicz and Ulysses.

13.   Cf. 'paraenesis', counsel-speech used often in the Inns of Court's *Gorboduc*. See Wolfgang Clemen, *English Tragedy before Shakespeare* (New York, 1961), pp. 52–3; Mark W. Edwards, *Homer: Poet of the Iliad* (Baltimore, Maryland, 1987), pp. 92–3 and *passim*. On the Elizabethan counsellor, see Mary T. Crane, '"Video et Taceo": Elizabeth I and the Rhetoric of Counsel', *Studies in English Literature* 28 (1988), 1–15. John Guy, 'The Rhetoric of Counsel in Early Modern England', in Dale Hoak, ed., *Tudor Political Culture* (Cambridge, England, 1995), pp. 292–310. A.B. Ferguson, 'The Problem of Counsel', *The Articulate Citizen and the English Renaissance* (Durham, North Carolina, 1965), pp. 70–90.

14.   In Jonson's *Hymenaei* (1606), order is both Reason's servant and the disposition of things. On *gradatio*, see Lausberg, *Handbook*, pp. 279–80, 672.

15.   Ulysses' degree speech suggests, in 'Take but degree away … / And hark what discord follows'! (I.iii.109–10), a lawyer's conventional 'parade of the horribles', woeful consequences of not following a particular rule. He thus recalls a traditional defence of law: for example that of Demosthenes (xxv.20),

who traces such ill consequences: 'If laws were abolished and each individual were given power to do what he liked ... our very life would be in no way different from that of animals'. See this law-espousing commonplace in Robert Crompton, *A Declaration of the ends of Traytors* (1587), sig. E ii.

16. Distinguishing causes and effects is a concern of the law, especially the law of torts and of negligence. Cf. the degree speech's opening cause-and-effect inversion, and Abraham Fraunce, *Arcadian Rhetorike* (1588), ed. Ethel Seaton (Oxford, 1901), p. 4. Fraunce notes of *Metonymia* of the cause, 'as when the cause is turned to signifie the thing caused, the thing caused to signifie the cause ...'. See Fraunce, *Lawyers Logic* (1588), pp. 12–12 v.

17. That Ulysses' degree speech is an expatiated political cliché, subject as such to ironic comment, has eluded commentators who pile up analogues. (Cf. other banal set-pieces in Shakespeare – for example, Jacques' 'Seven Ages', *AYLI*, II.vii.139–66) – to be interpreted in ironical dramatic contexts.) Cf. NVS, pp. 389–410; C.J. Ronan, 'Daniel, Rainolde, Demosthenes, and the Degree Speech of Shakespeare's Ulysses', *Renaissance and Reformation*, 21 (1985), 111–18; Tom Burvill, 'Ulysses on Degree: Shakespeare's Doctrine of Political Order'?, *Parergon*, 2 (1984), 191–203. See also V.K. Whitaker, *Shakespeare's Use of Learning* (San Marino, California, 1953), pp. 195–9; Whitaker, 'Philosophy and Romance in Shakespeare's "Problem Comedies"', in *The Seventeenth Century: Studies ... by Richard Foster Jones and Others* (Stanford, California, 1951), p. 342; E.M.W. Tillyard, *Shakespeare's History Plays* (1948), pp. 10–20; Tillyard, *Elizabethan World Picture* (1943), pp. 7–15, 82–4.

    Opposing such views, see Johannes Kleinstück, 'Ulysses' Speech on Degree as Related to the Play of *Troilus and Cressida*', *Neophilologus*, 43 (1959), 58–63; Elton, 'Shakespeare's Ulysses', pp. 95–111; Franco Ferrucci, *The Poetics of Disguise* (Ithaca, NY, 1980), pp. 140, 156–7; Stephen L. Collins, *From Divine Cosmos to Sovereign State: An Intellectual History of Consciousness and the Idea of Order in Renaissance England* (New York, 1989); David Norbrook, 'Rhetoric, Ideology and the Elizabethan World Picture', in Peter Mack, ed., *Renaissance and Rhetoric* (1994), pp. 140–64.

18. On the 'general' (versus 'special' or 'particular') as logical term, see Fraunce, *Lawiers Logicke*, fols 31v–37v. Cf. Maclean, *Interpretation*.

19. Cf. NVS, p. 52, citing William Warburton and Benjamin Heath. Perceiving the peculiar inversion of this 'hive' passage, Warburton (ed. 1747) notes:

> either it has no meaning, or a meaning contrary to the drift of the speaker. For either it signifies that 'the General and the hive are not of the same degree or species', as when the speaker's complaint is that the hive acts so perversely as to destroy all indifferences of degree between them and the general; or it must signify, 'that the General has private ends and interests distinct from that of the hive'; which *defeats the very end of the speaker, whose purpose is to justify the General, and expose the disobedience of the hive* [italics added].

While Johnson (NVS, p. 52) excuses the passage – 'The sense is clear, the expression is confused' – Heath (*Revisal*, 1765) concurs with Warburton on the oddity of Ulysses' lines: Ulysses would not directly inform his General that *he* is disliked by the hive: 'But I apprehend the artful and insinuating Ulysses would scarce tell Agamemnon bluntly, and in so many words, that he was not liked by the army ...' (NVS, pp. 52–3).

Like Ulysses' contradictory references to Troy as 'his' and 'her', the

counsellor's 'When that the general is not like the hive' (I.iii.81) sustains a
dramatic pattern of inversion.

20. Ulysses' speech favouring restraint against disorder summons up 'specialty of
rule' (I.iii.78), not only as moral doctrine, but also as a controlling device
against chaos. Hitherto, a chain of relationships based on a more-than-secular
'bond', *nexus et naturae vinculum*, degree comprises a containing alternative
to flux. Yet, from one perspective, the degree-speech passage suggests an
inversion of traditional dependence: the 'primogenitive and due of birth', as
well as 'Prerogative of age, crowns, sceptres, laurels', require the formality of
degree to 'stand in authentic place' (I.iii.106–8).

21. Ulysses' degree-speech justification of lawful order, set against its concluding
recognition of domination by power, recalls Cicero's antithesis (*De Officiis*,
1.2.34) between modes of argument, one belonging to a man, and another
(that of force), belonging to a beast. Cicero's antithesis is echoed in
Machiavelli's distinction (*The Prince*, ch. 18) between two kinds of combat,
'the one by right of the laws, the other merely by force'. Having espoused
order and justice, the degree speech in its closing recognition of *force majeure*
recalls numerous legal maxims on the subservience of law to force: for
example, Tilley, *Proverbs*, D624; see also Liebs, *Rechtsregeln*, C88, J14, S35,
V32.

Part II Academic

3.   Academic

> The wise and fool, the artist and unread
> I.iii.24

> Degrees in schools
> I.iii.104

This chapter examines the play's academic allusions (Chaucer's 'scole-matere'), suited to and recognizable by a student audience. Since a large proportion of Inns of Court students had also been to university, they shared with university students a common academic vocabulary.[1]

Act I scene ii

Question

Recalling Hamlet's 'That is the question' (III.i.55) are Cressid's mocking 'This is her question', and Pandar's 'That's true; make no question of that' (I.ii.160–1; cf. IV.i.13). 'Question' is also a topic of a disputation, or academic mode of 'commencing'. 'Question' is, moreover, among the play's terms familiar to students of rhetoric, logic, and the law: for example, cause, argument, proposition, theme.[2]

In addition to 'question', related words such as 'father' and 'sons', occurring in close sequence (I.ii.163), could for a student audience recall the academic sponsor and his candidates.[3] Along with 'determination' (II.ii.170), or verdict on a *disputatio*, such terms suggest a pattern of academic allusion.

In sum, such an academic pattern comprises 'The wise and fool, the artist [liberal arts student] and unread' (I.iii.24); 'Degrees in schools' (I.iii.104); 'in some degrees' (I.ii.68–9); glozing (II.ii.165; or glossing, commenting on a text);[4] tutor (II.i.44; II.iii.28, 239); discipline[d] (II.iii.29, 41); learn (II.i.18); mind (V.vii.17); erudition (II.iii.240); instructed (II.iii.248; V.vii.17); ignorance (II.iii.14); folly and ignorance (II.iii.27); 'wide unclasp the tables of their thoughts / To every tickling reader!' (IV.v.60–1); and such philosophical terms as 'per se' (I.ii.15), 'co-act' (V.ii.118), 'effect' (V.iii.109), 'negation' (V.ii.127) and 'cognition' (V.ii.63).[5]

Act II scene i

Knowledge, folly and ignorance

Despite Thersites' refusal to 'learn' Ajax 'the tenour of the proclamation' (II.i.90–1), Achilles starts to read aloud its challenge. As ability to read a proclamation tested elementary literacy, Ajax's ignorant plight could have amused a literate, especially academic, audience.

Although Tristram Shandy exclaims, 'But with an ass, I can commune forever', Thersites finds Ajax an incommunicable 'scurvy-valiant ass' (II.i.44). Indeed, Ajax has just had catalogued his incapacities: 'I think thy horse will sooner con an oration than thou learn a prayer without book' (II.i.17–18).[6]

Scourged by Thersites, Patroclus is claimed, like the illiterate Ajax, to be cursed with 'folly and ignorance' (II.iii.27).[7] Thersites' curses contain academic implications, as for a student audience: 'Heaven bless thee [Patroclus] from a tutor, and discipline come not near thee!' (II.iii.28–9) – tutors and discipline are inimical or irrelevant to your folly.[8]

As Thersites is a 'knower' of fools, the play itself comprises modes of 'knowing' folly. In an Erasmian sense, to know, as well as not to know, is to be a fool. To be a fool is to be part of folly's chain, and in that sense to 'know' and to be known. Thersites as 'Patroclus' knower' (II.iii.54) is still the deformed railer's act of knowledge; and Patroclus may be a fool, but he has other 'knowers', including Achilles. As Ulysses seems to know all, so does the gossipy Pandar, according to the wheedling Helen: 'you know all, Lord Pandarus' (III.i.140–1).

If the chain leads down to a fool, it also leads up to a fool. The fool 'knows' the other fools. Those in the rest of the chain, insofar as the relation is one of 'command', are also infected by folly: for example, when Patroclus calls Thersites knave, the latter calls him fool. Achilles insists that Thersites be allowed to complete his 'declining': 'He is a privileged man' (II.iii.57). 'I *know* that, fool'. 'Ay, but *that* fool knows not himself' (II.i.64–5).

Act III scene i

Pandar's song and grammar

> And nowe I will proceed to the applicacion of the gramer lecture to the Christmas tyme.
>
> Eccles, Francis Beaumont, *Grammar Lecture* (c.1601–05)

Propaedeutic to legal studies, as part of the trivium, is grammar. Among other recollections in the play of William Lily's standard school Latin grammar is the substantive that 'stands alone' (I.ii.16). (Cf. other grammatical terms, such as 'decline', II.iii.52; 'derive', II.iii.60; 'fool positive', II.iii.65.) Along with logic and rhetoric, the third member of the trivium, grammar, is reflected, for example in I.ii.16, on a noun that 'standeth by him selfe'.[9]

Notable also is Pandar's song (III.i.122–6), with its interjections of 'ha! ha! he!' and 'ha! ha! ha!' Pandar's 'Doth turn oh! oh! to ha! ha! he!' (III.i.122) recalls the grammarian Lily's subsection 'De Interjectione'. There, for the interjection to manifest grief, Lily notes 'Dolentis: vt Heu, hoi, hei, o, ah. Terentius. *I intro, hoi, hei.* Vergilius. *O dolor atque decus magnum*'. For the interjection to show laughter, the grammarian remarks: 'Ridentis: vt Ha ha he. Terentius. *Ha ha he, defessa iam misera sum te ridendo*'. Pandar's 'ha, ha, he!' could have been recognized from the standard Latin grammar book by an academic audience as a familiar school-allusion.[10]

Act III scene iii

Mock-tutorial: substance and accident

> And turnen substaunce into accident.
> Chaucer, *The Pardoner's Tale*

As I.i and I.ii comprise love tutorials, III.iii provides a Ulyssean mock-tutorial. Between these scenes, II.ii's illogic sends up an academic disputation. The public Greek and Trojan councils of I.iii and II.ii are succeeded by the private counselling of III.iii. Such mock-*enseignement* recurs: advice on life's choices is a revels' feature.[11]

While Pandar (in I.i and III.i) declines to perform, then performs (cf. III.i.115–26), Thersites declines *in* performing his declension. As he dismisses the question also by declining to participate, he mockingly mirrors the role of his war-abstaining interrogator, Achilles, who notoriously 'declines' the (military) question. Thersites' 'I'll decline the whole question' (II.iii.52) also implies: run through its forms. Paradoxically, to 'decline the whole question' is both to perform and refuse to perform, as well as to go through the forms of the play (the 'question') itself. As Polonius traces the 'declension' of Hamlet to madness (*H*, II.ii.149), Thersites 'declines the whole [epic war] question' (II.iii.52–4) to folly.[12]

For his part, Achilles agrees that man is describable not only by substance, but also by accidents – including attributes of fortune (III.iii.80–2). Earlier, I.ii's 'per se' (l. 15) helps initiate the play's probing of what is a man *per se* and what he is by attributes or accidents. Indeed, the play recurrently recalls the academically commonplace substance–accident distinction, along with questions on the authenticity (or substantiality) of degree. Accidents (such as external honours) comprise 'place, riches, and favour' (III.iii.82–3), 'Prizes of accident as oft as merit'. Logically, accidents may belong to a subject, but are not necessary to that subject, and are sometimes irrelevant, for example, to internal merit. Achilles' words may suggest that 'place' is *in*authentic, or unrelated to essential value.[13]

According to Ulysses, 'virtue' is among attributes which are themselves held to be transient (III.iii.169–74). The subject, 'man', Ulysses claims further, is describable by a series of such circumstances: 'And not a man, for being simply man' – 'a very man per se' (I.ii.15) – 'Hath any honour but honour for those honours / That are without him' (III.iii.81–2). Rehearsing the kinds of distinctions in logic textbooks, Ulysses removes from 'simply man' (III.iii.80) attributes such as inherent or ingrafted adjuncts and describes him in a series of accidental externals.

Like other sententious speeches (such as Agamemnon's and Nestor's), Ulysses' degree oration, and his utterance at III.iii.112–23, comprise expatiated clichés. Ulysses' mediating persuasion to Achillean action (III.iii) is ironical in relation to Achilles' own savagely reflexive eruption (V.viii). Ironically, too, that eruption is itself reported (V.v.30–5) by the Achilles-prodding Ulysses (III.iii).

Complementarily, Ulysses' speeches (in I.iii and III.iii) espouse antitheses: degree's 'authentic place' (I.iii.108) and rank versus potential relativism (III.iii.74–92) – are dependent on a fluctuating evaluative climate. In Ulysses' time–flux–oblivion prognosis (III.iii.145–79), 'identity' is related to external 'opinion'. Internal sense of self is insufficient: 'I do enjoy', complains Achilles, 'At ample point all that I did possess, / Save these men's looks' (III.iii.88–90). Value- and degree-concerns are transformed (between I.iii and III.iii) from man's identity (I.i.101), 'place' (I.iii.108), or 'estimate and dignity' 'precious of itself' (II.ii.54–5), to what is 'without him' (III.iii.82) in changing social opinion.[14] Ulysses' 'strange fellow' concurs: 'man, how dearly ever parted, ... / Cannot make boast to have that which he hath, / Nor feels not what he owes but by reflection' (III.iii.95–9; cf. *JC*, I.ii.52–3). Elaboratingly, Ulysses expands a similar commonplace, recalling the Aristotelian injunction to communicate one's virtues (cf. Appendix III). So Achilles remarks: 'As when his virtues, shining upon others, / Heat them and they retort that heat again / To the first giver' (III.iii.100–2). As Nestor (in I.iii) parrots Agamemnon and Ulysses, Ulysses' social-reflection commonplace is here elaborated in Achilles' repetitious deduction (III.iii.105–8).[15]

Achilles offers his own ponderous dictum: opening his speech with 'This is not strange, Ulysses', he closes it with 'This is not strange at all' (III.iii.102, 111). An effect is mock-academic *non mirandum est*, in pontificating tutorial deliberation. Like Helenus' 'No marvel' (II.ii.33), Achilles' 'not strange' recalls (as in III.i's demythologizing of Helen) the play's anti-marvellous motif. As Ulysses, parroted by Achilles, understates sententiously, the 'position ... *is* familiar' (III.iii.112–13).

'I was much rapt in this', notes Ulysses, 'and apprehended here immediately / The unknown Ajax' (III.iii.123–5). 'Apprehended' (sensed, especially in conjunction with Ajakes) is itself one of the 'perfumed' terms ridiculed by Elizabethan critics. As Ulysses unmediatedly and raptly 'apprehended' the wafted presence of Ajax (III.iii.124–5), so Thersites puts on the 'presence' of Ajax (III.iii.269).[16]

'Then marvel not, thou great and complete man, / That all the Greeks begin to worship Ajax' (III.iii.181–2). By mock-encomiastic device, Ulysses here would arouse the jealousy of Achilles against the newer idol, Ajax, as Ulysses had (in II.iii) inflated Ajax against Achilles.

Act V scene ii

Being and knowing: 'Bid "Oncaymeon" farewell'

In questioning Cressid's identity and truth (V.ii), Troilus brings to mind bases of academic metaphysics: the one (*hen*), the good (*agathon*), and the true (*aletheia*), as well as unity (V.ii.141), and what there is, 'what is or is not' (I.iii.183).[17]

In Troilus' apocalyptic fear (cf. V.ii.140–9) of a cosmic split, he also, in effect, questions 'what is or is not'. As the scholastic science of being includes the principle of identity, Troilus' V.ii intimates a crisis of identity: the being or *esse* of Cressid (V.ii.146) – 'What Cressid is' (I.i.101) – is again in question.

To summarize, while I.iii subverts school rhetoric, and II.ii inverts school logic, V.ii invokes, in its diction, academic philosophy. This chapter has noted academic allusions of relevance to, and comprehensible by, a student audience: for example scholastic terms, disputation references, allusions to knowledge and books, 'degrees in schools', 'the artist and unread', and references to mind, learning, ignorance, tutors, instruction, stupidity and folly, grammar (as well as logic and rhetoric), mock-tutorials and school philosophy. These academic reflections suggest an audience attuned and receptive to such allusions, as at a student revel.

Notes

1. Cf. academic concerns also in the Introduction and Chapters 4 and 5. See Maclean, *Interpretation, passim*.
2. On the *quaestio*, see Lausberg, *Handbook*, pp. 66–138 and 749–50. On 'question' and law, see S.E. Thorne, ed., *Readings and Moots at the Inns of Court*, vol. 2, Selden Society (1990), pp. xvi–xvii: on *quaestiones disputatae*, cf. the structure of a law disputation: (1) the *casus*, problem; (2) the *quaestio*, arising from the problem; (3) the *disputatio*, arguments *pro* and *contra*; (4) the *solutio, responsio*, or *determinatio*, the ruling in answer by the teacher – cf. 'determination', as in Hector (II.ii.170) ruling on the disputing participants. *Quaestio* in law was the issue, or *exitum*, the aim of pleading. A legal controversy existed in a proposition contradicted by a denial: a *quaestio*. See Selden Society, *Spelman Reports II*, 94 (1977), 143.
    Cf. M. Dominica Legge, '*Hamlet* and the Inns of Court', in M. Brahmer et al., eds, *Studies in Language and Literature ... M. Schlauch* (Warsaw, 1966), pp. 213–17. On the *quaestio* and the law, see also Hermann Kantorowicz, 'The *Quaestiones Disputatae* of the Glossators', *Revue d'histoire du droit*, 16 (1938), 1–67; Brian Lawn, 'The Use of the *Quaestio Disputata* in Legal Circles', in *Rise and Decline of the Scholastic 'Quaestio Disputata'* (Leiden, The Netherlands, 1993), pp. 3–5; Alfonso Maierù, *University Training in Medieval Europe* (Leiden, The Netherlands, 1994).
3. Cf. *OED*, s.v. *son* †3 '... at Cambridge, one presented for a degree by the "father" of his college'; *OED*, s.v. *father* sb. 7. Such terms as in I.ii were involved with the ceremony of commencement: 'questions' were 'dysputyde in the Commensment Day' as explained in George Peacock, ed., *Observations on the Statutes of Cambridge* (1841), pp. xxii–xxiii. Cf. *ibid.*, 'the Father shall ... gyve Benedyctyon to hys Chyldren ... The Father in Arte shall purpose ij Questyons ... After that the Father shall rede hys Comendatyon, hys Chyldren folowyng, & there whodys pluckydde on there Hedys ...'.
4. Cf. Barnabe Rich, *Opinion Diefied* (1613), p. 30: '[laws] wrested glosses and subtill expositions'. On the legal gloss, cf. Harold J. Berman, *Law and Revolution: The Foundation of Western Legal Tradition* (Cambridge, Massachusetts, 1983), pp. 129–31.
5. See, on cognition, Trimpi, *Muses*, pp. 230–40, 375–8 and *passim*. On negation, see L.R. Horn, *A Short History of Negation* (Chicago, 1989). Cf., among other of the play's academic echoes, 'Good words' (II.i.88), a well-known tag from Terence, 'bona verba quaeso', as a plea for moderation (NVS, p. 89). In addition, see recollection of the familiar school Euclid on parallel lines not meeting: 'as near as the extremest ends / Of parallels' (I.iii.167–8). (Cf. Andrew Marvell's 'The Definition of Love', ll.27–8: 'But ours so truly *Paralel*, / Though infinite can never meet'.) 'Parallel' was, in the War of the Theatres, a mocked word. Cf. Dekker, *Satiromastix*, IV.i.204: 'I hope he and I are not Paralels'; Jonson, *Poetaster*, I.ii: 'are wee paralells, rascall? are wee paralells?'
    The Trojan Hector's allusion to Aristotle (II.ii.166) is but one of a series of anachronistically-sounding references: for example, Trojan allusions to 'moral philosophy', to 'right and wrong' and to 'law in each well-ordered nation' (II.ii.171–80). Cf. such references regarding deities as Jove (I.ii.20; II.ii.45; II.ii.127; II.iii.11; III.iii.279; IV.i.19, 27; IV.v.129; V.i.46, 54, 105); Juno (I.ii.121); Jupiter (I.ii.61; I.ii.164; II.iii.196; IV.v.191; V.i.52); Mars (II.i.52; II.iii.242; III.iii.190; IV.v.177; IV.v.198; IV.v.255; V.ii.164; V.iii.52); Mercury (II.ii.45; II.iii.11); Neptune (I.iii.45); Venus (III.i.33; IV.i.24; V.ii.165); Vulcan (I.iii.168; V.ii.170).

In addition to Aristotle's anachronistic citation by name, and Aristotelian similarities noted in Appendix III, are other of the play's Aristotelian recollections: for example, Ulysses' 'things in motion' which 'sooner catch the eye / Than what not stirs' (III.iii.183–4), and Aristotle on 'things in motion', *Metaphysics*, Delta, 1020 b 1–25. Motion, in Aristotle is important to seeing. Cf. his *De Anima*, 435 a. On the eye, cf. III.iii.105–11.

6.   Cf. Manningham's Middle Temple diary, fol. 16b, February 1601/02, p. 54: '"He will reade as well as my horse"'. Thersites' 'con an oration' and 'learn a prayer without book' (II.i.17, 18), on Ajax's incapacities, recall Jonson's own escape by 'neck verse', and the relation of literacy to legal extenuation, as by benefit of clergy: pleading benefit of clergy to escape execution was allowed seculars who could read. Cf. Dekker, *Satiromastix*, I.ii.117.

7.   The large, brutish Ajax beating the smaller, clever Thersites could, for student spectators, recall Elizabethan schoolroom practice. Cf. Jonson, *Poetaster*, V.iii.265, on 'jerking pedants', teachers who beat their students. As Henry Peacham, *Compleat Gentleman* (1634; Oxford, 1908) complains, 'too many teachers beleeve with *Chrysippus* in *Quintilian*, that there is no other Method of making a Scholler, than by beating him' (p. 23).

8.   If addressed to a student audience, knowledge-and-ignorance jests would have been pointed. See 'ignorance', I.i.10, II.iii.14, 27, III.iii.312; 'knowledge', IV.i.43. Cf. jests on instruction and ignorance in the Middle Temple Hall-produced *Twelfth Night* (e.g. 'this house is as dark as ignorance', *TN* IV.ii.45); and Thersites' boast on ignorance, that he is 'bastard instructed' (V.vii.17). With these, cf. Francis Beaumont's Inner Temple burlesque (c. 1601–05) 'shew' referring (Sloane MS 1709, fol. 3, in Eccles, *Grammar Lecture*, p. 410) to this 'ill-instructed hall'.

9.   Ajax is described in terms also defining, near the start of William Lily's well-known Elizabethan grammar, a 'Noune Substantive' (*A Shorte Introduction of Grammar*, 1567 (ed. V.J. Flynn, 1945), sig. A5: 'A Noune Substantive is that standeth by him selfe, & requireth not an other word to be ioyned with him to shew his signification: as Homo, a man'). John Lyly, *Endimion* (III.iii.17–19): '... I am a noun adjective ... Because I cannot stand without another'. Cf. Jonson's *Cynthia's Revels*, IV, with its game of Substantives and Adjectives. See The Middle Templar Sharpham, *Cupids Whirligigg*, sig. K3, on the mentula as 'a nowne adiectiue', 'Because it stands not by himselfe, but requires another word to be ioyned with it'. Cf. Henry Wotton, *Reliquiae Wottonianae* (1654), p. 25: 'not that the Earl [Essex] meant to stand alone like a Substantive ...' On a 'man per se' and the noun that stands alone, see T.F. Crane, *Italian Social Customs in the Renaissance* (New Haven, Connecticut, 1920), p. 534: a courtiers' game: 'Substantives and Adjectives'. Grammatically, Pandar suggests a copulative conjunction, Thersites a disjunctive. See J. Brinsley, *The Posing of the Parts* (1669), p. 47, on 'Conjunctions, Copulatiues and Disjunctiues'. J.A. Alford, 'The Grammatical Metaphor: A Survey of Its Use in the Middle Ages', *Speculum*, 57 (1982), 728–60.

10.   Cf. NVS, pp. 143–4; Baldwin, *Small Latine*, I. 570; and Peter J. Seng, 'Pandarus' Song and Lily's Grammar', *Modern Language Journal*, 48 (1964), 212–15. The jest's academic status is recalled in *Gradus ad Cantabrigiam* (1803), p. 2 v: 'Some be of laughing, as ha, ha, he' 'Shakespeare citing Lilly, *Much Ado* ...'

11.   See *Gesta*'s speeches of advice, pp. 44–56, to a king concerning future policy; and *Prince*, p. 89, where the Prince receives recommendations on course of life

from his Council. Cf. Pandar's counsel to Troilus on success in love (I.i.13–28); Cressid's to women on love-strategy (I.ii.287–96); Pandar's to 'tongue-tied maidens', offering his services (III.ii.209–10); and Ulysses' to Achilles on course of life and worldly success (III.iii.150–90). In this play, the chief counsellor on love is a pander; and on self-advancement, traditionally a trickster-*eiron*, Ulysses.

12.   On 'decline' and 'undecline', cf. Eccles, *Grammar Lecture*, p. 441. 'Declined' reflects the opening to *A Short Introduction of Grammar*, the English version of Lily's standard grammar. In 'declining', Thersites recalls *Merry Wives*, where the boy is bade, 'Show me now, William, some declensions of your pronouns' (*MWW*, IV.i.74–5). Cf. Daniel J. Taylor, *Declination: A Study of the Linguistic Theory of Marcus Terentius Varro* (Amsterdam, 1974).

13.   So Milton's 'Substance' is told (*Vac.* 74), 'Your son ... / Shall subject be to many an Accident', or property of a substance. On substance and accident, cf. Thomas Wilson, *The Rule of Reason*, pp. 18–20, 25–6; E.L. Wiggins, 'Logic in the Poetry of John Donne', *Studies in Philology*, 42 (1945), 45–9. Thomas Blundevile, *The Arte of Logicke* (1619), sig. [D2 v], defines *substance* in relation to *accident*: the former is

> a thing consisting of it selfe, and needeth no helpe to sustaine the being thereof: and yet it is clad with accidents; for, otherwise we could not discerne it with our outward senses, whether it were any substance, or not: for we cannot see the substance of any thing with our bodily eyes, but only with the eyes of our mind & understanding.

14.   'The judgement which wee have to knowe our selves', concludes a speaker in Guazzo (*Civile Conversation*, 1574, I.115; cf. *Guizo*, in *Gesta*, p. 41), 'is not ours, but wee borrow it of others'. Similarly, James Cleland, *Propaideia, or the Institution of a Noble Young Man* (Oxford, 1607), observes: honour 'is not in his hand who is honoured, but in the hearts and opinion of other men ...' (Book V, ch. 6, p. 179). On the external 'otherness' of valuation, see also Hobbes, *Works*: 'The value or worth of a man, is ... his price ... a thing dependant on the need and judgment of another'. Further, 'not the seller, but the buyer determines the price. For [like Ajax and Achilles] let ... [men] rate themselves at the highest value they can; yet their true value is no more than it is esteemed by others' (III.76).

15.   Cf. Dent, *Index*, E 231 a, with analogues in Erasmus; and cited in *Julius Caesar*, and in 1600, Robert Cawdray, *A Treasurie ... of Similies*, pp. 428, 429, on 'Knowledge and sight of our selves'.

16.   While Achilles' 'evasion' 'Cannot outfly' the Grecians' 'apprehensions' (II.iii.113–4), Ulysses (II.iii.124–5) encounters Achilles' apprehensions.

17.   Ulysses' 'what is or is not' (I.iii.183) recalls an Aristotelian definition of metaphysics. (Cf. Faustus' 'On kai me on' (Christopher Marlowe, *Doctor Faustus*, I.i.12.) On Renaissance uses of 'what is or is not' (formulated also as 'being and not being' – Hamlet's 'to be or not to be', III.i.55) – see R.W. Dent, 'Ramist Faustus or Ramist Marlowe?' *Neuphilologische Mitteilungen*, 73 (1972), 63–74. Cf. Plato, *Sophist*, 263d; Aristotle, *Metaphysics*, IV. 7, 1011 b 26; VI, 4, 1027 b 20: 'To say of what is that it is not, or what is not, that it is, is false, while to say of what is that it is, and of what is not that it is not, is true'. Cf. E.A. Moody, *Truth and Consequence in Mediaeval Logic* (Amsterdam, 1953), p. 102.

See Petrus Ramus, *Dialectique* (1555), opening on 'being and not being ...'. Cf. Thomas Lodge in G.G. Smith, ed., *Elizabethan Critical Essays* (Oxford,

1904), I.67; Alexander Richardson, *The Logicians School-master* (1629), sig. S. Cf. Carl Karpf, *To ti en einei. Die Idee Shakespeare's und deren Verwirklichung* (Hamburg, 1869). Cf. A. Gaggi 'L' "essere" e il "non essere" nella sofistica graeca', *Atti della (R.) Accademia di Scienze di Torino, Classe di Scienze morali* ... 61 (1926), 215–30. G.B. Kerferd, 'Gorgias on nature or that which is not', *Phronesis*, 1 (1955), 3–25. R. Miceli, 'Dall' "essere" degli Eleati al "non-essere" dei Sofisti', *Archivio di Storia della Filosofia Italiana*, 5 (1936), 191–224.

Cf. Ulysses' 'what is or is not' (I.iii.184) and Hector's 'way of truth' (II.ii.189). Both phrases recall Parmenides' poem, which distinguishes, on the one hand, between an intelligible world ('That that is, is,' *TN*, IV.ii.14) and the Way of Truth, and, on the other hand, an unintelligible one, that which is, is not. Cf. W.N. King, 'Shakespeare and Parmenides: The Metaphysics of *Twelfth Night*', *Studies in English Literature*, 7 (1968), 283–306.

4.   Rhetoric

> Then would come some matter from him;
> I see none now
>
> II.i.8–9

> he raves in saying nothing
> III.iii.249

Rhetoric, with logic and grammar, was traditionally propaedeutic to legal studies. Rhetorical forms, involved in legal training as well as in forensic pleading, would have been recognizable by word-sensitive law students. This chapter examines rhetorical and mock-rhetorical patterns in *Troilus*.[1]

Act I scene iii

'Matter needless, of importless burden'

The play provides models of rhetorical solecism:[2] how not to argue, along with how not to orate. Such mock-rhetorical utterance recurs in King–General Agamemnon's 'matter needless, of importless burden' (I.iii.71). Mockery of rhetoric recalls Inns of Court revels' burlesque, including fustian and other rhetorical modes; see for example *Prince*, 'The Princes Orator having made a ridiculous and sensless speech unto his Excellency' (p. 37). That speech (pp. 37–40) suggests the farrago of a burlesque oration: 'The *Fustian* Answer made to a *Tufftaffata* Speech'. This fustian mode seems reflected in the play's own rhetorical excesses or deviations (of, for example, Agamemnon, Ulysses, Hector, Nestor).[3]

Act I scene iii displays rhetorical excess (Puttenham's 'Too full speech', *Poesie*, p. 257; cf. 'swollen' or 'high' style). As I.iii unfolds, the audience hears mis-evaluations, burlesqued banalities and subversive equivocations. As the monarch's errant generalities fail directly to address the main malady afflicting the Grecian army, the King 'apprehends a world of figures here, / But not the form of what he should attend' (*1H4*, I.iii.209–10). In such utterances, Renaissance ideals of the orator as combining eloquence and wisdom clash with the Greek command's divagations.

Agamemnon's 'protractive [military] trials' (I.iii.20) are recalled in his own speech's 'protractive' rhetorical 'trials'. Recurrent victims of confusion, Greek leaders clumsily utter (like Dull, Quince, Dogberry, the Hostess, Shallow or Elbow) the opposite of their apparent intentions: 'Bias and thwart, not answering the aim' (I.iii.15). In turn, the dotard Nestor damns his monarch's oration with loud praise.

As previous efforts at 'largeness' have 'come short' (I.iii.5, 11), the King–General remarks a disparity between men's expectations and results (I.iii.18–19). A cause of Grecian failure resembles infected 'sap' within the equivocal 'pine'.[4] The 'pine' is 'Tortive and errant from his course of growth' (I.iii.9), twisted (like the speaker's style) from its proper thrust. Hence, explains Agamemnon, '... we come short of our suppose so far' (I.iii.11). His oration-of-state, indecorously mingling equivoque and bowling metaphor, does 'come short' and is itself, like other speeches, 'not answering the aim' (I.iii.15; cf. Nestor, I.iii.343–6).

Following Cressid's strategy to retain love-command (I.ii.287–94), the Greek general considers strategies of military command (I.iii.1–30). In his deliberative oration, at issue now is not private withholding by a young girl, but performance-withholding by the Greek army. The King–General speaks first in the scene by rank-decorum, in an utterance which betrays a deficiency of decorum. His exhortation, aiming to rouse his army, is subverted by its rambling clichés, inadvertent equivoques, and instances contrary to his purpose. Intending to call his forces to order, he falls into verbal disorder, rhetorically paralleling his own military account.

For his part, Nestor supports Agamemnon's assertions by exemplary 'application': deferring to a platitude, Nestor shall 'apply' his king's 'latest words' (I.iii.32–3). Nestor's repetitions of his leader's 'latest words' are, like himself, *déjà vieux*. Rhetorically, Nestor concludes his clichéd illustration with a complacent moral (I.iii.45–54).[5] Incongruously, the play's dubious personages here prate of distinction and 'winnowing out' of men's abilities. Incongruously, as well, the decrepit Nestor – a challenging lover in I.iii.291–301 – equivocally praises the athletic Pegasus: 'Bounding between the two moist elements / Like Perseus' horse' (I.iii.41–42).[6]

In turn, addressing his king as 'nerve and bone of Greece' (I.iii.54–61), Ulysses is mock-encomiastic. In his royal salutation, he reverses crowned head for 'nerve' (I.iii.55) – and 'quite athwart / Goes all decorum' (*MM*, I.iii.30–1).

Much of *Troilus* is in the epideictic or mock-epideictic mode. Troilus' demonstrative oratory (involving praise or blame) includes his hopeful encomium of woman (III.ii.157–69), which complements his later diatribe (V.ii.137–60). Along with demonstrative oratory, the play exhibits deliberative oratory, concerned with expedience or inexpedience: in I.iii, the Greek council's deliberation on the progress of the war, and in II.ii, the Trojan council's debate on whether to return Helen. In the latter debate, judicial oratory considers the justice or injustice of Paris' deed and Helen's retention. Both Greek and Trojan council scenes follow conventionally deliberative topics, for example honour, advantage, safety and value.[7]

Act II scene ii

Trojan council: disputation[8]

Priam

King Priam opens the Trojan council (II.ii), as King Agamemnon does the Greek council (I.iii). Like the Grecian king's, the Trojan monarch's rhetoric is suspect. In one *senex*'s relaying of another's message – Nestor's by Priam – the report's sequence is itself scrambled: 'Deliver Helen, and all damage else – / As honour, loss of time, travail, expense, / Wounds, friends, and what else dear that is consumed ...' (II.ii.1–5). Nestor's reported 'damage'-sequence, beginning with the high value of honour and descending to loss of time, suggests anticlimax, and this lesser temporal loss is followed by 'travail, expense' (II.ii.4).

In the aged Priam's Nestor-transmission are thus words in a kind of senile zeugma: 'After so many hours, lives, speeches spent' (II.iii.1). Here, in confused anticlimax, 'lives' (the chief item) is inserted in mid-series. 'Deliver Helen, and all damage else –' (II.ii.3): ambiguously, 'else' joins Helen to 'damage'. Further, while honour, travail, expense and friends might be among 'what else dear that is consumed / In ... war', it is difficult in the same way for 'loss of time' and 'wounds' to be 'consumed'. Nestor's sequence jumbles major elements with relatively minor ones, rising confusedly to the miscellaneous 'Wounds, friends, and what else dear' (II.ii.5).[9]

Hector

Following King Priam, Hector, as eldest born,[10] speaks first in response to Priam's II.ii question, as in the same scene he also speaks last. Hector salutes 'Dread Priam', of whose dreadfulness the audience has experienced little (except his propensity to scramble terms). Recalling Hector's 'toucheth my particular' (II.ii.9), Troilus responds: 'For my private part, / I am no more touched than all Priam's sons' (II.ii.125–6). While Paris self-interestedly defends his 'particular' under guise of the general, the Greek (I.iii) and Trojan (II.ii) debates comprise both general and particular. Among the Greeks, it is the problem of degree, the General affecting Grecian disorder in particular. Among the Trojans, it is the pleasure of one in particular that leads to sacrifice of many in general (II.ii.142–5).[11] ('Why should the private pleasure of some one / Become the public plague of many moe?' *RL*, ll. 1478–9.)

Responding to Priam's 'Hector, what say you to 't'? (II.ii.7), Hector utters a reply not precisely 'to 't'. For Hector's response starts with a defence of his courage that had not itself been questioned. He also indecorously juxtaposes majestic salutation with personal bodily allusion: 'Yet, dread Priam, / There is no lady of more softer bowels', he claims, 'More spongy to suck in the sense of fear, / More ready to cry out "Who knows what follows?" / Than Hector is' (II.ii.10–14). What this seeming fustian has directly to do with Priam's Helen-return question is not made clear.

Following his father's disordered commencement, Hector's opening recalls the rhetorically disordered orations of his predecessors. So too Hector's confused overture (II.ii.8–25) foreshadows his contradictory verdict: 'Paris and Troilus, you have both said well, / *And* on the cause and question now in hand / Have glozed – but superficially ...' (II.ii.164–5). This abrupt praise–blame contradiction is capped by the Trojan Hector's anachronistic allusion to Aristotle (II.ii.165–7). Rhetorically, Hector's contradiction exemplifies the work's pattern of disorderly juxtapositions: inadequate connectives, sudden shifts, and anticlimactic descents into inadvertent double entendre. Hence, it is not merely at II.ii's end, where Hector's sudden reversal is conspicuous, but also in the play elsewhere, that rhetorical as well as logical anomalies recur.

While Hector's seemingly irrelevant response (II.ii.8–17) supports prudence, its syntax appears peculiarly imprudent. Like Agamemnon's, Nestor's and Ulysses' utterances, Hector's speech comprises clichés, with odd conjunctions and articulations. His '"Who knows what follows?"' (II.ii.13) brings to mind also his own lack of consequence, as well as the scene's instances of *non sequitur*. Transitionless, Hector's response is followed by a sententia: 'The wound of peace is surety, / Surety secure' (II.ii.14–15), which suggests the commonplace that peace breeds complacency. So Hector had reportedly found peace not falsely reassuring, but stagnating: He 'in this dull and long-continued truce / Is resty grown', and, in his reported challenge, demands conflict (I.iii.262–3). 'But', adds Hector 'modest doubt is called / The beacon of the wise, the tent that searches / To th' bottom of the worst' (II.ii.15–17). If peace breeds complacency, 'modest doubt' (as 'the tent that searches / To th' bottom of the worst', as wisdom's tool) does not seem a clear or direct alternative.

In his digressive opening response to his king, Hector thus recalls Ulysses' disordered degree-speech opening, in reply to *his* king. After ten lines of dubiously relevant exordium, Hector to Priam's question abruptly responds: 'Let Helen go' (II.ii.17).

Troilus

Lacking precision or subtlety in argument, Troilus is also deficient in prudent estimation. In his advocacy-plea for the abductor Paris, the furore exceeds the reason. Instead of the traditional orderly process of disputation, his II.ii speeches are exhortatory, rousing his hearers to action by threats and promises: His 'promised glory' (II.ii.204) by the scene's end sways Hector to a 'truth'-dismissive folly.

To Hector's apparent reasonableness (II.ii.17–25), Troilus replies first with an emotive side-issue, a reproach against filial impiety. Troilus holds that Hector is guilty of such defects in weighing his father's honour with mere 'counters' (II.ii.28). Troilus' response to Hector's opening speech includes asking a question in order to reproach. Later, in extenuation of Paris' rape, he employs the figure of apology for a friend's offence. As he lauds his prolific sire in terms of 'past-proportion of his infinite' (II.ii.29), Troilus' question-begging intrudes a distraction of shame and paternal honour. Arguing *ad hominem* as well as *ad verecundiam*, or shame, Troilus decries the weighing of such honour 'in a scale / Of common ounces' (II.ii.26–8).

Security versus honour

Hector's and Troilus' II.ii value debate opposes considerations of security to those of honour. While Hector is linked to security (cf. IV.v.73), elsewhere he would oppose the complacencies of security: 'The wound of peace is surety, / Surety secure' (II.ii.14–15). While Hector would (in II.ii) return Helen and maintain security, Troilus poses, against security, honour: 'There can be no evasion / To blench from this and to stand firm by honour' (II.ii.67–8); and he remarks 'the goodness of a quarrel / Which hath our several honours all engaged' (II.ii.123–4).[12] While Troilus argues against returning Helen, citing their royal father's honour, it is Priam himself who chides Paris for keeping Helen (II.ii.142–5), and who himself initiates II.ii's debate on her return.

Hyperbolically,[13] Troilus' 'O, theft most base', expanding complicity (II.ii.92) charges that the other Trojans were implicated: 'That we have stolen' (II.ii.92–3; but Paris has stolen). Paris, though 'still possess'd / Of those effects' (*H*, III.iii.53–4) for which he did the crime, would, like the usurping Henry IV, have his hearers now 'March all one way' (*1H4*, I.i.15). (The abductor Paris' inculpatory speech recalls complicitous overtures of usurpers: not only Henry IV's political consolidation-topos at the start of *1*

Debate on Helen - whole process

Henry IV, but also Claudius' opening oration, *H*, I.ii.1–39.) The Trojans are thus declared not only complicitous thieves, but also unworthy of their ill-gotten booty – 'thieves, unworthy of a thing so stol'n' (II.ii.94).

Troilus answers two of Hector's previous contentions: he denies that defence of Helen is an effect of hot blood (II.ii.115–16) or 'heaving spleens' (II.ii.196); and that in her cause lives are wasted (II.ii.18–25). Reinforcing Troilus' view is the self-interested Paris' assurance that no 'life were ill bestowed' in Helen's cause, 'or death unfamed' (II.ii.159). Proclaiming Helen's 'theme' a spur to honour (II.ii.200), Troilus' argument for 'honour' sounds oddly in defence of a notorious abduction. So also does his hope that, in such defence, 'fame in time to come' will 'canonize' them (II.ii.202).

Troilus' and Paris' use of 'fear of shame' to persuade the Trojans (II.ii.32, 151) anticipates Ulysses' use of fear of shame to persuade Achilles (cf. III.iii.209–13). Troilus combines Erasmian-rhetorical 'hope of renown', 'fear of shame', and 'greatness of reward'. In his summary on Helen as a 'theme of ... renown' (II.ii.199), he invokes 'So rich advantage of a promised glory' (II.ii.204).[14]

Troilus condemns Hector's argument against Helen's retention as dishonourable and shameful (cf. II.ii.32). Charging 'cowardice', he ends on a taunting personal note (II.ii.127–9). Troilus has shifted the grounds of the argument, from Trojan losses to their honour in a quarrel.

Act II scene iii

Argument and theme

The play offers differing perspectives on the Helen-war plot: Troilus' in I.i and II.ii; Ulysses' in I.iii and II.iii; and Thersites' in II.i and II.iii. These provide anticipations of what the spectators are to witness in III.i: Helen as Paris' 'Nell' (III.i.53, 138). Such perspectives also change: for Troilus, Helen's is 'an argument' (I.i.94), for others, a question; for Thersites, in II.iii, it becomes reductively an 'argument' (II.iii.71–2) – 'All the argument is a whore and a cuckold'.[15] While Hamlet 'will fight upon this theme' (*H*, V.i.289), Troilus cannot at first 'fight upon this [Helen's] argument' (I.i.94). For Troilus later, however, Helen is a 'theme of honour and renown' (II.ii.199).[16] Menelaus' 'deadly theme' (IV.v.181), Helen, is rejected by the contentious Thersites (II.iii.71–3), himself an 'argument'. In turn, Ulysses condemns Menelaus' pursuit of Helen: 'O deadly gall, and theme of all our scorns!' (IV.v.30).

In play-summarizing terms, quarrel, argument, theme, *Troilus and Cressida* is thus a quarrel about a 'quarrel' (Prologue, l. 10); thematically, an argument about an argument. As argument is a basis of legal practice and advocacy, the play itself, like the war, is the argument that 'is' the argument.

In parody of the plot's epic quarrel ('argument') over Helen's possession is II.iii's contest over the 'argument'. (In part, the contest is also an argument over possession of the argumentative Thersites.) As subject becomes object and the reverse, 'He *is* his argument that *has* his argument' (II.iii.95–6). Achilles is both object of argument and possessor of the argument (Thersites), both object and subject. So also, he (Achilles) is Thersites' argument that *has* his argument, as in identification by possession. (Paris *has* Helen, the war's argument.)[17]

Achilles' connection with 'argument' recalls the 'Achillean argument' (NVS, p. 117), one which is insuperable. In one sense, Ulysses denies that Ajax will lack 'matter', having lost his argument, Thersites. For Achilles *is* an argument or point of emulative dispute – and Achilles *has* his argument.[18] The 'argument Achillean' *is* an argument. Thus, Achilles *is* an argument and *has* Ajax's argument (Thersites). 'Then', concludes Nestor, ponderously punning, 'will Ajax lack matter, if he have lost his argument' (II.iii.93–4) – including Thersites, his provoking butt. Deprived of Thersites, Ajax will have no material for contention. Ajax bays at Achilles – Achilles has taken away Ajax's victimized fool, Thersites (II.iii.89–90). Thus, Ajax will lack matter (waste; rhetorical substance – both senses ironically correlated; cf. 'matter' as legal *res*) if he have lost his argument (his case; or Thersites); or if he have forgotten his argument, as an actor who is 'out' has lost his matter's cue or thread (cf. '"Who knows what follows?"', II.ii.14).

Ulysses tops Nestor's quibble by his own: 'No, you see, he is his argument that has his argument – Achilles' (II.iii.95–6). Ajax has not lost an argument (Thersites). He has, rather (in a possessing chain), gained the possessor of his argument, Achilles. Achilles is now the issue (argument) with Ajax. He (Achilles) has his (Ajax's) argument – a dubious acquisition – while he (Achilles) *is* Ajax's argument. But Achilles, having 'inveigled' Thersites (II.iii.90), is now also Thersites' argument (the argument's argument). Thersites notes Achilles' position in a chain of fools (II.iii.61–4). The possessing subject is the argument's object (of ridicule), while the object (Achilles) also possesses the controversial subject (the argument – Thersites).

Act IV scene v

Body-rhetoric

Cressid's body is a book in which Ulysses can read familiar matters. She is one of those who 'wide unclasp the tables of their thoughts / To every tickling reader'! (IV.v.60–1).

As Ulysses can recognize Diomedes by his bodily expression (IV.v.14–16), he claims to recognize Cressid by hers. If she can be read, she can, recalling the musically trained boy actors, be sight-read: 'And any man may sing her, if he can take her clef; she's noted' (V.ii.11–12). Ulysses' verbal manipulations are matched by Cressid's corporeal: Cressid uses not only body-language (IV.v.55–7), but also bodily persuasion – a rhetoric of movement, to arouse and withhold, excite and control. While her body speaks one language 'concupiscible' (desiring), her tongue speaks another 'irascible' (repelling) – or, in her terms, 'hold[ing] ... off' (I.ii.287). Cressid, currently in exchange, changes value, as she is herself changed in exchange. Her expressive body-language noted by Ulysses anticipates the same scene's theatrical body-inspections between Hector and Achilles – the latter, in turn, is to destroy Hector, Troy's 'body'.

Recurrently, Ulysses (grandson of Autolycus) is the contriver of dubious situations: for example in the relaying of slander to the Greek command; in the snubbing of Achilles; in directing the general Grecian kissing of Cressid, and in his snubbing of her; in conducting Troilus to witness his own betrayal – the traditional trickster Ulysses is present as manipulative stage-manager. His critique of Cressid parallels Diomedes' condemnation of Helen (IV.i.56–68, 70–6). Ulysses, who insinuates the scandal to the Greeks of Achilles' external heterosexual liaison (III.iii.193–4), comments also on Cressid's communicating her 'parts to others' (cf. III.iii.117).

Act V scene ii

Instance

> There is no worse torture, then the torture of the lawe, they are so full of *Instances*, of *Quidities* ...
>
> Barnabe Rich, *Opinion Diefied* (1613)

Examples of the play's use of rhetorical categories or topoi include 'Taking ... the world to witness', as in Troilus' appeal to the world: 'Instance, O instance', followed by another 'instance' – appeal to witness (V.ii.155–6).[19] 'Instance', itself also legal, recurs in Troilus' legal–rhetorical citation of examples. Pandar offers a final comic reduction of this proof method: 'What verse for it? what instance for it?' (V.x.39–40). 'Instance' occurs in *Troilus* at other times (cf. 'instant way', III.iii.153): for example Ulysses on Troy as having been down 'but for these instances' (I.iii.77). In Troilus' 'instance' (V.ii.153, 155), one pair of sentences rebuts the other.[20] Troilus' 'instances' are first positive: 'Cressid is mine ...' (V.ii.154), and then, as above, negative – a case adduced in objection. In the presence of a conventionally requisite two witnesses (Ulysses and Thersites), Troilus' 'instance' is sounded, with its appeal to witness. While the Greeks and Trojans are earlier concerned with 'argument', 'proposition' and 'theme', the play's last act thus dwells on 'instance' (V.ii.153, 155; V.x.40) and 'proof' (V.ii.113; V.v.5, 29). Troilus' 'Instance, O instance!' (V.ii.153, 155), proclaims the lament universally, *ad orbem*.

Act V scene x

Rhetoric of pity[21]

'Or if you cannot weep yet give some groans, / Though not for me, yet for *your* aching bones' (V.x.48–9). Pandar's is here invertingly parry and counter-thrust. To unweeping or mocking spectators at his plight, he offers what seems heartfelt, yet insulting, sympathy. Pandar thus (in one breath) manages insult, self-exculpation, and actor–audience reversal. As Troilus seems finally to forget his love wound in his grief for his brother, so the self-concerned Pandar ignores both: his last words evince no response to Troilus' 'double sorwe' (Chaucer, *Troilus and Criseyde*, I.i).

As pity and tears are wanting, woe or wonder is mocked: It is Pandarus he mourns for. Pandar's complaint is a *lugete*, an appeal to mourn, combined with a *plaudite*, an appeal to applaud. Pandar is also audience-complicitous: he salutes spectators as kindred 'Brethren and sisters of the hold-door trade' (V.x.50). Like Pompey addressing fellows in the flesh trade (*MM*, IV.iii.1–19), Pandar's ultimate tone is familiarly *primus inter pares*.

To summarize, this chapter has, inspecting the play's rhetorical expressions, suggested a rhetorically aware audience. Propaedeutic to legal studies, and basic to pleading, rhetorical forms here indicate an audience professionally attuned to such recognitions. As the work exhibits logical subversion, it displays as well rhetorical misrule – both modes suited to a world-upside-down revels occasion.

Notes

1.   See also Maclean, *Interpretation, passim*; Jody Enders, *Rhetoric and the Origins of Medieval Drama* (Ithaca, NY, 1992); see *ibid.*, 'Forensic Heritage of Medieval French Drama', pp. 162–245.
       Rhetoric in Aristotle and Cicero was directed to the law courts, with the orator prepared to dispute *in utramque partem*, on either side. On the law-rhetoric connection, see, himself a lawyer, Cicero, *De Inventione*, II.xl–li; and Cicero, *Topica*, aiming to show lawyers the utility of rhetoric. Cf. R.L. Enos, *The Literate Mode of Cicero's Legal Rhetoric* (Carbondale, Illinois, 1988).
       See also R.J. Schoeck, 'Lawyers and Rhetoric in Sixteenth-Century England', in James J. Murphy, ed., *Renaissance Eloquence* (Berkeley, California, 1983), pp. 274–91; Schoeck, 'Rhetoric and Law in Sixteenth-Century England', *Studies in Philology*, 50 (1953), 110–27; reply by D.S. Bland, 'Rhetoric and the Law Student in Sixteenth-Century England', *ibid.*, 54

(1957), 498–508. See Alessandro Giuliani, 'The Influence of Rhetoric on the Law of Evidence and Pleading', *Juridical Review*, 7 (1962), 216–51. Law's link to rhetoric is emphasized in the lawyer Thomas Wilson's *Arte of Rhetorique* (1553). Cf. Hardin Craig, 'Shakespeare and Wilson's *Arte of Rhetorique ...*' *Studies in Philology*, 28 (1931), 618–30.

Rhetoric was traditionally paired with logic, and both interrelated with law. Rhetoric and logic together recall Zeno's contrast: rhetoric resembles an open hand, logic a closed fist. On logic and rhetoric, see Christopher Hegendorf, *Libri Dialecticae Legalis* (Paris, 1535), pp. 12–14. On logic versus rhetoric, see Wilson, *Reason*, p. 11. On law in relation to rhetoric and literature, see Kathy Eden, *Poetic and Legal Fiction in the Aristotelian Tradition* (Princeton, New Jersey, 1986).

2.   Cf. Pope, *Sinking in Poetry*.

3.   Cf. Hoskyns, *Speech and Style*, 'Fustian Speech', pp. 108–13. *Prince*, p. 83: 'The Orator made a neat Tuftaffeta Oration, which was answered in a handsome Fustian speech ...'. Cf. William E. Miller, 'Fustian Answer to a Tuftaffeta Speech', *Notes and Queries*, n.s. 5 (1958), 188.

4.   Cf. Cotgrave, *Dictionarie*, s.v. *pine ...* member. See also R. Fletcher, *Ex Otio Negotium. Or, Martiall his Epigrams Translated* (1656), Lib. 4, Epig. 13, p. 32: 'Pine'.

5.   See Nestor's expatiated clichés in his application of his king's 'latest words' (I.iii.31–110). Nestor's instance of the ship tested by storms of fortune, contrasted with the ship on smooth waters, is recurrent in proverbs and emblems (cf. Curtius, *European Literature*, pp. 138–41). (Such proverbial clichés were guyed in the revels: for example *Prince*, pp. 78–79, one '... ran down amongst them, like a *Laocoon* ardens: and with a most furious and turbulent action uttered these two Proverbs, the one borrowed from a Smith, the other from a Clown'.)

6.   Nestor here anticipates Thomas Carew's 'A Rapture', which steers the lover's 'Bark into Loves channell, where it shall / Dance, as the bounding waves doe rise or fall' (*Poems*, p. 51, ll. 89–90).

7.   Recurrently, the play exhibits the rhetorical solecism of catachresis. This, John Smith, *The Mysterie of Rhetorique Unveil'd* (1665), pp. 41, 43, condemns as 'an improper kinde of speech, somewhat more desperate than a Metaphor ... the abuse of a Trope, when words are too far wrested from their native signification ...'. A standard example is: The sword shall devour (cf. Jeremiah 46.10). Recalling the devouring sword, cf. Hector's 'Rest, sword; thou hast thy fill of blood and death' (V.viii.4); and Achilles' 'My half-supped sword that frankly would have fed, / Pleased with this dainty bait, thus goes to bed' (V.viii.19–20). Cf. also Troilus' 'I cannot fight upon this argument; / It is too starved a subject for my sword' (I.i.94–5). If a sword eats, it may also be eaten: 'A should eat swords first' (II.iii.215–16). The sword is personified: 'the great Hector's sword had lacked a master' (I.iii.76).

The sword metaphor is criticized by the Inns of Court rhetoric-counsellor Hoskyns (*Life*, p. 121):

> ... for (swordes) desirous of blood, hee [Sidney] sayth hungry of blood ... the fittnes of bloudshed in a weapon usurpes the name desirous ... [of] a living creature ... it pledeth to thirst, & then to hunger. The rule of a Metaphor is that it be not too bold nor too ... farr fetch't ...

See also on catachresis, Lausberg, *Handbook*, pp. 255, 577.

8.   On the *disputatio* at Oxford, see S.G., 'The Order of Disputations', *Bodleian*

Quarterly Record, 6 (1930), 107–12. Regarding academic judgments on the *disputatio*, see Henry Gunning, *Reminiscences of Cambridge* (1932), p. 48; Christopher Wordsworth, ed. R. Brimley Johnson, *The Undergraduate* (1925), pp. 72–3; Christopher Wordsworth, *Scholae Academicae* (1877), pp. 220–23. On the disputation, see Harris F. Fletcher, *The Intellectual Development of John Milton*, 2 vols (Urbana, Illinois, 1956–61). Thomas Gilby, *Barbara Celarent* (1949).

9.   On zeugma, see Lausberg, pp. 309–15. Cf. Nestor's rhetorical confusions and Dogberry's '... they have committed false report; moreover, they have spoken untruths; secondarily, they are slanders; sixt and lastly, they have belied a lady; thirdly, they have verified unjust things; and to conclude, they are lying knaves' (*MAAN*, V.i.215–19).

10.   Hector as (II.ii) law-defender and eldest son, parallels Inns of Court barristers, many of them (like Shakespeare) elder sons – concerned with their own 'primogenitive and due of birth' (I.iii.106).

11.   Both eponymous lovers are given to generalities about the opposite gender (cf. Cressid's 'You men will never tarry' (IV.ii.16); and Troilus' 'Let it not be believed for womanhood!' (V.ii.129)). On generalities vs. particulars in law, see Maclean, *Interpretation*, pp. 72–3; as Coke noted, the law requires not generalities, but judgments on particular cases. On generalities vs. particulars in law cf. Liebs G2, G3, G4, G6, 172 ('In generalibus latet error'), L52, L67, M22.

12.   The *Rhetorica ad Herennium* (pp. 161–3) treats 'Advantage in political deliberation' (e.g. II.ii) with its 'two aspects: Security [cf. Hector] and Honour [cf. Troilus]'. That rhetorical manual explains: 'To consider Security is to provide some plan or other for ensuring the avoidance of a present or imminent danger'. Against such security-consideration stands honour: 'The Honourable is divided into the Right and the Praiseworthy. The Right is that which is done in accord with Virtue and Duty ...'.

Subordinating security and advantage to glory and honour, Troilus at II.ii's end welcomes Hector into his cause – advantage becomes glory. 'Hector would not lose / So rich advantage of a promised glory' (II.ii.203–4). As the *Rhetorica ad Herennium* (p. 161) puts Security and Honour under the heading of Advantage, Aristotle's *Rhetoric* (I.3, 1358 b) treats Honour under Advantage. Cicero's *De Inventione* (2.li.46) considers Honour and Advantage as coordinate aims. According to the Stoics, Honour and Advantage cannot be at odds (cf. Cicero, *De Officiis*, 3.2.9ff).

Cf. *Rhetorica ad Herennium* (pp. 171–3), recalling the Hector–Troilus security-versus-honour antithesis: '... if it happens that in a deliberation the counsel of one side is based on the consideration of security and that of the other on honour ...'.

The 'speaker who advocates security will use the following topics: Nothing is more useful than safety ... nothing ought to be deemed honourable which does not produce safety'.

On the other hand, 'One who prefers the considerations of honour to security will use the following topics: '... death ... is more tolerable than disgrace ... one must consider the shame which will ensue – neither immortality nor a life everlasting is achieved'. Here are recalled the honour-driven Troilus' motives: avoidance of shame, and desire for canonization in glory. Indeed, 'he who lives honourably, lives safely – whereas he who lives shamefully cannot be secure for ever'. Here also is heard Troilus' defence against cowardice, against 'fears and reasons? fie, for godly shame' (II.ii.32).

Defending 'Manhood and honour' (II.ii.47), Troilus hyperbolically proclaims, 'There's ... none so noble / Whose life were ill bestowed or death unfamed / Where Helen is the subject' (II.ii.156–60).

On debates concerning honour, security, glory and advantage, cf. Cicero, *De Inventione*. See also Rolf Soellner, 'Prudence and the Price of Helen: The Debate of the Trojans in *Troilus and Cressida*', *Shakespeare Quarterly*, 20 (1969), 255–63, citing a standard text on moral duty, Cicero's *De Officiis*.

13. Hyperbole, in Aristotle's view (as cited by Pope, *Sinking in Poetry*, sig. F4v) 'is an Ornament of Speech fit for young Men of Quality; accordingly we find in those Gentlemen a wonderful Propensity toward it ...'. Such 'wonderful Propensity' young Prince Troilus exhibits. On hyperbole, see also Lausberg, *Handbook*, pp. 363–4, 410–11.

14. Such usages follow Erasmus, as noted in Thomas Wilson's *Arte of Rhetorique* (1560), p. 100: 'Erasmus sheweth these to bee the most especial places ... [in exhortation]: Praise or commendation / Expectation of all men. *Hope of renown. Fear of Shame. Greatnesse of reward ...*' (italics added). Cf. II.ii.199–204.

   Troilus – like Paris – recalls *Rhetorica ad Herennium* (Loeb ed., p. 167), to 'show that what our opponent calls justice is cowardice ...'. Cf. Troilus' response to Helenus, II.ii.37–50.

15. On argument, see Lausberg, *Handbook*, pp. 518–19, 607–8; Trimpi, *Muses*, pp. 296–395 and *passim*. On argument and law, cf. evidence and proof as *argumentum*; and Cicero, *Topics*, 2.8: 'argumentum est ratio quae rei dubiae faciat fidem'. On argument and law, and the long tradition of proof as *argumentum*, see Alessandro Giuliani, 'The Influence of Rhetoric on the Law of Evidence and Pleading', *Juridical Review*, 7 (1962), 220–5.

   Arguments were in academic exercises concerned, for example, with Helen. Cf. Erasmus' *De Conscribendis Epistolis*, held to be Shakespeare's letter-writing text in grammar school (Erasmus, *Opera*, 1703, I.766ff.). See Erasmus' *Modus Conscribendi Epistolas* (trans. Baldwin, *Small Latine*, II. 240) concerning whether

   > Antenor should persuade Priam that he should not be unwilling to return the stolen Helen to her Menelaus, either because it was just in itself, or because it would be part of a very foolish ruler on account of the most shameful love of an effeminate youth and hardly a man Paris to cause that so many very brave men should enter battle; the fortunes and even the lives of so many people should be thrown into extreme jeopardy. But if Agamemnon should persuade his brother Menelaus that he should rather neglect Helen than that because of a woman unworthy in life, he should bring so many thousands of noble men into peril of life, and seek her again by a tumult of the whole world, who even if she should return, ought not to be received ... Or if Menelaus should reproach Paris with violated hospitality.

16. Dramatic allusions to rhetorical exercises, such as 'question', 'argument', or 'proof', include 'theme'. 'Theme' occurs in this play most frequently in the canon: II.ii.199; IV.v.30; IV.v.181; V.ii.131. 'Theme' was applied by the declamatory schools to the term 'thesis' ('fictional proposition;' cf. Gr., *thesis*, act of setting out discussion). Troilus fears lest Cressid become 'a theme / For depravation' (V.ii.131–2). 'Themes' were proposed by Erasmus (in *De Rationi Studii*); see W.H. Woodward, *Desiderius Erasmus: Concerning the Aim and Method of Education* (Cambridge, England, 1904), p. 170. Cf. p. 173, and

Menelaus and the Helen-return citation above: 'Amongst suitable subjects ... Menelaus before a Trojan assembly claims the restoration of Helen'. On theme and thesis, see Lausberg, pp. 497–8; Hermann Throm, *Die Thesis: Ein Beitrag zu ihrer Entstehung und Geschichte* (Paderborn, Germany, 1932).

17. 'Argument' or 'proof' alludes also to a syllogistic middle term; cf. 'proof' as evidence. Further, 'argumentum' is one of three types of literary narration distinguished by Quintilian (2.4.2), including 'fabula' and 'historia'. 'Argument' has other, more equivocal, meanings: cf. John Florio, *Queene Anna's New World of Words* (1611), s.v. *argomento*, glister. Cf. with this sense, 'bowels' (II.ii.11), 'collick' (Q, F, IV.v.90), and a pattern of similar terms relating to Ajakes.

18. On the *Achilleum Argumentum*, see Erasmus, *Adagia* (Oxford, 1666), p. 69: 'Rationem et Argumentum Achilleum vocabimus, quod sit insuperabile & insolubile'. (Ajax will have matter, also, because an Achillean argument is insuperable.) Cf. NVS, p. 227.

19. On Pandar's 'world! world! world!' (V.x.36), cf. Puttenham, *Poesie*, p. 212, on 'The figure of exclamation', or 'the outcry', so called 'because it vtters our minde by ... imprecation or cursing, obtestation or taking God and the world to witness ...'. He cites, 'as *Chaucer* of the Lady *Cresseida* by exclamation ... O *caytife Cresseid, for now and euermare*'. The Chaucerian allusion is proverbial (Tilley, *Proverbs*, K116). Troilus exhibits such emotive figures as 'exclamatio' and 'evidentia' (Lausberg, pp. 359–61).

20. In scholastic logic, 'instance' (*OED*, sb. †5) includes a case adduced in objection to, or disproof of, a universal assertion. ('Instance ... a new objection to School disputes to destroy the solution which the Respondent has made to the first Argument'.)

21. Pandar's epilogue, appealing to pity after *indignatio*, recalls a conventional part of the traditional epilogue. According to Aristotle's *Rhetoric* (III.19, 1419), the conclusion comprises the need to conciliate the audience, and to excite the emotions required by the case. As the *Rhetorica ad Herennium* (p. 145) explains, 'Conclusions, among the Greeks called *epilogoi*, are tripartite, consisting of the Summing Up, Amplification, and Appeal to Pity'. In Cicero's *De Inventione* (I.8), the *conclusio* is divided into summing up, invective or *indignatio*, and appeal to pity (*conquestio*). *Conquestio*, notes Cicero (I.iv.106), 'est oratio auditorum misericordiam captans'.

Pandar's concluding audience-address (or *peroratio*) suggests a parodic epilogic *conquestio* (see Lausberg, *Handbook*, pp. 207–208, describing the device 'as the winning of the judges' (audience's) sympathy for one's own party by awakening sympathy for the injustice or misfortune which has befallen. ...'). Thus, the play's epilogue complements the play's Prologue with its appeal ('Like or find fault', l. 30) to the audience judges.

There is rhetoric in pub. thea. plays - + parody (Falstaff.)

5. Logic

... the practice of Law to bee the use of Logike, and the methode of Logike to lighten the Lawe

> Abraham Fraunce, *The Lawiers Logike* (1588)

logike is necessary for obtaining of the knowledge of the Law

> John Doddridge, *The English Lawyer* (1631)

A meere Common Lawyer who has '*Logicke* enough to wrangle'

> Thomas Overbury, *Characters*

This chapter examines the play's reflections of issues of logic. Propaedeutic to legal studies, logic was involved in pleading, and its forms would have been comprehensible by a law-student audience.[1]

Act I scenes i and ii

Definition, identity and contradiction

Troilus' initial demand for definition or the *quid est* ('what Cressid is, what Pandar, and what we'?, I.i.101) recalls an academic, especially legal, mode:

scholastic works regularly initiated a question with reason's first logical act, definition. Regarding identity and contradiction, Pandar and Cressid (in I.ii.59–80) debate whether A is really A, or whether, in violation of logical rule, A 'is and is not' A: compare Pandar's 'brown and not brown',Cressid's 'true and not true' (I.ii.98) and Troilus' 'This is, and is not, Cressid!' (V.ii.146). Identity questions recur (e.g. in II.iii.42–67), where Thersites is quizzed on the identities of Agamemnon, Achilles, Patroclus and himself. Such preoccupation with identity (and its unmasking) is itself (as in *Comedy of Errors* and *Twelfth Night*) a conventional comic concern.[2]

If Ajax, is 'a very man per se' (I.ii.15), 'per se' introduces problems of identity and relation. Ajax himself subverts logic textbook definitions of man – opposed to horse – as a rational animal. 'I think thy horse', taunts Thersites, 'will sooner con an oration than thou learn a prayer without book' (II.i.17–18). The horse, rather than Ajax, Thersites considers *animal capax*, 'the more capable creature' (III.iii.307).[3] That Ajax is a 'very man per se' raises the question of what is a 'man per se' – 'the thing itself' (*KL*, III.iv.106). It recalls also the familiar scholastic distinction between what is *per se* and what is *per accidens*. This duality foreshadows the play's substance–accident antithesis, as well as its extrinsic–intrinsic value debate, and the Ulysses–Achilles exchange (III.iii) on what belongs to 'man' – a Renaissance question of what is intrinsic to the definition of man, and what is mere accident or attribute. (Cf. III.i.37; III.iii.112–30.)

As I.i debates identity, I.ii comprises contradiction and comparison. Juxtaposing names, implying cross-correlations, I.ii invokes shifting identities: Helen and Cressid, Troilus and Paris and Hector, Hector and Ajax.

From her uncle's assertion of the law of identity, 'Troilus is Troilus' (I.ii.65), Cressid develops the law of contradiction: 'he is not Hector'. Thereupon, Pandar reverses the formula: 'Hector is not Troilus', qualifying it with 'in some degrees' (I.ii.68–9). Reaffirming the law of identity concerning 'each of them', Cressid asserts of Troilus, 'he is himself' (I.ii.70). Punning upon identity and self-possession, she retorts that Troilus *is* himself, insofar as, by the law of identity, A = A.

Asserting identity and claiming Troilus' superiority to Hector, Pandar brings to mind Troilus' circular 'woman's answer' (I.i.108)[4]: as in Pandar's identity-formulation that 'Troilus is Troilus' (I.ii.65). This is deflated by Cressid's playfully commonsensical 'Then you say as I say: for I am sure he is not Hector' (I.ii.66–7).

While I.i and I.ii invoke the law of identity, I.ii subverts identity, casting it into the conditional. When Cressid echoes Pandar's claim that Troilus is Troilus, 'he is himself' (I.ii.70), Pandar qualifies this identity-statement: 'Condition I had gone barefoot to India' (I.ii.74). As, in the first scene, Troilus asks the Trojan characters' identity (I.i.101–2), the second scene questions the law of identity, a basis of metaphysical being – and of value, hierarchy and degree.

Pandar tries to escape the 'true and not true' dilemma (I.ii.98) by returning to what Helen said: she praised Troilus' complexion 'above Paris'. Translating 'above' as 'intenser than', rather than 'superior to', Cressid responds that, if Paris' colour is high enough, 'above' that, Troilus' would be too high. (Here and elsewhere, the play employs equivocation, which logic manuals termed *aequivocatio* or *homonymia*.)[5]

Troilus reckons Helen's 'fairness' cost in copious and continual bloodshed: 'Helen must needs be fair, / When with your blood you daily paint her thus' (I.i.92–3). So the Middle Temple's John Ford in his paradoxes (*Honour Triumphant*, 1606) intimates how this fairness was reckoned: 'Helen was counted *faire* because many affected her, procur'd by her enticing wantones, inviting allurements'.[6] If Helen's beauty exists in the test of reaffirmation, it needs reapplications of paint/blood. So Time's 'wallet for oblivion' (III.iii.145–6) requires continual replenishment: as swiftly as 'blood decays' (III.ii.162), an aim is to move faster than decay, to outrace the runner Time.

Act I scene ii

Relations: Ajax; Pandar and Cressid

> all in pieces all coherence gone,
> All just supply, and all relation.

John Donne, 'First Anniversarie'

The play examines bonds and their failures (erotic, socio-political and military), relationally – for example, 'the general is not like the hive' (I.iii.81): the general and the particular, the military general and the individual warriors. Relation recurs problematically: for example, in love, marriage and war, as well as in the degree speech's relations of rank levels – or 'specialty of rule' (I.ii.78). Ulysses' degree-speech, indeed diagnoses a potential failure of relation.

Logical concepts involving descriptions of an object include, as in Aristotle's *Categories*: relation, substance, action, passion, time, place, position, state, quantity, quality.[7] Employed in the play also in other senses are most of these categorical terms; for example 'relation' (III.iii.201); 'substance' (I.iii.324); 'quality' (IV.i.46); 'passion', 'action', 'state' (*passim*); 'place' (I.iii.108); 'position' (III.iii.112).

While Ajax 'hath the joints of everything, but everything so out of joint ...' (I.ii.27–8), and is internally unrelational, Thersites, like him, is also externally unrelational. Anticipated in Agamemnon's unrelational speech-opening to I.iii, Ajax's and Thersites' contest in the next scene is an acting out of Grecian failure of relation.[8] Ajax has been described by his family 'relation' and categorically by relation: 'Nephew to Hector ... a very man per se and stands alone' (I.ii.13–15).[9] (Ajax is nephew to Hector as Cressid is niece to Pandar.) As it inspects the relation of 'relation', the play scans the relation of degree levels: the relation of value to the object and the self, and of perception to the object – the relation of audience to the action, and to itself.[10]

In contrast to Ajax's use in logic as relational symbol, Ajax himself is said to be a monstrous disunity, and constitutionally unrelational: 'This man, lady, hath robbed many beasts of their particular additions' (I.ii.19–20). Not only beasts have been ill-assortedly despoiled, but also the virtues and vices of men: 'There is no man hath a virtue that he hath not a glimpse of, nor any man an attaint but he carries some stain of it' (I.ii.24–6). As Ajax's Greekish persona is relationally qualified: 'A lord of Trojan blood, nephew to Hector' (I.ii.13), his is, moreover, an incoherence external as well as internal. What makes him (with delusions of grandeur) 'stand alone' is, on the one hand, his bad eminence, as Ajakes: on the other, his stolen or borrowed parts from beasts and other men. His asserted uniqueness is thus ludicrous self-delusion: and what he claims as uniquely his are others' ill-assembled and dysfunctional pieces. Antithetical to equable-Horatian stability, Ajax, in Alexander's 'character' (I.ii.19–30), reveals a 'churlish' and mixed personality, ridiculous and (cf. Ajax's 'humours', I.ii.22) – 'humorous'.

As he comprises *disjecta membra*, stealing his parts from others, Ajax is said also to be of mingled blood. Hence, Ajax, if he glances at Jonson, suggests questions regarding the latter's self-vaunted 'unity', coherence and integrity. (We may contrast, with the depiction of Ajax, Jonson's self-congratulatory images as Asper (*Every Man out of His Humor*) and Crites (*Cynthia's Revels*).) Yet, like Thersites, who survives in his bastardy, the Greek–Trojan Ajax emerges unscathed from the aborted Hector-duel (IV.v) *because* he is a mongrel (II.i.13). Reflecting ironically on degree, mongrels (like bastards) paradoxically survive.

Relationally, from Pandar's and Cressid's conditionally advanced exchanges (I.ii), bases are recurrently removed. Assertions are related by 'ifs', or conditions, hypothetically articulated in a dependent chain. The latter anticipates Ulysses' (I.iii) degree chain as well as Thersites' chain of folly (II.iii.61–4), and Troilus' apocalyptic chain (V.ii.138–60). Not only is the uncle–niece dialogue (I.ii) a denial of absolute truth. It is also a mode of conditional dependence, in which almost nothing, relationally, 'stands alone' (I.ii.16): as the series of pile-ups in the work suggests, rather, unreliable dependencies. These anticipate Ulysses' degree speech, where dependent relations are defended, yet are undermined during the play.

Cressid denies Pandar's assertions: when her uncle reports Helen's praise of Troilus' complexion, she responds conditionally (I.ii.105, 107). What emerges is a series of assertions conditionally dependent on prior assertions, themselves questionable. If Pandar depends on his niece to remedy Troilus' love-sickness, she depends 'on my back to defend my belly; upon my wit, to defend my wiles; upon my secrecy, to defend mine honesty; my mask, to defend my beauty' – and her uncle 'to defend all these' (I.ii.261–4). Yet this paradoxical dependence is conditional upon Pandar's questionable prior discretion.

Pandar's Cressid-exchanges (I.ii) are articulated by a series of 'ifs' (or 'ands'). Those joinings, like the lovers', suggest a mode not finally, but conditionally, disposed. Such speculative conditions also surround Troilus' love, whose survival proves (in V.ii) contingent – as seem identities and values themselves. On the insecure basis of 'thy Daphne's love' (I.i.100) – which eluded the god – Troilus appeals to the oracular Apollo to answer essentialist questions: 'what Cressid is, what Pandar, and what we?' (I.i.101). Cressid's and Pandar's series of contingent 'ifs' anticipates Troilus' series of 'ifs' regarding Cressid (V.ii.138–42), as the lover strives to connect cosmic meaning and personal identity. Souls here do *not* guide vows, and yet this *is* she. As Troilus substitutes conditionals and dependencies, such 'slippery standers' (III.iii.84) recall the degree-speech pile-ups (I.iii.109–34) and similar effects through the play: 'Take but degree away' (I.iii.109), and social interdependencies collapse. The indicative is transposed to the conditional or subjunctive; declarations shift to indirect reports; simple truths are qualified; little can be accepted as itself, for itself. So Troilus' apocalyptic discharge (in V.ii.137–60) projects, at witness of Cressid's dallying, a cosmic consequence upon one young girl's fickleness.

Act I scene iii

Misrecognitions

The ambassador Aeneas fails (after the degree speech) to recognize King–General Agamemnon (I.iii.223–5), and (following the Grecians' III.iii.38–71 snubbing) the celebrated Achilles (IV.v.75–6). Such ambassadorial non-recognitions are, during a protracted war, extraordinary: first, because Agamemnon would be pre-eminently placed and accoutred as King and General; and second, because Achilles had ranked as famous Greek champion.

Act II scene ii

Disputatio ad absurdum

And … [in] the thirteene Fallacies had praise.[11]

Francis Lenton, *The Young Gallants Whirligigg* (1629)

And prethee, noble *Ignorantio* Sirnam'd *Elenchi*; wilt thou prove Pandar and procurer to any man ...

Richard Zouche, *The Sophister* (1639)

[in] the train of opponents and respondents ... [one] sweat and foamed at the mouth for very anger his adversary had denied that part of the syllogism which he was not prepared to answer ... [another] gasped and gaped for wind and groaned in his pronunciation as he were hard bound with some bad argument ...

Thomas Nashe, *The Unfortunate Traveler* (1594)

Disputations, scholastic exercises, were rhetorical–logical contests required for graduation from the universities. Law disputations were among required Inns of Court exercises: the regular bolt- or moot-exercise was itself a type of mock-disputation.[12]

Traditionally, inversions of logic and consequent nonsense (as in parodic disputations) were features of academic festivities and the *festum stultorum*. Further, mock-disputations (or *Scherzdisputationen*) themselves comprised a recognizable academic genre, echoed, for example, in Rabelais (cf. Gargantua in *Pantagruel*, chapter 3; and Jonson's mock-disputation in *Bartholomew Fair*, V.v).[13]

In II.ii, Hector and Troilus recall opponents at the start of a disputation: the thesis' *defendens* versus his opponent, the *obieciens* (or *arguens*).[14]

Unlike the intemperate Troilus or the self-interested Paris, conventional disputants were to argue decorously in order, by logic and proof. After Troilus' dismissal of reason (II.ii.37–50), the Defender, Hector, once more takes up the main issue: he repeats his first speech's conclusion, that Helen is not 'worth what she doth cost / The holding' (II.ii.51–3).

The Objector, Troilus, seeks to undermine the Defender's argument by striking at the basis of evaluation itself (II.ii.51–2): 'What's aught, but as 'tis valued?' In doing so (and in his dismissal of reason, II.ii.46–50), Troilus contributes confusion to a traditionally orderly form supposed to discover truth. As disputation Objector to Hector's thesis, 'Let Helen go' (II.ii.27), Troilus, while asserting Helen as a basis of absolute value, subverts his own position by his relativistic value-question (II.ii.52): in effect, what's Helen but as *she* is valued?

Troilus and Cressida comprises a series of deliberations. These include: I.iii, Greek council, on progress of the war; II.ii, Trojan council – whether and how to continue the war; whether to keep Helen and protract the war; III.ii, whether one gender is the superior in love, plus other questions of love – for example can one simultaneously love and be wise? (III.ii.154–6). Compare IV.i's debate whether husband or lover deserves Helen more: her husband (then) or her 'husband'-lover (now). Despite I.ii.161's 'make no question of that', the play 'makes' several 'questions' of such matters.

Traditionally, the disputation was to comprise sequential arguments displaying orderly distinctions, syllogistic reasoning and logical consequence. Yet *Troilus* presents a mock-disputation (II.ii) in which the more rational Defender concludes the scene by embracing his opponent's folly – as with Hector (II.ii, end): 'The issue is embracement' (IV.v.148). If, in scholastic tradition, human action's essential nature is related to the outcome of rational deliberation, the present scene seems parodic of such process. Generally, II.ii's Trojan debates sound like so much fiddling before Troy burns.

Troilus' digressions and judgments are of dubious or inadmissible pertinence, a defect censured in law-maxims. As Troilus intrudes his irrelevancies, there is little *reditus ad propositum*, or return after digression to the main subject. Regarding Helen, the scene lurches from 'explanation' to peculiar explanation: for example, 'Why keep we her? – the Grecians keep our aunt' (II.ii.80). To Hector's speech (II.ii.8–25), Troilus' response is a *heterogenium*, an irrelevant listener-distracting reply. II.ii ends with Hector's peroration, joining Troilus – confirming the triumph of folly. In this 'Fooles play', folly, having beaten down wit (among the Greeks, II.i; among the Trojans, II.ii), is shown in both Trojan and Greek camps triumphant – 'Fools on both sides!' (I.i.92).

Anti-reason[15]

> Raison, nous e'en usons point céans
>
> Rabelais, *Gargantua*

Analogous to II.i's Grecian *argumentum ad baculum* (appeal to violence) is II.ii's Trojan argument through illogic. Indeed, the two scenes are juxtaposed in their world-upside-down display of domination through folly. As Ajax's argument had been *ad baculum* (II.i), Troilus' argument is (in II.ii) *ad odium*, *ad honorem*, and recurrently *ad hominem*. Troilus also wields the *argumentum ad ignorantiam*, which includes browbeating the opponent. Further, Troilus' first speech in the Trojan-debate scene employs the appeal *ad verecundiam* – to shame (cf. *JC*, III.ii.29–30).

As in the appetitive Troilus' own terms, the lust-impelled Tarquin dismisses as weak, 'reason and respect': 'Reason and respect wait on wrinkled age' (*RL*, l. 275). So, for Troilus, 'Reason and respect / Make livers pale and lustihood deject' (II.ii.49–50). In addition, II.ii sets Troilus, lacking prudence and marked by unbridled appetite, against the order of natural law.[16]

Troilus (II.ii.37–50) uses speech (*oratio*) against reason (*ratio*), foreshadowing his further illogicality. If law is a kind of practical reason or prudence (cf. *phronesis*), Troilus' arguments are particularly imprudent. 'Should not', demands Helenus concerning their philo-progenitive sire, 'our father / Bear the great sway of his affairs with reasons', this, despite Troilus' lack of reason: 'Because your speech hath none that tells him so' (II.ii.34–6).

As the Grecians invert the common discourse (of truth, identity and reason) which makes up man, so Troilus dismisses reason while defending Paris' transgressions as reasonable (II.ii.32, 35). Troilus' unreason subverts not only law, but also the community of language itself.

Fallacy of 'indignant language'

Another symptom of logical breakdown is the fallacy identified in Aristotle's *Rhetoric* of angry language.[17] Troilus' initial II.ii speech is directed first (cf. II.ii.25–36) against Hector. Still more indignant is the response of Troilus to his brother Helenus, whom he accuses of cowardice (II.ii.37–50). Troilus brings to mind the counsel in the *Rhetorica ad Herennium*[18] to 'show that what our opponent calls justice is cowardice ...'.

As Paris' tactic is to implicate and upbraid his accusers who, he claims, encouraged him to the deed, Troilus supports Paris in his brazen charge against the Trojans: 'O, theft most base / That we have stolen what we do fear to keep!' (II.ii.92–3). In turn, Troilus engages in sarcasm, angry taunts and derision. Troilus' abuse of his brother Helenus, and his own anger and irrelevance in argument, mark him (cf. II.ii.165–7) as among Aristotle's 'young men' not fit for rational debate.[19]

Against the Defender, the Objector or opposer is Troilus, who holds Hector's argument untenable: Helen should *not* be yielded up. Troilus rejects Hector's use, in regard to Priam's honour, of such unworthily small matters as 'fears and reasons' (II.ii.31–2). This reply of Troilus' suggests multiple irrelevancy: Priam's honour is not the issue in dispute; Hector has already rejected fear as a motive (II.ii.8–14); and the debate is presumably grounded on 'reasons'. Thus, in one short speech, Troilus (as he does in II.ii.52), subverts the rational basis on which he himself is supposed to be arguing.

On various grounds, which relativistically contrast with each other, Hector advocates returning Helen: she causes many deaths; she is not worth what she costs; the 'moral laws / Of nature and of nations' (II.ii.184–5) argue that she be returned to her husband as 'nearer debt' (II.ii.175). Hector's bases are multiple and inconsistent: expediency is mingled with principle – cutting the cost, as expedient: sacred vows of marriage, as principle.

'What's aught, but as 'tis valued?'

On the basis of his 'What's aught, but as 'tis valued?' (II.ii.52), Troilus' own value arguments would seem themselves vulnerable. In terms of its logic, his value question suggests a faulty conversion from the particular to the general, as well as an additional *petitio principii* and *ignorantio elenchi*. In reply to Helenus' charge that Troilus avoids reasons, Troilus retorts *ad hominem* (II.ii.37–50). Once more appealing to emotion, he rejects reason as weakening 'Manhood and honour' (II.ii.47). As Troilus complains of measuring their father's honour by mere reasons, and connects reason with fear, he commits a similar fallacy (II.ii.25–32).

Shifting the burden of proof, as Paris and Troilus do, is an instance of *ignorantio elenchi*, including the assumption that something has been contradicted when it has not been. Modes of *ignorantio elenchi* (cf. Aristotle, *Topics*, Book 6) include evading (as do Paris and Troilus) arguments on the opposite side; shifting the ground of argument to the irrelevant, or from one premise to another; and evasions (cf. II.i.68; 'his evasions have ears thus long') through general or complex terms (e.g., Paris' and Troilus' 'honour'). Like Marlowe's Faustus rejecting reason on behalf of appetite, Troilus in II.ii commits himself to Helen and a promised glory.

Fallacy of false conversion

Troilus, by fallacy of consequent confusing tenses, argues by false conversion: 'If you'll avouch 'twas wisdom Paris went – / As you must needs, for you all cried "Go, go"' (II.ii.84–5). No logical necessity exists for acknowledging the wisdom of an action from the fact that one may previously have encouraged it. Such *non sequiturs* recur: the valid argument, 'It is wise, therefore we will do it', is converted by Troilus to 'We did it: therefore it is wise'. So also his reply, 'the goodness of a quarrel / Which hath our several honours all engaged / To make it gracious' (II.ii.124–5), contains a conversion of the major premise, 'a quarrel that is gracious and good should engage our honours', into 'a quarrel that engages our honours is gracious and good'. The goodness of the quarrel is thus made gracious by commitment of our engaged honours to it. Mistaking hyperbole for literal statement is also a fallacy of *secundum quid*. Among overstaters is Troilus – voice of hyperbole, in his idolization of Cressid, in his championing of Helen (II.ii), and in his would-be 'canonization' in fame (II.ii.202).[20]

Like Hector and Troilus, Paris (violating the legal principle of interest-disqualification) disavows self-interest. Paris' illogic comes through his misleading inversion of tenses: Helen has *already* been Paris' private pleasure, but he alleges such pleasure as a future condition ('I propose not merely to myself / The pleasures such a beauty brings with it', II.ii.146–7). Only one of the contestants for her 'has' Helen: and Troilus is shortly (IV.ii.69), with his brother Paris' collaboration, to be deprived of his own Cressid-'achievement'.

Reminding the Trojans of their commitment, Troilus seeks by inverted logic to bind his hearers to results: *If* they agree that it was wisdom for Paris to go ('As you must needs') – agreement then must be agreement now – ('you all cried "Go, go"', II.ii.85): *if*, further, they 'confess he brought home worthy prize – / As you must needs, for you all clapped your hands / And cried "Inestimable"'! (II.ii.84–8) – approval then must be approval now – Trojans should not now reject their former wisdom. The two 'if' constructions involve the fallacy of the consequent, deriving from a false conversion.

In addition, Troilus (like Paris) argues from a fallacy of consistency: an action in the past requires one in the future, and consent in the past provides a blank cheque for the future.

At every point, Troilus generalizes to the common concern what is merely the particular pleasure of Paris – indeed, the war-plot partly rests on this discrepancy. Having been accused, Paris reverses the case so that it becomes a necessity of Trojan honour to keep the victim of this 'fair rape' (II.ii.148). He refuses, like Falstaff or Hotspur, to deliver up his booty on terms of 'base compulsion' (II.ii.153). As Paris operates by fallacy of consequence (Aristotle, 167 b 1–20; 168 b 27–169 a 5; 181 a 22–30), he also implies that delivering up something through compulsion is base. Hence, delivering up Helen through compulsion is base. But this ignores the circumstance and qualifications which should precede the premise.

Literal interpretation in an unintended sense is related to the logical fallacy of *secundum quid*: a statement taken more broadly or narrowly than meant, leading to an irrelevant conclusion. This includes the fallacy of taking the part for the whole, *fallacia a dicto secundum quid ad dictum simpliciter*. As Falstaff (on honour) and Iago (on reputation), or Shylock and Cassius, nominalistically reduce abstract value to the material or physiological, or to one aspect of its meanings, so does Paris, reporting Pandar, reduce love (III.i.129–34). So, too, the fallacy *secundum quid* characterizes Thersites in his generalizations based on partial views: 'Nothing but lechery!' (V.i.95). Being 'nothing but' Thersites, he is aptly labelled 'fragment' (V.i.8). Thersites' 'nothing but' echoes reductively Paris' report of love's diet: Pandar 'eats nothing but doves, love' (III.i.129), recalling Pandar's song, 'Love, love, nothing but love' (III.i.115).

In the Trojan council scene (II.ii), Troilus' dichotomizing reflects the fallacy of faulty opposition: either one champions Helen *or* one is a coward. Such pseudo-opposition or false exclusiveness is based on faulty division, setting Helenus in the camp of cowards, and Hector (at II.ii's end) in the camp of glorious heroes. Similarly, Paris misleadingly divides the Trojans into those of 'generous bosoms' (II.ii.155) and those who meanly would deliver Helen up 'On terms of base compulsion' (II.ii.153). Although Troilus implies relative value (II.ii.52), he clings to absolute 'honour'. Hence, by a type of fallacy *secundum quid*, he confuses the relativist partial for the absolute whole.

Like Marlowe's Faustus, Troilus shapes logic to conform to desires, and both appetitive figures pervert reasoning to suit their goals. So Troilus and Paris, like shifty debaters, alter the grounds at issue, affirming what is not, in fact, in dispute. (So in his opening II.ii speech, Hector affirms his fearlessness, which was not in dispute.) In so doing, both brothers commit the fallacy of *ignorantio elenchi*, or irrelevance: denying or disproving what the question need not assume, or proving what is not denied.

Troilus includes arguments *ad hominem*: arguments by *petitio principii*; arguments from wrong premises, from silence or compliance wrongly interpreted, and false analogies, running counter to the arguments' general intent. Troilus charges the Trojans with 'theft most base / That we have stolen / What we do fear to keep!' (II.ii.92–3). In II.ii's world-upside-down dispute, it is not the abductor Paris but the Trojans who are deemed culpable.

Here, Troilus intrudes into his *ignorantio elenchi* a Falstaffian appeal to honour among thieves – immorality is ascribable not to theft, but to cowardly theft – fear to hold on to one's loot. He compounds his illogic by a faulty or irrelevant *a fortiori*: If the Trojans had the courage to rob in a foreign country, they should have still more the courage to keep their plunder in their own, where less boldness is required.

Illogic in blunderland

In II.ii, fallacies suggest, amidst reductiveness and errors of argument, a feast of unreason. Troilus' notion of reason guided by will – 'my election / Is led on in the conduct of my will' (II.ii.61–2) – inverts such traditional priorities as 'Reason ... the marshal to my will' (*MND*, II.ii.120). Instead of reason guiding will, 'When the compulsive ardure gives the charge ... reason panders will' (*H*, III.iv.86–8). Troilus' unreason is related to his upside-down views: Renaissance thought connected 'election' with reason rather than with will. If Troilus' 'election' is 'led on' by his will, which is 'enkindled by mine eyes and ears – / Two traded pilots 'twixt the dangerous shores / Of will and judgement' (II.ii.63–5), he subverts the reasoned deliberation which Aristotelian commentators attributed to 'election'. *Prohairesis*, rational choice, yields to *epithumia*, the appetitive impulse that drives Troilus and other personages.

Appetitively impelled as well, Cressid extenuates her fickleness by a specious plea of gender-fallibility (V.ii.109–10). Her generalization anticipates Troilus' hyperbolic fear (V.ii.129–33) lest adverse critics generalizingly indict a whole gender. As both lovers leap illogically from an individual instance to a general indictment, they invert customary legal procedure which applies a general rule or law to a particular case.

Logically and rhetorically, Troilus' matrimonial 'put case' (II.ii.61–8)[21] is among the worst he could have chosen. It reminds his audience both of

Paris' extra-matrimonial adventure and persistent violation of the marital oath. Troilus inquires, 'how may I avoid / Although my will distaste what it elected, / The wife I chose?' (II.ii.65–7). Mingling the relativistic 'distaste' with the rational 'elected', Troilus' analogy is contrary to Paris' circumstance: Paris is being asked to return *someone else's* wife he had *abducted*.

Troilus next argues from precedents and commitment. His euphemistic 'some vengeance' cloaks (with an impersonal passive) the actual misdeed: 'It was thought meet / Paris should do some vengeance on the Greeks' (II.ii.72–3). Further, Troilus invokes the topos, all nature concurs: the elements themselves conspired on Paris' behalf. 'The seas and winds, old wranglers, took a truce / And did him service' (II.ii.75–6). Arguing by false analogy regarding election of a wife (II.ii.61), Troilus inverts a chain of faculties: election is conducted by will: will is aroused by eyes and ears: eyes and ears are 'traded pilots' (II.ii.64), familiar mediators between opposed faculties of will and judgment. Hence, contrary to rational choice implied by 'election', Troilus' election is invertedly led on by will, aroused by his senses, which in turn connect judgment to will.

Remarking that Paris brought home worthy prize, Troilus persistently euphemizes Paris' action – irrelevantly. Why do you do what Fortune did not do, when it brought you such a rich prize? Why do you deny, degrade or 'beggar' it? If Fortune did not refuse you Helen *then*, why should you reject Helen *now* (II.ii.84–96)? Yet Troilus' speech contrasting Trojan 'then' and Trojan 'now' is based on a pseudo *a fortiori*, and a claim for consistency inflexible to changing conditions. The circumstances of Trojan approval *then* are unlike those *now*, as Troilus' 'I take today a wife' (II.ii.61) is unlike Paris' previous abduction of *another's* wife.

Troilus' argument here confirms Hector's imputation of a doting will, which values 'Without some image of th' affected merit' (II.ii.60). Troilus' is a confused defence of the will, his faculty overcome by sense, rather than governed by reason. His self-subversive analogy of food remnants (II.ii.70–2) matches his argument on taking a wife (II.ii.61). Helen analogized to food remainders or 'soiled' 'silk' (II.ii.69, 70) hardly supports Troilus' argument to keep her for 'honour'.

Cassandra

Responding to Hector's plea on behalf of Cassandra, Troilus' argument throws Hector's arguments back at him: 'Cassandra's mad' (II.ii.122). In a speech raising questions about 'sanity', Troilus argues that because she is mad, she ought not swerve them from commitment to honour – 'distaste the goodness of a quarrel' (II.ii.123). Previously, Troilus used a similar argument and the same term, 'distaste', with the analogy of soiled silks and food remnants (II.ii.69–72). Although values may seem *de gustibus*, 'Now good or bad', like 'the chance of war' (Prologue, l. 31), or relatively, 'as 'tis valued' (II.ii.52), they are also for Troilus paradoxically a matter of absolute choice. Ignoring objections, Troilus also shifts from the question of returning Helen to the promise of glory.

In contrast, Hector's is, as soliciting 'Some touches of remorse' (II.ii.115), an *argumentum ad misericordiam*. Hector will later, in vain, appeal to Troilus' pity (V.iii.37–49). Yet in V.iii compassionate appeals to the supposedly merciful Hector by the same sister elicit no 'touches of remorse' (II.ii.115).

Cassandra's entrance highlights the scene's aberrancy: her insane yet prescient foreboding contrasts with the sane Troilus' clouded imprudence. In II.ii, Hector defends their mad sister's insight against the 'reasons' Troilus and the 'besotted' Paris (II.ii.143) 'allege' (II.ii.168). Yet, at II.ii's end, Hector himself joins the 'besotted', and, later, having dismissed Cassandra's prophetic pleading, he is slain.

Eventual ironies

Not entirely to Hector's point is Troilus' reply (to Hector's 'fear of bad success in a bad cause', II.ii.117): 'We may not think the 'justness of each act / Such and no other than event doth form it' (II.ii.119–20). But this formulation is not precisely responsive to Hector's objection – Hector had suggested that a bad consequence may be feared in a bad cause.

While Troilus rejects with Hamlet the 'craven scruple / Of thinking too precisely on th' event' (*H*, IV.iv.41), both youthful princes are ironically victims of the 'event'. Eventual ironies are implicit in the play's '"Who knows what follows?"' (II.ii.13).[22] Despite Troilus' exaltation here of 'ends' (for example, II.ii.198–206), irony inheres in his dismissal of the event in relation to an act's justness. For events contingently afflict Troilus, including his displacement by Cressid, and his brother's death through Achilles' revenge – in the event. Amidst a costly war fought as an unjust abductive act's event, Troilus opposes an act's 'justness' being judged only by the 'event' (II.ii.119–20). Indeed, the II.ii debate scene (like the play) is itself ironically a judgment of the Judgment of Paris, and a judgment of Paris' abductive act by its event.

Cressida has, declares her uncle, 'no judgment' (I.ii.92). Traditional symbol of Henrysonian poetic justice, Cressid will indeed in the play have 'no judgement' – she will here escape final judgment. The 'judgment' of Helen (the prize of Paris' Judgment), like Cressid, in the play, to escape final judgment, is summoned (in I.ii.150–5) to be mocked by Cressid. The judgment of Paris soliciting Diomedes' judgment (cf. IV.i.56–76), as it recalls Paris' Judgment of goddesses effecting Helen's war, is also in question.

Paralleling the 'event' debate (II.ii.120) is the motive dispute. An act which is wrong, argues Hector against Troilus, cannot be justified by a glorious motive: Adultery and rape remain what they are, despite extenuations (II.ii.186–8). Peculiarly, Troilus equates right given through marriage with rape's 'privileges' – 'fair rape' (II.ii.148), as Paris euphemizes his act, is an instance of *synoeciosis*, a composition of contraries. Such paradoxes or oxymorons in the play include 'virtuous sin' (IV.iv.81) and 'secretly open' (V.ii.25).

Troilus' argument against the sole criterion of the event or outcome – or judgment of an act solely by its consequences – suggests further ironies. For, in the event, he himself will ask for judgment in the event: 'Praise us as we are tasted', he pleads with Cressid, 'allow us as we prove' (III.ii.89–90). At III.ii's close, Troilus and Cressida, as well as Pandar, stake their 'reputations' on the event.

Ironically, to Troilus' objections might be counterposed his own 'What's aught, but as 'tis valued?' (II.ii.52). Troilus opposes Hector's warning of 'bad success in a bad cause' (II.ii.117) by a self-defeating *ignorantio elenchi*: he cites, irrelevantly to Hector's objection, 'the justness of an act' in defence of Paris' war-instigating abduction. Legally, an action wrong in itself cannot be absolved by special appeals (permitting questionable means for desired ends); for example Troilus' dubious excuse that in the event the stolen and unjustly retained Helen is 'A spur to valiant and magnanimous deeds' (II.ii.200).

For his part, Paris would universalize complicity, so as sophistically to make wrong right, and right wrong. If Paris can euphemize his abduction as 'fair rape' (II.ii.148), and inculpate the other Trojans, then values seem (as in Troilus' II.ii.52 query) indeed at the disposal of the valuer. Like Brutus' assassination of Caesar, Paris' abductive crime, in whose benefits all are supposed to share, could be thus no crime, but a publicly benevolent intervention. To Priam's charge that Paris' valour is linked to his own pleasure (II.ii.142–5), Paris counters with his own social benevolence-plea, justifying means by ends – a social justification echoed by Andromache who would rob 'in the behalf of charity' (V.iii.22). Paris evades the issue by rejecting (like Hotspur) 'base compulsion' (II.ii.153). The abductor refuses to yield Helen on, anticlimactically, three grounds: 'treason to the ransacked queen'; disgrace to the Trojans; and shame to himself. By a *petitio principii*, Helen's retention is through 'war logic' implicitly defended: Men have, by dying for an ideal (Helen), confirmed its value.

Act II scene ii's *Wonderland* logic thus inverts argument, subverts reason in a mock-disputation, discards reason, and (with Hector, II.ii.189) dismisses the 'way of truth'. As 'compliments' turn into insults, so Trojan logic, like Grecian rhetoric, turns to self-defeating confusion. Hence, on the Greek side, factional disintegration; on the Trojan, faction related to unreason. In this 'Fooles play' (Q, F; V.iii.43), Grecian rhetorical disorder is ruled by folly, while folly's chaos marks Trojan logical fallacy. Paris, with self-interested logic, claims that by 'honourable keeping' what has been stolen (II.ii.149), the misdeed would be 'Wiped off'. Helen's theft, if once endorsed by the Trojans, now commits them, through 'honour', to keeping her – and to protracting in her behalf a costly 'honourable' war (II.ii.68). A transgressive action thus justifies and reinforces, as 'honourable', a dishonourable one. Her abductor Paris with peculiar logic and effrontery argues: 'I would have the soil of her fair rape / Wiped off in honourable keeping her' (II.ii.148–9). Within such an inverted universe of discourse, 'honourable' (as in *Julius Caesar*) mocks its conventional significances.

Paris' 'proof' begins formally enough. Paris uses a scheme (cf. *proecthesis*) defending one's actions by reasons for having done what has been done. In arguing the legitimacy of Helen's abduction, Paris emphasizes the necessity of his act: he (II.ii.130–42) confesses 'the thing done but excuses it by necessity'. The action was impelled, claims Paris, by the Trojans' 'full consent' which 'Gave wings to my propension' (II.ii.133). So Troilus earlier argued, 'your breath of full consent bellied his sails' (II.ii.74). Paris, expanding on such complicity, adopts the 'affected modesty' formula: 'For what, alas, can these my single arms?' (II.ii.135).

Paris' and Troilus' defences of Helen's retention for the sake of the 'general' echo other dubious defences of the 'general good'. (Cf. Brutus on the 'general good', *JC*, I.ii.85; *R3*, III.vii.68.) Paris' self-exculpatory formula (II.ii.146–9), removing himself from 'interest', is a rhetorical device dubiously rendered, since Paris is, of all parties present, most interested (II.ii.146–7). Should the Trojans not support the abductor in retaining his prize, Paris remarkably holds, the world would convict them of 'levity' (II.ii.130).

Once again, Paris has shifted ground from the original question: Should Helen, because of her disproportionate cost and her little worth to the Trojans, be returned? Although Priam accuses Paris: 'You have the honey still, but these the gall' (II.ii.144), it is Paris' 'gall' which permits him to accuse the Trojans in defence of his stolen 'honey'. The abductor marvels at the Trojans exhibiting 'so degenerate a strain as this' (II.ii.154).

Hector's verdict and palinode

Evaluating his fraternal disputation, Hector as disputation-moderator in his summing-up verdict (II.ii.163–73) appears judiciously authoritative. (Hector is given to didactic legal maxims; for example II.ii.173–4: 'Nature craves / All dues be rendered to their owners'; II.ii.186–8: '... to persist / In doing wrong extenuates not wrong, / But makes it much more heavy'.)

Hector's connectives in his summary judgment (II.ii.end) seem, unlike those of his first speech (II.ii.8–17), relatively coherent: 'for', 'now', 'if' –

'then', 'thus', 'but' (II.ii.171, 174, 176, 183, 186, 188). Yet such connectives mark a coherence abruptly to be subverted, not only by Hector's contradictory compliment–insult (II.ii.163–4), but also by his sudden scene-end switch to views he has just rationally opposed.

Traditionally, the disputation was academically in the guidance of a master, who decided the question at issue, and, following presentation of sides, offered a judgment, solution, or 'determination'. Following his brothers and himself in their inverted disputation, Hector takes on the questionable role of judge in his own cause.[23] Hector provides a mock-determination or judgment:

> The reasons you allege do more conduce
> To the hot passion of distemper'd blood
> Than to make up a free determination
> 'Twixt right and wrong ...
>
> II.ii.168–71

As Moderator, Hector replies contradictorily in successive lines, in one breath commending his brothers' 'determination' and negating the praise: 'Paris and Troilus, you have both said well' (II.ii.163) – a *bene disputasti*, you have disputed well, which a student might receive after a disputation or determination.[24] Yet, self-cancellingly, Hector's verdict continues (II.ii.164–5): 'And on the cause and question now in hand / Have glozed – but superficially ...'

Both Hector and Ulysses contradict their own counsels: Hector, having defended natural law, and law itself, qualifies truth and justice in favour of glory (II.ii.186–93).[25] So Ulysses, following his degree encomium, plots, contrary to degree, to inveigle Achilles into the war through a lottery prearranged (I.iii.373–5) to be won by Ajax.

For Hector, at II.ii's end, instead of honour and glory depending on reason and truth, reason and truth depend on honour and glory. In his reversal, moreover, Hector recalls a conventional method of legal dialectic. Argument on opposite sides of a question took place in universities, where the process was a step to a degree, as well as in the bolts, moots and other exercises of the Inns of Court. A law-student audience could recognize in Hector's turn-about an echo of its own exercises – a basis of legal training – arguing both sides of a question.[26] His antithetical positions abruptly exchanged recall the law's traditional training in *dissoi logoi*, speaking on either side.[27]

In the inverted arguments of II.ii are preposterous reliances: 'it hath no mean dependence / Upon our joint and several dignities' (II.ii.192–3). 'The glory of our Troy' depends on Hector's 'fair worth and single chivalry' (IV.iv.147–8), but, despite his 'fair worth', Hector finds trusting Achilles' chivalry (V.viii.9) a singularly fatal dependence.

Hector and Troilus, in their military contradictions, exchange places.

Hector himself is first described contradictorily: his 'patience / Is as a virtue fixed, [yet] today / ... He chid Andromache and struck his armourer' (I.ii.4–6). He is reported to have been 'coped' by a Greek in battle, the shame of which has kept him 'fasting and waking' (I.ii.33–5). Yet he is next reported as challenging the Greeks (I.iii.260–3), to which Achilles in the following scene alludes (II.iii.20–25). Despite such previous military challenge, Hector, through most of II.ii, is opposed to the war.

Troilus, for his part, is first opposed to participation in the war – it is 'too starved a subject for my sword' (I.i.95). Yet, throughout II.ii, he emerges as the war's champion.

At II.ii's end, the brothers' military positions converge. Hector, recalling his earlier challenge to the Greeks, embraces Troilus' war-like commitment (II.ii.206–210).

As Troilus performs a change regarding Helen, Hector turns more than twice, as does Achilles.[28] First, Achilles is out of the war: then, admonished by Ulysses, he fears his reputation is imperilled (III.iii.227–8). Warning Hector that he plans to kill him (IV.v.242–6), Achilles seems to be back in the war. Yet Thersites delivers to him a letter from Hecuba containing a token from her daughter Polyxena, recalling to him his pledge not to fight. Achilles agrees (V.i.36–43), thus reverting to his previous withdrawal. When Patroclus is slain, however, Achilles plunges into revengeful battle. Such changes help orchestrate the plot's contingent, mutable relationships. The eponymal lovers' alteration is adumbrated in such changes as those of Hector, Troilus and Achilles: and echoed even in the sudden anticlimaxes (and 'pretty abruption', III.ii.65) within speeches.

Among Hector's contradictions is his defence of 'fair play' against Troilus' 'Fooles play' (Q, F; V.iii.43). Hector, Troilus complains, allows the captive Grecian foe, 'Even in the fan and wind of your fair sword ... rise and live' (V.iii.41–2). Shortly thereafter, Hector is shown sparing the Grecian Thersites (V.iv.29) – not through mercy, however, but through the latter's claimed lack of 'blood and honour' (V.iv.26). And shortly after that, the 'merciful' Hector is described as destroying the foe: 'Here, there and everywhere he leaves and takes ...' (V.v.24–7). So also the 'merciful' Hector slays both Patroclus (V.v.46–7), and, covetously for his 'hide', the Greek in shining armour (V.vi.27–31; V.viii.1–2).

Hector's 'resolution' (II.ii.191) is his scene-end revolt against reason, coming at a point of alteration from reason to will (cf. *RL*, l. 352: 'My will is back'd with resolution'). At the end of II.ii, Hector snatches defeat from the jaws of victory: the errors he had persuasively condemned, he now adopts. All three Trojan brothers thus exhibit logical subversion: while Troilus and Paris have the knack of supporting the worse cause, Hector has the trick of turning victory into defeat.

Act III scene ii

Tertium quid

In the play's logic of relationships, a *tertium quid* is Pandar, sponsor of amorous pseudo-absolutes, masking transience in the commitments of love. As a dialectic ensues among terms (true, false, and seeming true), Pandar is an intermediary middle term, confidant of 'truth', but kin (uncle) of falsity. Meddling Pandar as mediating middle term, himself at length by Troilus rejected, ultimately becomes 'excluded middle'. If his niece recalls the 'whetstone' (V.ii.76), or sharpener, traditional liar's award,[28] can she be believed even in her own (potential) falsity? Cressid offers herself, if she be false, as a standard of falsity (III.ii.188–95). On this standard, it is Pandar who ironically provides his peculiar seal of 'authenticity' (III.ii.196).

Paradoxically, the truthful and plain Troilus (III.ii.168–9) commits (as in II.ii) the most fallacies, and voices its most arcane diction: maculation (IV.iv.64); recordation (V.ii.116); credence (V.ii.120); deceptious (V.ii.123); orifex (V.ii.151); constringed (V.ii.173); rejoindure (IV.iv.36); (Q, F) embrasures (IV.iv.37). In his world, true Troilus' simple truth, unsubtle and undialectic, is tried, tired, and 'un-trued'.

'To be wise and love': 'Fools on both sides!'

Cressid's 'logic' is a defence against Troilus' charge that she speaks too wisely for one in love (III.ii.151). Compare (1) his claim that she may be wise and thus not love; (2) her counter-charge that *he* is wise and thus loves not; (3) Troilus' rejoinder: would that she could be all he hoped for in a woman. To be wise and simultaneously to love are held to compose a contradiction – forming a (literally) self-stultifying proposition. The lovers' dialogue (a type of Trojan *Dunciad*, like the play itself), composes a contest of unwisdoms: 'Fools on both sides!' (I.i.92). Responding to Troilus' 'Well know they what they speak that speak so wisely', Cressid turns the implication to a *tu quoque*: 'but you are wise, / Or else you love [not]: for to be wise and love / Exceeds man's might: that dwells with gods above' (III.ii.154–6).[29] Each lover thus indicts in advance – and inhibits – the other's potential deviation into sense. The result finds the lovers threshing about in a quagmire of accusatory folly. At the play's centre, the paradox of inability to 'love and be wise' thus rehearses the imprudent or foolish Choice of Paris – of beauty, not wisdom.

But Cressid's ability to formulate her dilemma suggests that she herself is 'wise' and thus cannot love. What results is a logical impasse or tautological circularity – the formulation turns (as in a 'generation of vipers', III.i.134) upon the formulator. Troilus cannot respond on the discrepancy between love and wisdom without seeming 'wise', and therefore incapable of loving. That Troilus may either be wise, *or* love Cressid, is also an implicit insult to Cressid by her own logic. (Insofar as Troilus has already dismissed reason (II.ii.32, 35, 49), he is eligible for the unwisdom of loving her.) Logically, Troilus cannot 'win at the odds' (*H*, V.ii.211–12). For any sign of intelligence – any deviation into sense – subverts his lover's claim to greater unwisdom, or to greater folly. In this bind, unwisdom undoes him, while any hint of rational capacity declares him love-ineligible. As the Cressid–Troilus love debate in III.ii correlates love and folly, the dispute echoes parodically the work itself: in this 'Fooles play' is implied (appropriately to an academic misrule occasion) the Erasmian or *festum stultorum* commonplace that 'it is folly to be wise'.

Troilus' unwisdom contest with Cressid is, moreover, set in military terms: as Cressid claims greater simplicity, she challenges, 'In that I'll war with you'. To this, Troilus retorts, 'O virtuous fight, / When right with right wars who shall be most right!' (III.ii.170–1) – a contest in which adversaries each claims a greater simplicity and a 'most right' just war.[30]

Act V scene ii

'Doubt truth to be a liar'

> Shall I not lie in publishing a truth?
> (V.ii.119)

Patroclus is either a 'slanderer' (I.iii.150) who, by mimetic derision, maligns the Greek leaders, including Agamemnon and Nestor; *or* he demeans by ineptness the profession of 'imitation' (or acting) – or both. His slanders, if 'true', may be 'honest slanders' (*MAAN*, III.i.84). Patroclus as false 'gilt counterfeit' (II.iii.24) falsely or truly slanders the 'true' King Agamemnon who is also, as indecorous (if 'true') king, 'false' ruler. If true, then false; if false, then true: thus is the Liar's paradox (cf. V.ii.119) implicated.[31] The 'true' Troilus, a naïvely unskilled (hence 'false') lover, is himself to suggest that paradox. This occurs as he observes a true/false vision of the false but truly seductive Cressid, played by a boy as counterfeit girl – (as in V.ii) theatrically, and in her *légende*, both 'there' and 'not there'.[32]

At midplay, 'truth tired with iteration' (III.ii.175) evokes the relation of outworn language to truth. Marriage troth or truth is a subject of III.ii, along with the relation of vows to troth and truth themselves. As discrepancies of words with truth emerge, the concluding act probes the truth of words as vows, the violations of sworn troth/truth. Truth there 'Fails in the promised largeness' (I.iii.5). Ironically, it is the True-ilus character, with his echoic name, true to Cressid, and as Troy-ilus, true to Troy, who inquires: 'Shall I not lie in publishing a truth?' (V.ii.119).

As in his hope for 'a winnowed purity in love' (III.ii.166), Troilus' outbursts suggest an 'untutor'd youth, / Unlearned in the world's false subtleties' (Sonnet 138). Despite his subversive value-question (II.ii.52), he is unprepared for 'truth' as related to subjectivity, or for truth as contingent truth: or a coherence view of truth. Troilus' traditional correspondence view of truth (*adequatio*) involves a relation of conformity of knowledge and the thing known.[33] Insofar as Troilus perceives truth undialectically, as iterative or 'persistive constancy' (I.iii.21) – 'something of great constancy' (*MND*, V.i.26) – or as predictable correspondent regularity, for him Cressid's dallying implies cosmic disorder: 'Chaos is come again' (*O*, III.iii.92).

'Deceptio visus': 'This is, and is not, Cressid!'

As 'Cressid' is identified by Troilus with 'Cressid' of an earlier stage, it is not Cressid's earlier 'forms, moods, shapes' that can here and now 'denote' her 'truly' (*H*, I.ii.82–3). 'This is, and is not, Cressid!' (V.ii.146) recalls not only the play's confused recognitions, but also the inconsistencies of dramatic dialectic, as well as discrepancies between the character as here and as traditionally portrayed. Troilus' exclamation paradoxically undermines both the law of contradiction and the reliability of perception, joining logical subversion with epistemological doubt. So Cressid's 'show' and Cressid's 'worth divide / In storms of fortune' (I.iii.46–7). Troilus moves from illusion – that Cressid is 'a pearl' and 'her bed is India' (I.i.102) – to delusion: 'rather think this not Cressid' (V.ii.133) – if not *his* Cressid, not Cressid – has the parodic-extreme logic of 'If not Achilles, nothing' (IV.v.76).

If Pandar's 'will shall here be made' (V.x.51) implies local witnessing, spectators 'here' as attesting, V.ii suggests a *récit spéculaire*: a theatrical watching of the process of witnessing: how various witnesses react to a scene, and perceive differently. Clinging, despite discrepancies, to his 'reality', witnessing Troilus, like Quixote and the Knight of the Burning Pestle, suffers the buffeting of the 'real' world. Complementing Don Quixote, Sancho's 'realistic' world seems here suggested by the boor Thersites and the *eiron* Ulysses. Indeed, V.ii recalls *Quixote*'s opposition between a love-delusional protagonist and a prosaic 'reality'.

As in I.i Troilus queries identity, and in II.ii value, in V.ii he questions identity and value in 'cognition' (V.ii.64). Troilus confronts his dilemma by doubt and denial – by cognitive dissonance and self-alienation. In a play of misrecognitions, Troilus' 'I will not ... have cognition / Of what I feel' (V.ii.64–5) threatens a failure of cognition in re-cognition.

Generalizing Troilus

Troilus leaps illogically from extremes of overvaluing Cressid, to undervaluing (V.ii.129), from the insufficient individual case to the dubious general induction. If believing Cressid were 'there' would produce such calumny (ll.129–37), Troilus prefers to credit the alternative: 'rather think this not Cressid' (V.ii.133). Troilus generalizes from one instance *secundum quid*, 'to square the general sex / By Cressid's rule' (V.ii.132–3). Hyperbolically, Troilus' denial implies: if this *were* Cressid, women would all be seen to be false (cf. *KL*, III.vii.102). Ergo, this is not Cressid. Troilus' addiction to generalization as in 'Let it not be believed for womanhood! / Think we had mothers' (V.ii.129–30) is punctured by Ulysses' wry 'What hath she done, prince, that can soil our mothers?' (V.ii.134).

Troilus' 'That cause sets up with and against itself!' (V.ii.143) suggests a paradoxical dispute assuming both sides. 'Cause' is also subject of litigation, a matter before a court for decision, the case of one party in a suit. Troilus' 'with and against itself!' echoes the play's paradoxical 'true and not true', 'brown and not brown', 'This is, and is not, Cressid'! (I.ii.97–8, V.ii.146) – contrary to logical rules, these, indeed, 'strain at the position' (III.iii.112).

As Troilus' first scene questions identity (I.i.101), his last act inquires the relation of identity to perception (V.ii.133). Witnessing Cressid with Diomede brings into question, for Troilus, premises of thought: laws of identity, contradiction, and excluded middle. 'Bifold authority!' (V.ii.144) here capitulates to 'madness of discourse' (V.ii.142–4).

As Troilus begins by bearing witness against himself (I.i.7–12; I.i.9–12; cf. IV.iv.85–8), he later bears witness against Cressid: 'Instance, O instance!' (V.ii.153, 155). By fallacy of *secundum quid*, he attributes to the general, absolutely, what may be true in particular, relatively. His chain of 'if's' (V.ii.138–42) thus depends by fallacious generalization from the relative instance. His repeated 'instance' (in V.ii.153–5) suggests that, rather than viewing Cressid in her particularity, he perceives her also as an 'instance' of some generality.

Unity and division[34]

Logical issues pervade both *Troilus* and Shakespeare's contemporary poem, 'The Phoenix and the Turtle' (in *Love's Martyr*, 1601).[35] The dramatist has Troilus see division, where that poem rather 'Saw division grow together'. 'Reason', which rules distinction, is in the poem 'in itself confounded' by love. Reason seems irrationally subverted. 'Love has reason, Reason none, / If what parts, can so remain' ('Phoenix', ll. 47–8).

Troilus' 'What's aught, but as 'tis valued?' (II.ii.52) subjectively separates value from the unity and principle of identity, of 'Being'. Troilus, who had himself thus subverted unity, now complains, 'If there be rule in unity itself, / This is not she' (V.ii.141–2). Such outbursts suggest the opposite of love as unitive force – the latter view celebrated in 'The Phoenix and the Turtle'. There, constancy is praised, along with love, beauty and truth, while unity is a keynote, in contrast to division. Indeed, in that poem (unlike V.ii.148–9), union was so close that space was not seen, and distance was absent (l. 30).

As 'martyrdom' (martyr, Gr. witness) includes witnessing, Troilus is by *mise en abyme* witnessed (by Ulysses, Thersites and, in turn, the audience) as he witnesses his own love's martyrdom. Thus, he (like Pandarus) exemplifies, in more than one sense, the collection-title, *Love's Martyr*: Troilus as witnessed witnessing victim of love.

Like *Troilus*, that collection's 'The Phoenix and the Turtle' comprises scholastic concepts and terms, for example, division, property, distinct, essence. 'The Phoenix and the Turtle' observes, 'Two distincts, division none: / Number there in love was slain' (ll. 27–8). 'Either was the other's mine. / Property was thus appalled, / That the self was not the same' (ll. 36–8) – as in the case of Troilus 'appalled' that Cressid's 'self was not the same', that 'This *is*, and *is not*, Cressid' (V.ii.146). While Single nature's 'Reason, in itself confounded, / Saw division grow together' (ll. 41–2), the less reasonable Troilus (II.ii.38–49) sees division grow apart (V.ii.149).[36]

As Troilus' speech (V.ii.138–42) contains a 'degree chain' built on questionable 'if's, he leaps by *secundum quid* fallacy from relative conditions and individuals to absolute conclusions. Troilus' present series of conditional assertions has already been undermined: '*if* beauty have a soul' – a question subverted in III.i, where the vapid Helen is introduced as 'love's indivisible [Q, F invisible] soul' (III.i.33–4); '*if* sanctimony be the god's delight' (V.ii.140). ('*If* souls guide vows' has been subverted in Cressid's own unsoulful vow-violation, and her admission (V.ii.110–12) that 'The error of our eye directs our mind …'.)

To summarize, this chapter has examined logical significances, and illogicalities, including logical inversions (as in mock-disputations), recognizable by an academic–legal audience. Recognition of standard fallacies is also here relevant to dramatic comprehension. As logic was propaedeutic to legal study and basic to forensic pleading, expressions of logical inversion and misrule would have been perceptible and suited to a festive law-student occasion.

Notes

1. Logic was traditionally preparatory to legal studies and pleading. On law and logic, see Paul Vinogradoff, *Outlines of Historical Jurisprudence* (Oxford, 1920), I.3–27. Cf. I.15: '... all the principal operations of juridical thought necessarily contain elements of logical analysis'. Cf. I.5:

    > ...juries attending to the arguments of parties have to be careful not to be misled by fallacies ... [e.g.] the sophistical trick called *ignorantio elenchi* (irrelevant conclusion) from its frequent use by barristers. This sophism consists in substituting for the proposition to be proved some other proposition irrelevant to the problem of proof. Another fallacy much favoured by sharp pleaders is the substitution of the absolute affirmation for a conditional one (*a dicto secundum quid ad dictum simpliciter*).

    On legal pleading, and (as with Troilus, especially in II.ii) wandering from the point at issue, cf. Vinogradoff, I.8: 'It was important in a contest before the Court that the parties not be allowed to ... confuse the jury by irrelevant assertions and arguments. Historically, the growth of Common Law procedure was chiefly directed towards keeping pleadings within reasonable bounds and conducting them along definite logical avenues'.

    On law and logic, cf. V. Piano Mortari, *Diritto, Logica, metodo nel secolo XVI* (Naples, 1978); Mortari 'Dialettica e Giurisprudenza: Studi sui trattati di dialettica legale del XVI secolo', *I Annali di storia del diritto* (1957). Gerhard Otte, *Dialektik und Jurisprudenz* (Frankfurt am Main, 1971); Cesare Vasoli, *La Dialettica e la retorica dell'umanesimo* (Milan, 1968). Aldo Mazzacano, *Scienza, logica e ideologica nella giurisprudenza tedesca del sec. XV* (Milan, 1971). Cf. Cyprianus Regnerus, *Demonstratio logicae verae iuridica* (Leiden, 1638), ed. Georges [Jerzy] Kalinowski (Bologna, 1986).

    On logic and law, and the relations of rhetoric and logic, cf. Cesare Vasoli, 'La Dialettica umanistica e la metodologia giuridica nel secolo XVI', in *La Formazione storica del diritto moderno in Europa*, vol. 1 (Florence, 1977); Alessandro Giuliani, 'L'élément "juridique" dans la logique médiévale', *Logique et Analyse*, n. 6 (1963), 540–70. Cf. L.A. Knafla, 'The Influence of Continental Humanists and Jurists on English Common Law in the Renaissance', in R.J. Schoeck, ed., *Acta Conventus Neo-Latini Bononiensis, 1979* (Binghamton, NY, 1985), pp. 60–71. See handbooks on legal logic and rhetoric: for example Matteo Gribaldi, *De Methodo ac ratione studiendi* (Lyons, 1541). As Francis Bacon, himself a lawyer, pointed out ('Of Studies', *Essayes*, p. 153): '*Logick* and *Rhetorick* [make men] Able to Contend'.

    Cf. also Hardin Craig, 'Shakespeare and Formal Logic', in Kemp Malone, ed., *Studies in English Philology* (Minneapolis, Minnesota, 1929), pp. 380–96; A.H. Gilbert, 'Logic in the Elizabethan Drama', *Studies in Philology*, 32 (1935), 527–45; E.L. Wiggins, 'Logic in the Poetry of John Donne', *Studies in Philology*, 42 (1945), 41–60. See also W.S. Howell, *Logic and Rhetoric in England 1500–1700* (New York, 1956); E.J. Ashworth, 'Logic in Late Sixteenth-Century England: Humanist Dialectic and the New Aristotelianism', *Studies in Philology*, 88 (1981), 224–36.

2. On definition, see Lausberg, pp. 51–7. On definition and law, see Cicero, *De Inventione*, I.viii.2. See Ian Maclean, 'The Place of Interpretation: Montaigne and Humanist Jurists ...', in Graham Castor and Terence Cave, eds, *Neo-Latin and the Vernacular in Renaissance France* (Oxford, 1984), pp. 257–8: 'Law must ... proceed by definition, and medieval glosses are made up ... of

definitions in the scholastic mode, by *genus, differentia, species, proprium, accidens'*. See Wilson, *Reason*, pp. 92–3. On definition, see Claudius Cantiuncula, *Topica* (Basle, 1520), pp. 13–16, 21–5. Thomas Gilby, *Barbara Celarent* (1949).

3.   On the man–horse comparison as a pre-Swiftian topos (cf. II.i.17; III.iii.126; III.iii.306–7), see traditional logic-textbooks' distinction, following Porphyry. Such conventional man–horse antithesis is examined in R.S. Crane, 'The Houyhnhnms, the Yahoos, and the History of Ideas', in Crane, *The Idea of the Humanities* (Chicago, Illinois, 1967), II.261–82.

4.   Troilus remarks a 'woman's answer' (I.i.108). This, or 'woman's reason' (cf. *TGV*, I.ii.20–2; Tilley, *Proverbs*, B179), recalls a term in logic for a fallacy of circularity, or begging the question. Alexander Richardson's *Logicians School-master* (1629) describes the 'woman's reason' or cuckold's fallacy: 'The fallacian of the common Logicians of *Coxismus*, or *petitio principiis*, or *cuculi cantus* ... this is commonly the woman's reason ... as they will say it is so ... because it is so' (p. 58). Apropos to that *cuculi cantus*, or cuckow song, Troilus' 'woman's answer' comes ironically at a point where he mocks the cuckold (I.i.113–14), whom he is himself eventually to recall. On the 'Cuckoes Song' as related to fallacy, cf. Wilson, *Reason*, pp. 198–9.

      'Woman's reason' or 'answer' (I.i.108), in the sense of a fallacy of circularity, suggests relevance to Inns of Court usage, as indicated in the Middle Temple diary of John Manningham for 1602–03. In an entry for February 1602, Manningham (Sorlien, p. 186) cites Enoch Clapham (a popular preacher who appealed (*Diary*, p. 13) to Inns of Court students), on local usage: '"I will not believe it, because I will not" is Tom Sculs argument, as they say in Cambridge, and a woman's reason as they say here' – 'here' concerns a local term for circularity. 'As they say here' suggests, in Manningham's Middle Temple diary, 'woman's reason' or 'answer' as suited to the diction of Manningham's 1602–03 Inns of Court.

5.   Regarding complexion, cf. Pandar's and Cressid's exchange: 'To say the truth, brown and not brown ...' (cf. I.ii.96–105). This dialogue echoes, regarding complexion, Aristotle, *Metaphysics*, 1005 b 24–25 on the form according to which 'it is impossible for any one to believe the same thing to be and not to be'. Cf. Jan Lukasiewicz, 'On the Principle of Contradiction in Aristotle', *Review of Metaphysics*, 24 (1971), 538 ff.

6.   Ford, *Nondramatic*, p. 49.

7.   Cf. Edward Brerewood, *Tractatus quidam logici de praedicabilibus et praedicamentis*, ed. Thomas Sixesmith (Oxford, 1628); D.P. Henry, 'Predicables and Categories', in *Cambridge History of Later Medieval Philosophy*, pp. 128–42.

8.   On relation, see Julius R. Weinberg, 'The Concept of Relation: Some Observations on its History', *Abstraction, Relation, and Induction* (Madison, Wisconsin, 1965), pp. 61–119. See also A. Krempel, *La Doctrine de la relation chez St. Thomas* (Paris, 1952); Mark G. Henninger, *Relations: Medieval Theories 1250–1323* (New York, 1989); Rolf Schönberger, *Relation als Vergleich. Die Relationstheorie des Johannes Buridan ...* (Leiden, The Netherlands, 1994).

9.   Cf. Ajax's relational description (I.ii.13–15) and that in Wilson, *Reason*, sig. D7, pp. 32–3, on the 'category of relation ... he is a father, that hath a sonne, he is a maister, that hath a seruaunt ...'. Relation is a term, 'referring, comparing or applying of one thing to another, for some respect of affinity or likenesse, wherewith they are so knit together, as the one may not be well understood without the other' (Thomas Blundevile, *The Arte of Logicke* (1619), p. 36).

10. 'Relation' is a performer in Milton's 'At a Vacation Exercise in the College', and one of the ten sons of Ens, whose eldest was Substance. Cf. Wilson, *Reason*, p. 32. According to a correspondence theory of truth, 'truth is a relational concept consisting in a relation of correspondence to a fact: ... (A man is an uncle in those and only those cases where there is a matching niece)', Stephen Read, *Thinking about Logic* (Oxford, 1994), p. 7.

Ajax as 'a very man per se' (I.ii.15) contains an academic term 'per se' opposed scholastically to *per accidens*. See Kretzmann, *Translations*, index, *per se, passim*. On modes of *per se*, cf. J. Stierius, *Praecepta* (1659).

On Ajax's use in logic as relational symbol, cf. Peter of Spain, *Tractatus ... Summule Logicales*, ed. L.M. De Rijk (Assen, The Netherlands, 1972), in Tractatus VIII, 'De Relativis'. That logic manual cites, p. 187, the grammarian Priscian, who uses Ajax's name as symbol. See Radulphus Brito, *Quaestiones super Priscianum Minorem. Grammatica speculativa*, ed. H.W. Enders et al. (Stuttgart, 1980), II.253, 256: Quaestio 45, on grammatical relation, involving 'Ajax'. Connecting Ajax with logic instruction is, as noted above, *The Summule Logicales of Peter of Spain* (Notre Dame, Indiana, 1945), ed. J.P. Mullally, pp. 24–5, citing Priscian (*Institutione grammaticae*, ed. Heinrich Keil, pp. xvii, 56): 'Ajax came to Troy and Ajax fought courageously; it is doubtful whether "Ajax came to Troy and the same fought courageously", one immediately understands that numerically the same Ajax is meant'. On Ajax's and Hector's nominal employment in early logical treatments, see also Sten Ebbesen, 'Porphyry's Legacy to Logic: a Reconstruction', in Richard Sorabji, ed., *Aristotle Transformed* (1990), pp. 141–79. Cf. Zeno of Elea's paradox of Achilles and the tortoise. Hector's and Achilles' names were used also in medieval logic: for example in Anselm, Archbishop of Canterbury, *De Veritate*, ch. 8.

11. On fallacies, cf. Richard Zouche, *The Sophister: A Comedy* (1639), with Fallacy as a central character; and Sten Ebbesen, *Commentators ... on Aristotle's 'Sophistici Elenchi' ... Ancient and Medieval Writings on Fallacies*, 3 vols (Leiden, The Netherlands, 1981). See also Hans V. Hansen and R.C. Pinto, eds, *Fallacies* (University Park, Pennsylvania, 1995). Charles L. Hamblin, *Fallacies* (1970). L.M. de Rijk, *Logica Modernorum* (Assen, The Netherlands, 1967), 2 vols. For an instance of Elizabethan theatrical use of fallacies, cf. Marlowe's Faustus, whose illogic would have been recognizable by an academic audience: A.N. Ankerlund, 'The Intellectual Folly of Dr. Faustus', *Studies in Philology*, 74 (1977), 258–78.

12. On disputations, see J.H. Baker, *The Legal Profession and the Common Law* (1986), pp. 16–22; Brian Lawn, *The Rise and Decline of the Scholastic 'Quaestio Disputata'* (Leiden, The Netherlands, 1993); L.M. de Rijk, *Die Mittelalterlichen Traktate de Modo Opponendi et Respondi* (Münster, Germany, 1966). On legal relations of the *quaestio* and the *disputatio*, see Olga Weijers, *Terminologie des Universités au XIIIe Siècle* (Rome, 1989), pp. 335–9.

13. Academic mock-disputations are catalogued in Wilhelm Erman and Ewald Horn, eds, *Bibliographie der deutschen universitäten* (Leipzig, 1904), I, 353–69, listing numerous *Scherzdisputationem*, including those from the Renaissance. On the academic mock-disputation, cf. Erich Kleinschmidt, 'Scherzrede und Narrenthematik im Heidelberger Humanistenkreis um 1500 ...', *Euphorion*, 71 (1977), 47–81, 281. See Konrad Vollert, *Zur Geschichte der lateinischen Facetiensammlungen des XV. und XVI. Jahrhunderts* (Berlin, 1912), pp. 40–3. On the mock-disputation, see also the

Epistolae Obscurorum Virorum, satirizing the disputation in a letter (A XXXVII: 95, 5ff.) of Lupoldus Federfusius: Reinhard P. Becker, *A War of Fools: The Letters of Obscure Men. A Study of the Satire and the Satirized* (Bern, 1981), pp. 115–17. See also Milton's *Sixth Prolusion*, containing elements of a parodic disputation. Disputations are echoed in John Heywood's *The Spider and the Fly*; Robert Greene's *Friar Bacon and Friar Bungay*, sc. 9; the gravediggers' scene in *Hamlet* (V.i); and Thomas Middleton's *A Chaste Maid in Cheapside* (IV.i). See L.A. Beaurline, *Jonson and Elizabethan Comedy* (San Marino, California, 1978), pp. 219–24.

Troilus' abusive manner recalls that of traditionally combative 'barking dogs' intemperate in disputations: Alexander Murray, *Reason and Society in the Middle Ages* (Oxford, 1978), pp. 234–7. See *Juan Luis Vives against the Pseudodialecticians: A Humanist Attack on Medieval Logic*, ed. Rita Guerlac (Dordrecht, The Netherlands, 1979), pp. 4–5, 143–53, 179–91. On disputation and 'determination' (II.ii.170) – judgment on the disputation – see Jody Enders, 'The Theater of Scholastic Erudition', *Comparative Drama*, 27 (1993), 344–5, 355–7.

14.   'That is called a disputacion ... when certein persones debate a cause together, and one taketh parte contrarie vnto another, the one answering, and denying, and the other stil apposing and confirming ...'. The result is 'after harde holde, and long debating, the trueth either appeareth, or elles thei rest bothe upon one poincte, leaving the matier to bee adiudged ...' (Wilson, *Reason*, p. 153).

On the disputation, see also W.T. Costello, *The Scholastic Curriculum in Early Seventeenth-Century Cambridge* (Cambridge, Massachusetts, 1958); pp. 14–31. Hermann Schüling, *Die Geschichte des Axiomatischen Methode im 16. und beginnenden 17. Jahrhundert* (Hildesheim, Germany, 1969); J.E. Seigel, *Rhetoric and Philosophy in the Renaissance* (Princeton, New Jersey, 1968); J.B. Altman, *The Tudor Play of Mind* (Berkeley, California, 1978). See also Harris F. Fletcher, *The Intellectual Development of John Milton* (Urbana, Illinois, 1961), II. 238–70. Alfonso Maierù, *University Training in Medieval Europe* (Leiden, The Netherlands, 1994). Thomas Gilby, *Barbara Celarent* (1949).

15.   Anti-reason is linked to Troy in Petrarch (*Opera*, Basle, 1554, pp. 872–3): Troy, the voluptuous city, symbolizes the body in sleep, its gates opened by sins. Cf. Cristoforo Landino, *Disputationes Camaldulenses* (1508), Book 3: 'the youthful life of man when reason slumbers and the senses rule'. '... Troy is that first [state] of nature in which corporeal pleasures chiefly thrive ... reason is not yet able to arouse itself ...'. See Don Cameron Allen, *Mysteriously Meant* (Baltimore, Maryland, 1970), pp. 150 and *passim*. Allen, 'Some Observations on *The Rape of Lucrece*', *Shakespeare Survey*, 15 (1962), 89–98.

16.   Cf. Troilus' reason-rejection versus an audience professionally concerned with relating reason and law. (On the relations between and law and reason, see also Liebs C24; L15; L50; R4; U 7). Cf. 'from logicke to law (both grounded on reason)', Francis Lenton, *Characterismi* (1631), sig.F4. On law as right reason, cf. Cicero, 'est enim lex nihil aliud nisi recta ratio ...', *De Legibus*, I.6.18, I.2.4; Cicero, *Philippics*, xi.28. See Robert Hoopes, *Right Reason in the English Renaissance* (Cambridge, Mass., 1962).

17.   On the fallacy of indignant language see Aristotle, 1401b, 3–9.

18.   III.iii.6 (ed. H. Caplan, p. 167).

19.   Cf. NVS, pp. 106–8.

20.   On the fallacy *secundum quid*'s juridical misuse, cf. Aristotle's *De Sophisticis Elenchis*, 167 b 8.

21. 'Put case': see S.H. Thorne, ed., *Readings and Moots at the Inns of Court*, v.II (Selden Society, 1990), pp. lxxiii–lxxiv: the 'put-case' was among Inns of Court learning exercises, including a short case of an arguable point.

22. '"Who knows what follows?"' (II.ii.13) recalls the concern of logic itself. 'Logical consequence is the central concept in logic. The aim of logic is to clarify what follows from what. ... The consequence relation relates a set of given propositions to those ... conclusions which ... validly, follow from them'. – Stephen Read, *Thinking about Logic* (Oxford, 1994), p. 35. Troilus' argument, 'We may not think the justness of each act' to be estimatable solely by its 'event' or consequence (II.ii.119–20), recalls Socrates (*Apology*, 28 d 10–29 a 4): the justness of an act should be decided on, and the act performed, without fear of consequence. So Plato's *Republic* (cf. Book 2) tries to show a just act is good apart from consequences. (In contrast, the pragmatic Henry IV argues for judgment by the event, 'that nothing can seem foul to those that win', *1H4*, V.i.8.) Troilus here recalls a platonic absolute; his attitude to an act's justness seems deontological (necessary/dutiful), as opposed to teleological (consequential/utilitarian).

Aristotle (*Nicomachean Ethics*) carries Plato's *Republic* view further, holding that the virtuous man will choose virtuous actions for their own sake (1105 a 31–3 1144 a 19–20), or, even should the event prove personally disastrous, for the sake of admirable actions (1115 b 11–13, 1169 a 6–11, 1169 a 19–b 1).

23. Hector's role as a judge in his own cause recalls the legal maxim that no one may so act. Cf. *TN*, V.i.354–5, 'Thou shalt be both the plaintiff and the judge / Of thine own cause'. Cf. Richard Hooker, *Works*, general ed., W. Speed Hill (Washington, DC, 1977), V. 337, 819–20. '*No man can be a competent judge of his own right*'. On this legal commonplace, cf. Thomas Aquinas, *Summa Theologica*, 2a 2ae, 64.5 ad 2. See Liebs, N53; N56; N 75; N 82.

24. Hector's praising and condemning the same thing recalls an exercise in logic. Cf. Aristophanes, *Clouds*, l. 1336. Protagoras taught to praise and blame the same thing, 'making the worse argument seem the better' (Cf. Aristotle, *Rhetoric*, 1402 a 24–5). See Christopher Wordsworth, *Scholae Academicae* ... (Cambridge, England, 1877), p. 38, citing eighteenth-century verdicts on disputations: 'Tu autem ... satis et optime quidem, et in Thesi et in Disputationibus, tuo officio functus est'. Or '... summe ingenii acumine disputatisti ...'.

25. Cf. Hector's and Troilus' dispute (II.ii), with Hector capitulating, and Aristophanes' Right and Wrong debates: *Clouds*, ll. 889–104, 1321–452; and *Frogs*, ll. 905–1098. Cf. the *Clouds*' victory of Unjust Logic, after Just Logic deserts, like Hector, to the opponent's side.

26. Lawyers, complains Thomas Becon (*The Catechism*, ed. J. Ayre, Parker Society, XI, 1844, p. 108) 'make a good cause to seem bad, and a bad cause to appear good'.

27. Hector's changes include his earlier reported challenge (I.iii.260–83) to the Greeks. Hector 'in this dull and long-continued truce / Is resty grown' (I.iii.262–3; F rusty). On 'peace' as a 'wound' inducing 'security', cf. II.ii.14–15.

28. See traditional punishment for a liar of standing in the pillory with a whetstone around his neck. Cf. M. Mayr, 'Der Gebrauch des Lastersteines in der alten Strafrechtspflege Voralbergs', *Forschungen und Mitteilungen zur Geschichte Tirols und Voralbergs*, 1 (1904), 75–8. Cressid's confession of errour (V.ii.110), and Troilus' avowal as simple truth (e.g. III.ii.179–82), recall the False–True antithesis in Renaissance iconography as well as in Spenser and Milton (cf. *Prolusion* IV), of Errour versus Truth.

29. Such capacity 'to be wise and love' among the 'gods above' seems questionable in Apollo's failed pursuit of Daphne; cf. I.i.100. Cf. John Marston's *Dutch Courtesan*, II.ii: 'The gods themselves cannot be wise and love'. Castiglione, *The Book of the Courtier*, trans. Thomas Hoby (1900), p. 352: 'the opinion of many is, that it is impossible for love to stand with reason'. Cf. Tilley, *Proverbs*, L494: 'Love and knowledge live not together'. Henkel, *Emblemata*, col. 1741 '... Amori cum prudentia non convenit'. Arthur Henkel and Albrecht Schöne, eds, *Emblemata* (Stuttgart, Germany, 1967). See Schlumbohm, *Jocus und Amor*.

30. On just war, and the issue of right claimed on both sides, cf. Alberico Gentili, *De Jure Belli* (trans. J.C. Rolfe, Oxford, 1933), II.31–3. See Alfred Vanderpol, *La Doctrine Scolastique du Droit de Guerre* (Paris, 1919).

31. On the Liar's Paradox, see the bibliography in Paul Spade, *The Medieval Liar: A Catalogue of the Insolubilia Literature* (Toronto, 1975). See R.L. Martin, ed., *Recent Essays on ... the liar paradox* (Oxford, 1984). Cf. Aristotle, *Ethics*, VII.3; *De Sophisticis Elenchis*, 25; *Metaphysics*, IV, 4 and 5. See Stephen Read, ed., *Sophisms in Medieval Logic* (Dordrecht, 1993).

32. Thersites' 'Will 'a [Troilus] swagger himself out on's own eyes?' (V.ii.136), the denying lover brings to mind a Jonsonian response to self-willed *deceptio visus*. In Jonson's *Every Man Out* (1599), performed by Shakespeare's company, Macilente conducts Deliro, the uxurious husband, to witness his wife as she is kissed by the fop Fastidius Brisk. Cf. Ulysses' conducting Troilus to witness Cressid's dallying with Diomede, and Troilus' similarly defensive response: 'This is, and is not, Cressid!' (V.ii.146). Like Jonson's uxurious husband, the faithful Troilus would indeed 'swagger himself out on's own eyes'.

33. Cf. Thomas Aquinas, *De Veritate* l. 1c. Thomas von Aquin, *Von der Wahrheit. De Veritate (Questio I)*. (Hamburg, 1986). Günther Pöltner, 'Veritas est Adequatio Intellectus et Rei', *Zeitschrift für Philosophische Forschungen*, 37 (1983), 563–76.

34. 'Ens est unum, bonum, verum' (Aquinas). Unity and love are correlated in Aquinas: union as cause of love, founded on similitude regarding a love of others: union as love (*Summa Theologica*, 1–2, 28.5).) On unity and division, see citations in J.V. Cunningham, '"Essence" and the *Phoenix and Turtle*', *ELH*, 19 (1952), 265–76.

35. *Love's Martyr* was a collection planned by Robert Chester. If this is the Robert Chester of Royston, he was admitted to the Middle Temple on 14 February 1600 (*Register of Admissions to the Middle Temple*, ed. H.F. Macgeagh, 1949, I. 76) shortly before the publication of the volume. Such a Middle Temple figure may be linked to Shakespeare's own associations there – a favourite Inn of Warwickshire men – and influenced his contribution to that collection.

36. 'A thing inseparate' (V.ii.148), is a phrase both legal and logical. See a law-students' manual near the time of the play: W. Fulbecke of Gray's Inn, *A Direction* (1600), held to have been known to Shakespeare. (See Guy Butler, 'A New Shakespeare Source?', *Notes and Queries*, n.s. 33 (1986), 363–5.) Fulbecke, *Direction*, fol. 77 v, declares: 'A thing may be said to be ... inseperable' according to legal circumstances, including 'the nature of the thing; as when a thing will not suffer a particion ...'. On 'inseparate,' see also Ferne, *Blazon*, (1586), p. 293, linking 'incidents (as the Lawyers call them)' and '"inseparable" accidents (as Logicians do terme them)'.

6. Value

> he that preferred *Helena* quitted the Gifts of *Juno* and *Pallas*.
> Francis Bacon, 'Of Love'

> Lo here, the wrecched worldes appetites!
> Chaucer, *Troilus and Criseyde*

This chapter examines the play's value concerns, which would have engaged the legal–economic interests of a law-student audience. Traditionally, value considerations were closely involved with problems of jurisprudence.[1]

Valuations

Troilus' plot derives from Paris' evaluation of Venus and of Helen. The play's scenes, raising questions of how value is estimated, present a sequence of valuers and valued, its Prologue appealing to spectators as evaluating judges: 'Like or find fault' (l. 30).

Act I scene i exhibits Troilus' adulation of Cressid, while the lover is accompanied by her uncle Pandar, symbol of transiency of value. While in I.i Pandar and Troilus compete in extolling Cressid, in I.ii Pandar and Cressid discrepantly evaluate Troilus. The opening paired scenes, juxtaposing estimates of Cressida and of Troilus, thus set up opposed evaluating perspectives. In I.iii, the Greek commander initially appraises the Greek army; and Ulysses plots with Nestor to revalue Ajax against Achilles. For their part, according to Nestor's and Ulysses' recountings (I.iii.109–210),

Achilles and Patroclus also devalue the Greek leaders. Further, this devaluation of the commanders, with Patroclus' mimetic derision, is infectious: the Greek camp generally is also devaluing them. Ajax reportedly sets Thersites 'To match us in comparisons with dirt' (I.iii.194). In II.i, Thersites and Ajax devalue each other. In II.ii, the Trojans revalue Helen; against Troilus' championship of Helen, and Paris' defence, Hector re-estimates her advocacy by his brothers; and at II.ii's end, revaluingly reverses his own position. In III.i, the audience revalues Helen. In II.iii, the Greek command revalues Ajax and Achilles. In IV.v, Achilles and Hector evaluate each other. V.ii exhibits Troilus' revaluing of Cressid, followed in V.iii by his further devaluation of her. In V.x, Troilus dismissingly devalues Pandarus.

While the Trojans are fighting to retain a Helen Troilus claims is beyond price, he nevertheless implies (II.ii.52) that valuations are ascribable by the valuing process. Yet he continues to proclaim Helen's value as absolute, as well as a requisite to honour and other absolutes (II.ii.199–206). Hence, Troilus is in the paradoxical position of implying relative valuation (II.ii.52) while urging that men commit themselves to die to preserve absolute honour and his own value views.

While Troilus in the first scene estimates Helen as 'too starved a subject for my sword' (I.i.95), in the second act he emerges, without warning, as her champion. Such reversals or contradictions throw valuation into the hypothetical–conditional, relativistically depending on time and place.[2] Among other instances of reversal are the following: As Pandar refuses in I.i to woo, then woos, and as Troilus there declines to fight for Helen, then fights, Hector in II.ii will not fight to retain Helen, but abruptly on her behalf joins his combative 'sprightly brethren' (II.ii.190). For her part, Cressid swears she will not leave Troy, but departs for the Greeks virtually as soon as summoned. So, suddenly, in V.v, the previously recalcitrant Achilles plunges into retaliatory battle.

Value of 'value'

If *Lear* questions what authenticates the gods above, *Troilus* scans what authenticates 'degree' (or 'place') below. What basis or *Letztbegründung* validates degree, or, indeed, the valuing process? From the Prologue on, the value of valuation is examined until the epilogue, with value's inflater, Pandar, there deflated. The play revalues what men prize: love, honour, fame, glory – values also within other Shakespearean plays, whose modes of valuation are here questioningly revalued. (Ulysses and Pandar show how norms of value are manipulated: public and private reputations are, like the value-deflater Thersites' preposterous 'opinion' (III.iii.263), wearable on either side.) At issue is the value of such valuation: for example the various Trojan estimates of Helen; Troilus' estimations of Cressid;

Cressid's estimate of Troilus, then of Diomedes; Diomedes' of Helen, then of Cressid; Cressid's of herself.

In the play's unfolding, scepticism of traditional values is temporarily – as in a revel's holiday interim – privileged (II.iii.57). From the Prologue's inflated 'orgulous' (l. 2), the play tends to deflation in both war and love plot-lines, accompanied by a rhetoric of mock-inflated devaluation. That rhetoric comprises mock-heroic equivoques regarding bodily functions, as well as low kitchen-process (I.i.14–28); the latter helps initiate the play's devaluing love-concerns.

Devaluations

Following her lover's and her uncle's inflationary Cressid-estimates (I.i), their object enters (I.ii), offering her own deflationary perspectives. Her effect is mock-heroic derogation. Comical also, in praise of Troilus, is an epicene bawd lauding masculine traits to a girl (played by a boy) (in I.ii). As Marlowe's Faustus (sc. 2) would 'liue and die in Aristotle's works', Pandar, finally to be rejected by Troilus, would, with dramatic irony, 'live and die i' th' eyes of Troilus' (I.ii.243–4). To Pandar's encomia on Hector's valour and looks, Cressid responds with the deflationary 'O, a brave man!' (I.ii.203). Similarly, on Troilus' 'becoming' smile, Cressid mock-applauds his valour: 'he smiles valiantly' (I.ii.125), while reducing Pandar's Troilus by anticlimactic scorn: 'O yes, an 'twere a cloud in autumn' (I.ii.127).

For his part, against communities of value, Thersites poses the axiological negative. His 'fools' include Ajax, Agamemnon, Achilles; 'and [as in legal attestation], as aforesaid, "Patroclus is a fool"' (II.iii.59). In the 'faction of fools' (II.i.118), Thersites is himself both anti-social 'fool' (II.i.64) and 'knave' (V.iv.28), while he condemns Diomedes as a knave 'unjust' and 'false-hearted' (V.i.86, 87), reputed breaker of promises (V.i.88–92).

Act II scene ii

Value debate[3]

> O shame to knighthood and to shining arms!
>> *RL*, l. 197

Hector's counting the disproportionate cost of many dead to retain one woman, valueless to all but one Trojan, elicits Troilus' objection: 'What's aught, but as 'tis valued?' (II.ii.52).[4] Troilus' value question is ironical in regard to his own continual misevaluation, for example of Pandar, of

Cressid and Helen, and of the war itself. Throughout II.ii, Troilus begs the question, as his dismissive value query (II.ii.52) does here: The war's slain are objectively dead, whether valued so or not. There are facts, like the war itself, which are there unalterably; thinking (or valuing) does not make them so – or not so.[5]

For his part, Hector's defence of the 'estimate and dignity' (II.ii.54) within the object valued, as well as in the prizer,[6] ironically anticipates his discovery of the internal corruption of the knight in shining armour. Such bodily degradation as Hector himself there foreshadows (V.viii.1–2) is a proleptic mirroring of his own physical fate. Chasing the shining suit of armour, Hector recalls the phantom gleam of an evanescent decayed chivalry. Upon the slain knight, Hector moralizes: 'Most putrefied core, so fair without', / Thy goodly armour thus hath cost thy life' (V.viii.1–2) – what is meant to protect, instead causes death – externals (as with Helen) may prove fatal. Exposing chivalry, 'valour's show' versus 'valour's worth' (I.iii.47), in the same scene as Hector uncovers the knight's internal corruption, he discovers Achilles' unchivalric retribution (V.viii.9). As the play unmasks internal deficiencies (cf. V.viii.1–2), 'vizarded' exteriors of 'degree' (I.iii.83) or so-called 'authentic place' (I.iii.108) may themselves conceal (cf. the Greek King–General, II.i.6) 'a botchy core'.

As Troilus brings to mind Lincoln's Inn's John Donne and his value relativism, his value question (II.ii.52) recalls a relativistic Renaissance maxim: as cited critically in Agrippa of Nettesheim's sceptical *De incertitudine* (1530; ch. 91), among views accepted by lawyers: 'Tantum valet res quanti vendi possit' (A thing is worth as much as it can be sold for).

On Helen's value, Hector holds, 'she is not worth what she doth cost / The keeping' (II.ii.51–2). Hector's cost-accounting value test here recalls Troilus' own cost-evaluative critique: 'Helen must needs be fair / When with your blood you daily paint her thus' (I.i.92–3). Yet the issue of cost, as in men's lives, is not met by Troilus on the relativity of value. Indeed, as used by him, Troilus' 'What's aught, but as 'tis valued'? (II.ii.52) has something of the dismissive sophistry of jesting Pilate's 'What is truth?' Neither figure stops for answer – such questions' own terms themselves preclude necessary answers. Further, as in II.ii Troilus dismisses 'reason', Hector at scene's end qualifies 'the way of truth' (II.ii.188–9). Suppressing rational distinctions or degrees of difference, Troilus here brings to mind Hotspur, who dismisses fear of danger on the ground that many things are dangerous (*1H4*, II.iii.6–10). Neither Hotspur nor Troilus prudently recognizes degrees of difference, or makes rationally qualifying distinctions.

Paradoxically, even as Troilus intimates relative value, he is committed to yearning for the 'absolute' Cressid; or extolling as absolute ideal, Helen. (Troilus (*MND*, V.i.11) 'sees Helen's beauty in a brow of' Cressid.) 'Let not my love', bids Sonnet 105's speaker, 'be call'd idolatry'. But the idolators are here also contradictorily relativist: Pandar who idolizes Troilus within a transient-coupling concern (I.ii.243–4); and the idolizing lover Troilus with his subversive value-question (II.ii.52).

Yet, in contrast to Troilus' implication of value as the estimation of the valuer, the evaluator as his own value judge, how would state and throne, oaths or established religion, protect their authority against subjective relativism? 'How could ... / Prerogative of age, crowns, sceptres, laurels, / ... stand in authentic place?' (I.iii.103–8).[7] Both Hamlet and Troilus recall a climate of Renaissance scepticism, and a Renaissance-revived Pyrrhonism, including Sextus Empiricus and Montaigne.

Inadvertently, Troilus' rhetoric devalues Helen while attempting to extol her: 'she is a pearl', he exclaims, 'Whose price hath launched above a thousand ships / And turned crowned kings to merchants' (II.ii.81–3). No longer Marlowe's face that 'launched ... a thousand ships', it is relatively her *price* (or their bidding for her) that reduced monarchs to merchants. (As merchant, Troilus early casts himself (I.i.105), followed in that role by Ulysses and the Greeks (I.iii.358–9).)

As Cressid finds her own value reflected in what 'men prize' (I.ii.290), Helen's 'value' is ironically implied in blood shed and lives sacrificed on her behalf (I.i.92–3). What men will give, her market price, Cressid renegotiates, by distributing or withholding her kisses among the exiled Greeks (IV.v), and by the competition and rivalry she excites.

Value norm

'What many men desire' (*MV*, II.ii.175), Helen is regarded as a generally coveted good, but possessed only by Paris. Yet, as Shakespeare's work had demanded, 'Why should the private pleasure of some one / Become the public plague of many more?' (*RL*, ll. 1478–9).

Regarding Helen's value, Troilus' argument for her is echoed in the Middle Templar John Ford's paradoxical *Honour Triumphant* (1606): '*Beautie* is the maintainer of Valour', '*Beautie*! which prickes on the slowest, encourageth the faint-harted ...', and '*Beauty* is the spur to Honor ...'.[8] If, to Troilus, Helen's beauty is 'a spur to valiant and magnanimous deeds' (II.ii.200), to Thersites she inspires 'war for a placket' (II.iii.19–20). To Diomedes, she is beneath contempt (IV.i.70–6), while to Hector she is 'a thing not ours, nor worth to us' (II.ii.22).

Helen, like Cordelia, mainly absent though in the audience's mind continually present, is a figure around whom the play's value questions revolve. As V.ii suggests a spectrum of attitudes towards Cressid, II.ii suggests, depending upon 'interest', a spectrum of estimates towards Helen. Analogously, what the audience hears variously in Cassandra's entrance

(II.ii) as ear-piercing screams, Hector lauds as 'high strains of divination' (II.ii.113–14), while Troilus perceives these as (II.ii.122) 'brainsick raptures'. Such perspectivism culminates in the diverse eavesdropping responses to Cressid of V.ii.

Hector's value response: against 'particular will'

Opposing Troilus' relativist value-notion, Hector questions 'particular' individual estimate and a subjective value-stance:

> But value dwells not in particular will:
> It holds his estimate and dignity
> As well wherein 'tis precious of itself
> As in the prizer.
>
> II.ii.53–6

Hector's II.ii opposition to Troilus' individualistic value-view recalls traditional scholastic attitudes. These stress value as dependent not on valuation by a single individual, but on communal estimation.[9]

In contrast to Hector (in II.ii), Troilus is governed by a faculty inferior to reason: his will 'enkindled by mine eyes and ears' (II.ii.63), excited by sense, and unguided by prudence. His 'eyes and ears' are (like the 'sailing Pandar', I.i.105) his pilots ''twixt the dangerous shores / Of will and judgement' (II.ii.63–5). 'Traded', these sensory pilots – 'traders [traitors] in the flesh' (V.x.45) – are also considered 'deceptious' (V.ii.123–4).

Recurrently, Troilus seems at odds with his own implication of value as personal or subjective (II.ii.52). Regarding, for example, his case of a hypothetical wife, Troilus demands (some dozen lines following his II.ii.52 value-question): 'How may I avoid, / Although my will distaste what it elected, / The wife I chose?' (II.ii.65–7). Will, not reason, here invertedly 'elects'. Yet here, Troilus' individual valuation or 'will' is checked by something outside itself – value here does reflect more than Troilus' 'particular will' (II.ii.53).

The Defender (Hector) of the thesis, let Helen go, retorts to the Objector (Troilus) and his implication (II.ii.52) that value is at the disposal of the evaluating process. Troilus' objection, however, does not meet Hector's argument that many Trojan lives have been forfeited; and that Helen is, proportionately to her cost, lacking in Trojan value. As well as at Troilus' dismissal of reason (II.ii.49–50), at this point the brothers' disputation achieves an impasse.

Act II scene iii

Ajax on value

'What is he [Achilles] more than another?' (II.iii.141) – Ajax's levelling inquiry suggests questioning of a degree-ordered society. Further, 'Great Hector was as good a man as he [Achilles]' (V.ix.6) is Ajax's equalizing last line in the play. Spokesman for this claim is the brutal, illiterate braggart, who peers through the solipsism of self-glory. To Ajax's 'What is he [Achilles] more than another?' Agamemnon responds, 'No more than what he thinks he is' (II.iii.141–2). Yet Achilles, according to the rigged market in honour, seems *less* than he thinks he is (III.iii.74). As Achilles' 'imagined worth' (II.iii.170) poses the correlation of self-estimate and 'worth', his rival, Ajax, swollen with flattery, is at once a monstrous conceit and a caricature of Achilles.

Correlating degree and value, Ulysses' advice to Achilles (III.iii), like Ulysses' degree speech and Troilus' value question, raises issues (cf. III.iii.80–2): whether values are imputed or inherent, whether they are ascribed by external 'honour' or social place; whether (as in the Renaissance 'True Nobility' debate) rank makes man, or man makes rank.[10] The issue concerns the degree of value or the value of degree.

As II.ii turns upon the value of Helen, III.iii points to the necessity of Ajax. Paradoxically, in conditions of need, the 'necessary house' may be esteemed more dearly than conventionally more valued objects. Regarding Ajax, Ulysses' mock-encomium exclaims, 'Nature, what things there are / Most abject in regard and dear in use!', adding 'What things again most dear in the esteem / And poor in worth!' (III.iii.127–30). Even 'Ajax goes up and down the field asking for himself' (III.iii.244–5).[11]

On another level, Agamemnon alludes to Achilles' 'attribute' (II.iii.115) in terms of subject and adjuncts. He implies a distinction between 'attribute', which others ascribe to the hero, and his self-evaluation. Achilles is greater in 'self-assumption' (II.iii.123), taking unto himself more than is warranted in others' judgment. Those 'worthier than himself' (II.iii.124), King Agamemnon and his court, attend Achilles' uncivil behaviour, or foreshadowingly, 'the savage strangeness he puts on' (II.iii.125).

Act III scenes i and ii

'Love, love, nothing but love'

The sequence between III.i and III.ii suggests a reversal of Sonnet 129: 'Before a joy proposed, behind a dream'. In *Troilus* are inversions of 'before' and 'after', as well as a juxtaposition of post- and pre-consummatory attitudes. This midplay diptych of III.i and III.ii provides, by ironical inversion, its own commentary on the brothers and their beloveds, first Paris and Helen, then Troilus and Cressid: 'Look here upon this picture, and on this' (*H*, III.iv.53). In a play of 'preposterous discoveries' (V.i.23), as III.ii displays the 'before' of the pre-connubial Troilus and Cressida, its predecessor III.i is anticlimactic: the sated 'after' of the world's great lovers. That Paris–Helen–Pandarus scene (parodic of Mars–Venus–Cupid) shows Helen, 'a theme of honour and renown, / A spur to valiant and magnanimous deeds' (II.ii.199–200), as vain, trivial and bored. The vacuous 'Nell's' emergence in III.i, amidst the sacrificial conflict on her behalf, is itself anticlimactic. Following II.ii's heated debate over Helen and the locus of value is (concerning Helen as legendary value-absolute) her III.i in-the-flesh devaluation.

Act III scene iii

Parodies of value

> The art of our necessities is strange
> That can make vild things precious
> *King Lear*

Ajax, used and disesteemed, parodies value, as Pandar, used and disesteemed, parodies love – each intermediary of physical convenience provides a qualifying perspective. The Trojan value-debate of II.ii foreshadows Ulysses on the paradox of value in III.iii.

In response to the Grecian embassy to Achilles, Achilles plots a counter-embassy: 'Thou [Thersites] must be my ambassador to him [Ajax]' (III.iii.265). Declining this mission, Thersites mockingly assumes the role of Ajax, with Patroclus as Achilles' emisssary to *him* (Thersites as Ajax).

Recalling Cressid's mockery of heroic anger (I.ii.58), Achilles is in III.iii reduced in his physical pride. Parodying an epic–heroic sense, the work plays on the Homeric Achilles' 'pride' – he is not only vain, but also an inflatedly 'proud' man. Hector's 'Stand fair, I pray thee; let me look on thee' elicits (as actor from spectator) Achilles' proud 'Behold thy fill' (IV.v.235–6). Reports of Achilles note his inflated 'pride': 'Things small as nothing ... / He makes important' (II.iii.167–8). In contrast, Achilles is now an 'ebb'd man' (*AC*, I.iv.43).

Act IV scene v

Love's market-place

> Greet prees at market maketh deere ware,
> And to greet cheep is holde at litel prys
>   Chaucer, *The Wife of Bath's Tale*

Following III.ii's amatory exchanges, Act IV exhibits the transported Cressid, exchanging and being exchanged on the exiled Grecians' market. If value, according to an influential Aristotelian view (*Nicomachean Ethics*, Book V, ch. 5) is estimable in exchange, valuations (through I.i, I.ii, I.iii, II.ii, III, IV and V) are shown transformed in and through the process of exchange. Passing from the Trojans to the Greeks, Cressid has in Act IV experienced distance in exchange: her market-identity and value-estimate reflect a comparable transformation.[12]

After her idealized valuation by Troilus, Cressid moves, by monopolistic exhibition, to her *cambio* or exchange for kisses. Troilus cannot hold her (cf. Sonnet 87) as she becomes a displayed and more widely desired commodity. Cressid has been transported among the exiled love-starved Greeks, where her gender-unique monopoly and increased demand allow her to name her own terms.[13]

Seeking Cressid's kiss, for example, Menelaus is rebuked ('You fillip me o' th' head', IV.v.45) when he attempts to 'horn in'. Such horned argument is appropriately the downfall of the cuckold. To Cressid's 'In kissing, do you render, or receive?', he responds: 'Both take and give' (IV.v.35–6). Yet, as Lady Anne retorts to Gloucester (*R3*, I.ii.202), 'To take is not to give'. Insofar as Menelaus' reply contains logically contradictory or 'repugnant' alternatives, the trading Cressid rejects him on grounds of unequal exchange: that 'the kiss you take is better than you give' (IV.v.38). Cressid's is a market-quantification of quality, a cost-accounting of personal value. Since Cressid does 'as [her] ... pleasures are' (Prologue, l. 30), her denial of Menelaus (IV.v.37–9) reflects hedonic exchange: Menelaus cannot repay in pleasure-terms what he would receive.

Diomedes' response to Troilus – to Cressid's 'own worth / She shall be prized' (IV.iv.133–4) – anticipates the Grecian lover's relation to Cressid's variable self-worth. Reacting ineffectively to Cressid's removal and his Grecian rival's insult, Prince Troilus is devalued, diminished in his knightly 'estimate and dignity' (II.ii.54). He descends to further chivalric dishonour when he pursues Diomedes, not for his abducted beloved, but for his purloined horse (V.vi.7).

Troilus' early identification of Cressid as a 'pearl' who lies in 'India' (I.i.102) removes her from flesh-and-blood exchange. Later, Cressid, entering a market among the Greeks (IV.v), assays *quantum in mercato vendere*. Like Cressid, Helen is exchanged, brought from one place to another, her condition, transfer and distance affecting price.

Paralleling the war-plot's exchange of Ajax for Achilles, the love-plot movements depend on the credit and valuation bestowed on two reversedly exchanged 'exogamic' women. As Paris has a monopoly of Helen in Troy, Cressid (IV.v) among exiled Grecian warriors has her own masculine monopoly. Recalling the war of the many for the one, for Paris' sole possession of Helen, both Paris and Cressid evoke the topos of the one against the many, a disproportion to be rehearsed in the assault of the many Myrmidons on the solitary Hector (V.viii).

Tending to dissolve degree- and hierarchical structure, fostering an accumulative ethic, the market translates 'trust' (or 'troth') into transient and fluctuating estimates, along with honour, truth, and value itself. Where everything is on the market, everything is by exchange-value exchangeable, including the exchangers ('the parties interchangeably', III.ii.57). Insofar as commodity-transfer exchanges alter prices, and 'identity' is in process of exchange, nothing 'is' or 'stands alone'. (Not even Ajax – or if Ajax does 'stand alone', as Ulysses 'apprehended' (III.iii.124), it is for unflattering reasons.) 'Nothing is good I see, without respect' (*MV*, V.i.99). As market economy relativizingly agitates value, it transforms, by waves of desire, needs and satisfactions: Its infinite appetite creates a perpetual yearning for 'more' and 'others' ('That all with one consent praise new-born gawds', III.iii.176), as it instantly consumes and forgets gratifications 'devoured / As fast as ... made, forgot as soon / As done', III.iii.148–50).

'Weigh him well'

> in matters of Weight
> *Gesta Grayorum*

As dimensions are moralized, moral notions are weighed. Diomedes' Helen-verdict (IV.i.67–8) is apropros: 'weight' as judicial, evaluative, as well as literal, 'poising'. In weighing who more deserves Helen, Diomedes implicitly insults Paris, celebrated judge of women – indeed, of goddesses.

Troilus dismisses common scales for his father (II.ii.26–8). Diomedes' Helen-weighing imagery (IV.i.67–8) is returned upon him in Troilus' own Diomedes-weighing imagery (V.ii.167–8). In I.iii, the Greeks 'weigh' the progress of the war. In II.ii is Hector's weighing of the case of Paris, who had himself weighed the choice of goddesses. In III.ii, Cressid's Court of Love weighs men's promises against performance. Protracted Trojan weighing (II.ii) of Helen's return to the Greeks contrasts with Cressid's exchange to the Greeks (cf. III.iii), promptly dispatched. Paris weighs with Diomedes (IV.i) the issue of who 'merits ... most' to have Helen. 'Scruple'

(IV.i.58), as both weight and moral qualm, poses a quantitative–qualitative irony.

To Paris' judicial-sounding and ironically-posed question of 'Who … merits [Helen] … most' (IV.i.55), Diomedes responds, applying his argument to a topic of invention – comparison of equals, larger, and smaller. Both topic and argument contradict the absolute valuing of Helen: She is to Diomedes the 'lees and dregs' (IV.i.64), swilled by the 'puling cuckold', Menelaus (IV.i.63). Indeed, Diomedes' condemnatory verdict on Paris' choice and judgment is itself injudiciously extreme – a weighing without measure.

Ironically, the Helen devaluer, Diomedes, is to pursue her younger analogue, Cressid. The relativism of Troilus' value question (II.ii.52) is ironically elaborated through the play – characters continually, through appetite, project values which are shown to be discrepant with their desired objects' estimates. Such estimates and their value discrepancies suggest an infinite regress: recalling Erasmus' *Praise of Folly*, valuations, to the play's end, are thus recurrently set up and subverted.

Act V scene ii

Commodity transformations

Such concepts as degree and natural law are invoked in ironic contexts by questionable defenders, as are vows themselves. Conditional value-estimations dissolve to find their own price level, according to qualifying market factors: place and time, competition, exchange, supply and demand.

In this mock-epic 'traders' play, Homeric virtues seem incongruous where deeds are forgotten as fast as made (III.iii.148–50). Like identity in exchange-value, individual worth is subject to fluctuating price. As the play's transactions suggest a self-consuming process, persons become tokens of their own pleasure-giving capacities – not as ends in themselves, but as commodities (Pandar's 'parties interchangeably', III.ii.57, or a 'generation of vipers', III.i.134), purveyors of self-consuming gratifications.

In the commodity fetishism of market valuation, personages are themselves transformed to exchangeable objects. Lovers' pledges (glove, sleeve) ambivalently mimic genders. Having snatched, from Cressid, Troilus' detachable sleeve, Diomedes is identified anonymously as 'that Greekish whore-masterly villain with the sleeve' (V.iv.6–7). Thersites would like to see Troilus send his rival back to Cressid 'of a sleeveless errand' (V.iv.7–9). Diomede promises to wear the detachable sleeve on his helm (V.ii.94) – the sleeve which for Cressid sums up the detachable Troilus: 'You look upon that sleeve [cf. slave]', she incites Diomedes; 'behold it well. / He loved me' (V.ii.70–1). Her 'tempt me no more to folly' (V.ii.19) makes

Diomedes the tempter, while she both puts him off – like a glove or sleeve – and draws him on (cf. *AWEW*, V.iii.277–8). Cressid's excitation of Diomedes, eavesdropped by others, is a fragment of a comic *agon*: its private ebb and flow mimic the tide of military conflict.

While, in Jonson, Cynthia's 'Who's first in worth, the same be first in place' (*Cynthia's Revels*, V.vi.107) unites value and degree, *Troilus'* conclusion subverts this edict of Cynthia on value and degree, and appropriate rewards. Unlike Jonson's comical satires, *Troilus* has no 'reasonable' close. Instead, it ends in poetic injustice, blustery threats (V.x.25–31) and panderly self-pity (V.x.35–47). In the 'event', Troilus contradicts Puck's prediction, that 'Jack shall have Jill' (*MND*, III.ii.461–3): here, finally, 'Jack' does *not* 'have Jill' (reversing Tilley, *Proverbs*, A 164). In contrast to Puck's 'Nought shall go ill', 'nought' does go well. And appositely to Troilus' equine deprivation, 'the man' does *not* 'have his mare again' (*MND*, III.ii.463). Troilus fails to oblige Diomedes to restore his honour, his beloved, or his 'horse' (V.vi.7). If Puck's prophecy mocks a conventional happy ending, *Troilus'* close evades that formula. Instead of a romantic-comedy marital-coupling finale, the plot rotates further – its 'wooing doth not end like an old play' (*LLL*, V.ii.874) – to post-consummatory displacement. Such patterns of inversion are appropriate to the world-upside-down universe of a revel.

To summarize, this chapter has examined the play's value reflections, including valuation of 'value'. Such legal–economic and ethical value-issues would have been comprehensible to, and engaged, a law-student audience.

Notes

1. Cf. Donald R. Kelley, 'Hermes, Clio, Themis: Historical Intepretation and Legal Hermeneutics', *Journal of Modern History*, 55 (1983), 644–68: legal hermeneutics as anthropomorphic and subject-centred, and not value-free; legal interpretation as concerning not only facts, but also questions of values. For changes in the legal senses of 'estimate' and 'estimation' see Pierre Michaud Quantin, "'Aestimare' et 'Aestimatio'," *Archivum Latinitatis Medii Aevi*, 22, (1992), 171–82.
2. In terms of relativist mutability, Hobbes (after Montaigne) observes, 'the same man, in divers times, differs from himself; ... one time praiseth, that is calleth good what another time he dispraiseth, and calleth evil'. (Hobbes, *English Works*, ed. Molesworth, III.146.)
3. Cf. Hector's and Troilus' value-oppositions, and John Donne, 'To the Countess of Bedford', ll. 1–4, posing naturally intrinsic valuation against circumstantial market estimate. In addition, Donne's 'Love's Progress', ll. 11–15, counterposes intrinsic qualities against trade or market considerations. Cf. Nicholas Lemos, *Intrinsic Value* (Cambridge, England, 1994). Aristotle himself (*EN*, 1094 a) allows an intrinsic good. Defending this, see Robert Audi, *Moral Knowledge and Ethical Character* (Oxford, 1997). See also

Whitney J. Oates, *Aristotle and the Problem of Value* (Princeton, New Jersey, 1963). Robert Audi, 'Intrinsic Value and Moral Obligation', *Southern Journal of Philosophy*, 35 (1997), 135–154.

On valuation as a legal-commercial issue, cf. Liebs, *Rechtsregeln*, P 92: 'Pretium non ex re, sed propter negotiationem percipitur'. (Price is obtained, not from the thing, but because of negotiation.) On Renaissance value-debates, see Charles Trinkaus, 'Protagoras in the Renaissance: An Exploration', *Philosophy and Humanism*, ed. E.P. Mahoney (Leiden, The Netherlands, 1976), pp. 190–213. On Renaissance 'value', cf. Elton, 'Shakespeare's Ulysses'; 'La Valeur', in Philippe Desan, *Les Commerces de Montaigne* (Paris, 1992), pp. 199–225. On Renaissance value-relativism, see Z.S. Schiffman, *On the Threshold of Modernity* (Baltimore, Maryland, 1991). On Shakespeare and value, see Graham Bradshaw, *Shakespeare's Scepticism* (Ithaca, New York, 1987).

On the play's value debate, cf. Rolf Soellner, 'Prudence and the Price of Helen: The Debate of the Trojans in *Troilus and Cressida*', *Shakespeare Quarterly*, 20 (1969), 255–63.

4. Cf. Tilley *Proverbs*, M254, N298; cf. value relativism in John Donne, *Progresse of the Soule*, ll. 518–20: 'Ther's nothing simply good, nor ill alone ... / The onely measure is, and judge, opinion'. Fluctuating relativity of value, suggested in Thersites (III.iii.263–4), recurs in Marston's contemporary *What You Will* (1601, I.i): 'All that exists takes valuation from Opinion, / A giddy minion now'.

Against Troilus' relativist value-query, Hector holds value dwells not alone in 'particular will', but also in its own 'estimate and dignity / As well wherein 'tis precious of itself / As in the prizer' (II.ii.54–6). *TC*'s value-antithesis recalls a Stoic distinction between relative price and dignity. That distinction is made in Seneca (*Epistolae morales*, LXXI, 33), noting of bodily goods, 'His *pretium* quidem erit aliquod, ceterum *dignitas* non erit' (Loeb edition, 1970, II.92–3). (Cf. Seneca, 'De Beneficiis', in *Moral Essays*, ed. J.W. Basore (Loeb, 1975), III.393: '... the price paid for some things does not represent their value ... the price of everything varies with circumstances ...'.)

Troilus' versus Hector's value debate, recalling the Senecan opposition between value as *pretium* (price) and value as *dignitas* (inner worth), recurs from the Stoics to Kant. Cf. on Kant, H.J. Paton, *The Categorical Imperative* (1967), pp. 188–9; and Kant's *Groundwork of the Metaphysic of Morals*, trans. H.J. Paton (New York, 1956), p. 102, sections 77–8:

> In the kingdom of ends everything has either a *price* or a *dignity*. If it has a *price*, something else can be put in its place as an equivalent [cf. 'the parties interchangeably', III.ii.57]; if it is exalted above all *price* and so admits of no equivalent, then it has a *dignity*. What is relative to universal human inclination and needs has a market price; ... that which constitutes the sole condition under which anything can be an end in itself has not merely a relative value – that is, a *price* – but has an intrinsic value, that is, *dignity*.

Price and value recall a medieval dichotomy of *pretz* and *valour*. Cf. Moshe Lazar, *Amour Courtois* (Paris, 1964), pp. 32–3: '*Pretz* est l'estimation subjective, dont une personne jouit; *Valeur*, la valeur objective qu'une personne possède'. Cf. A.H. Schutz, 'The Provençal Expression *Pretz e Valor*', *Speculum*, 19 (1944), 488–93, concluding (p. 493): '*pretz* carries over from its economic use the idea of an estimation of personal worth by common consent within a given *milieu* and under given circumstances ... mutable and extrinsic.

Valor is the basic worth of a person, the sum of inherent qualities, hence intrinsic and not subject to common estimation'.

On price, cf. Hobbes' view that 'The value, or worth of a man, is as of all other things, his price; that is to say, so much as would be given for the use of his powers; and therefore is not absolute, but is a thing dependant on the need and judgement of another' (*Works*, III.76). So Achilles complains of his estimation, i.e. his price: 'What am I poor of late? / 'Tis certain, greatness once fallen out with fortune, / Must fall out with men too. What the declined is / He shall as soon read in the eyes of others ...' (III.iii.74–7). So Hobbes (III.76) explains, '... in men, not the seller, but the buyer determines the price. For let a man as most men do rate themselves at the highest value they can; yet their true value is no more than it is esteemed by others'.

5.   See Agrippa, *Of the Vanitie*, p. 334. 'What's aught, but as 'tis valued?' (l. 52), recalls the related maxim, 'Res tantum valet quantum vendi potest' (A thing is worth as much as it can be sold for). Such relativistic value-dicta are critically linked in Agrippa of Nettesheim's sceptical *De Incertitudine* (1530, xci). On 'Res tantum valet quantum vendi potest', see Kenneth S. Cahn, 'The Roman and Frankish Roots of the Just Price of Medieval Canon Law', *Studies in Medieval and Renaissance History*, 6 (1969), 35, 41–3. Cf. that maxim and Seneca, *De Beneficiis*, VI.xv.4, 'though you have praised your wares, they are worth only the highest price at which they can be sold' (Hobbes, ed. Molesworth, III.137).

Troilus' individualist claim recalls Rainolde's *Foundacion*, fol. xxxv, condemning a polity of merely individualistic judgment: '... euery man must bee a ruler. Their owne will is their Lawe: there luste setteth order, no Magistrate, but every one to hymself a Magistrate'. *Ibid.*, fol. xxxvi: '... there would bee neither Prince, Lawe, nor subiecte ... but every manne his owne hedde, his alone lawe ...'. 'Euery manne his owne hedde' suggests not only anarchic subversion of degree, but also the subversive subjectivism implicit in Troilus' 'What's aught, but as 'tis valued?' (II.ii.52).

6.   Bacon, 'Of Truth', *Essayes*, p. 7.

7.   Cf. Troilus' value-question ('What's aught, but as 'tis valued?' II.ii.52), and Hamlet's 'There's nothing good or bad, but thinking makes it so' (*H*, II.ii.250). Both value-remarks, with their pivotal 'but', uttered by youthful princes in plays near the same date, suggest sceptical value-questioning, as well as emphasis on the individual estimator: 'Thinking', for both, makes values 'so', as the valuer asserts his individual, subjective priority.

Cf. Sextus Empiricus, 'Against the Ethicists' (Loeb, Cambridge, Massachusetts, 1968, III.71: 'there is nothing good or evil which is common to all ... therefore there does not exist anything good or evil by nature'; III.89: 'each must necessarily regard as good that which appears so to himself. But what appears good to each man is not good by nature'. Cf. Nashe, *Works*, III.332: 'So that our opinion (as *Sextus Empiricus* affirmeth) giues the name of good or ill to euery thing'. (See Luciano Floridi, 'The Diffusion of Sextus Empiricus's Works in the Renaissance', *J. History of Ideas*, 56 (1995), 65–85.) Cf. Hobbes (III.41): '... there being nothing simply and absolutely so [good or bad]; nor any common of good and evil to be taken from the nature of the objects themselves ...'

Such sceptical questions were disputed at Oxford in the later sixteenth century; see C.B. Schmitt, 'Philosophy and Science in Sixteenth-Century Universities', in J.E. Murdoch and E.D. Sylla, eds, *The Cultural Context of Medieval Learning* (Dordrecht, The Netherlands, 1975), p. 501; see Richard

Popkin, *The History of Scepticism from Erasmus to Spinoza* (Berkeley, California, 1979), pp. 18–86. See Graham Bradshaw, *Shakespeare's Scepticism* (Ithaca, New York, 1987).

See also Julia Annas and Jonathan Barnes, *Modes of Scepticism in Ancient Texts and Modern Interpretations* (Cambridge, England, 1985); J.C. Laursen, *The Politics of Skepticism in the Ancients, Montaigne, Hume, and Kant* (Leiden, The Netherlands, 1992). See C.B. Schmitt, 'The Recovery and Assimilation of Ancient Scepticism in the Renaissance', *Rivista Critica di Storia della Filosofia*, 27 (1972), 363–84, revised as 'The Rediscovery of Ancient Skepticism in Modern Times', in Myles Burnyeat, ed., *The Skeptical Tradition* (Berkeley, California, 1983), pp. 225–51. See Julia Annas, 'Doing Without Objective Values: Ancient and Modern Strategies', in Malcolm Schofield and Gisela Striker, eds, *The Norms of Nature: Studies in Hellenistic Ethics* (Cambridge, England, 1986), pp. 3–29.

On the relations of prize, praise, price (analogous to those between taste and test, III.ii.90), cf. C.C. Barfoot, '*Troilus and Cressida*: "Praise us as we are tasted"', *Shakespeare Quarterly*, 39 (1988), 45–57. On price, cf. J.W. Baldwin, 'The Medieval Theories of the Just Price', *Trans. of the American Philosophical Soc.*, Part 4 (1959), 1–92.

8. Ford, *Nondramatic*, pp. 37, 41.

9. For this anti-individualistic view, see the medieval glossator, Accursius. Like Hector, Accursius opposes mere individual estimation. 'Non debent res aestimare ex affectu … singulorum, sed communiter' (Estimates are not to be derived from individual affects, but commonly). Accursius qualifies his value-dictum ('res tantum valet quantum vendi potest', a thing is worth what it can be sold for) with 'scilicet communiter' – by common estimation. Cf. Accursius, Gloss to Digest, xxxv, 2, 63.

Stressing the common interest, the medieval San Bernardino of Siena's views contrast with the Paris-inspired and self-interested Trojan War. 'Nothing is more iniquitous than to promote private interests at the expense of general welfare'. (R. de Roover, *San Bernardino of Siena …* (Boston, Massachusetts, 1967), p. 21 n.100.) On valuation and the common good, see San Bernardino, *De Evangelio aeterno* (*Opera Omnia*, IV.196).

Closer to *Troilus*' date, supporting communal estimate and common good, see Leonardus Lessius, c. 1600, on the just price (*De justitia et jure*, lib. 2, cap. 21, dub. 2, no. 7): 'either that which is fixed by public authority in consideration of general welfare or that which is determined by common estimate'.

Three legal-valuational maxims echoed in *Troilus* are also reflected in Odd Langholm, 'Economic Freedom in Scholastic Thought', *History of Political Economy*, 143 (1982), 260–83: (1) 'No man is beaten voluntary' (II.i.98): 'volenti non fit iniuria' – the willing man receives no injury. (2) Related to 'What's aught, but as 'tis valued?' (II.ii.52) is the maxim 'Res tantum valet quantum vendi potest' – a thing is worth what it can be sold for. (3) 'But value dwells not in particular will' (II.ii.53). This recalls the maxim in Justinian, *Digest*, 9.2.23, 35, 63: a thing is worth what it can be sold for – 'scilicet communiter', 92.3 – that is, in common estimate, communally, not by 'particular will'. Common vs. private good was emphasized by scholastic economists. See André Lapidus, 'Metal Money, and the Prince: John Buridan and Nicholas Oresme after Thomas Aquinas', *History of Political Economy* 29 (1997), 28–42. See also Odd Langholm, *The Legacy of Scholasticism in Economic Thought* (Cambridge, England, 1998).

10.   Regarding 'True Nobility' and the law, cf. John Fortescue, *De laudibus legum Anglie* (ed. S.B. Chrimes, Cambridge, England, 1942, p. 119).

11.   That necessary house is remarked in Caspar Dornavius' *Amphitheatrum* (Hanoviae, 1619), pp. 348–9: poem by Carol Liebhard entitled 'Latrina querela', with its complaint against its obscure domestic location, and its assertion of nothing being more useful. See A.A. Stephenson, 'The Paradox of Value: A Suggested Interpretation', *History of Political Economy*, 4 (1972), 131, 132.

12.   Cf., on such change, Thomas Aquinas (*Summa Theologica*, II-II, 77, 4 ad 2): 'the value (*pretium*) of the thing has changed with the change of place or time'. Cf. also Aquinas in relation to the play's pattern of buying and selling, and the ethics of 'just price' – topics of scholastic legal–economic debate. See Aquinas on buying and selling (*Summa Theologica*, II.ii. Q77. Art. I).

13.   Monopoly was, close to the play's date, a controversial issue in Parliament, which met from 27 October to 19 December 1601. (Cf. Milton's *Paradise Lost* with its infernal debates reminiscent of Parliament, and analogously this play's possible reflections of its own contemporary parliament, 1601.) Parliamentary complaints against monopolists at this time reached a crescendo. In particular, leaders of anti-monopolistic parliamentary protest conspicuously included lawyers of the Middle Temple. Among the most vehement of these Middle Temple lawyers opposing monopoly was Richard Martin, prominent also as Prince d'Amour in the Middle Temple revels, 1597–98. (On Richard Martin's anti-monopoly views, see also P.W. Hasler, ed., *The House of Commons, 1558–1603* (1981), III.22–3.) (Martin also attacked monopolies at James' accession: *A Speech delivered to the Kings Most Excellent Majestie in the Name of the Sheriffes of London and Middlesex* (1603).) Such links between Middle Temple revels and contemporary parliamentary monopoly-controversy could have been recognizable by a law-revel audience.

    On the 1601 parliament and monopoly, see J.E. Neale, *Elizabeth and Her Parliaments 1584–1601* (1957), pp. 376–93. See Jonson's *Poetaster* (1601), V.iii.118–20. Cf. David H. Sacks, 'Parliament, Liberty, and the Commonweal', in J.H. Hexter, ed., *Parliament and Liberty from the Reign of Elizabeth to the English Civil War* (Stanford, California, 1992), pp. 85–21; also Sacks, 'The countervailing of benefits: monopoly, liberty, and benevolence in Elizabethan England', in Dale Hoak, ed., *Tudor Political Culture* (Cambridge, England, 1995), pp. 272–91. See also Sacks, 'Private Profit and Public Good: the Problem of the State in Elizabethan Theory and Practice', in G.J. Schochet, ed., *Law, Literature, and the Settlement of Regimes* (Washington, DC, 1990), pp. 121–42. The pro-monopolist argument (noted in Sacks, *ibid.*, p. 130) recalls the Helen-monopolizing Paris and his public-benefit defence: 'I propose not merely to myself / The pleasures such a beauty brings with it ...' (II.ii.146–7). Like Paris, monopolists claimed their private benefit would, accruing 'not merely to' themselves, promote the common good.

Part III   Law revels

7. Revels

> Why, I have been a reveller, and at my cloth of silver suit and my long stocking in my time ...
>
> Ben Jonson, *Poetaster*

> His Honour's learned Revels
>
> *Gesta Grayorum*

This chapter concerns the play's revels reflections. Law students were trained not only through moots, bolts (cf. Prologue, l. 18; I.i.19, 21), and similar exercises, but also through compulsorily attended Inns of Court revels.[1]

Prologue and Act I scene i

'Digested in a play'

From the Armed Prologue's epic start, he draws to a close – with the Horatian 'Beginning in the middle' (l. 28). His proposal, 'What may be digested in a play',[2] anticipates a pattern of interrelated theatrical and culinary allusions. In *Troilus* (appropriately to a festive occasion) have been estimated twice as many images of food, cooking and related matters as in any other of its author's works. Lovers themselves suggest 'dainty bait' (Q; V.viii.20; 'bait' was also refreshment for lawyers).[3]

Such food allusions are introduced by a love tutorial in the form of

Pandarus' baking instructions. The occasion is also suggested in Achilles' address to his king: 'for your health and your digestion's sake, / An after-dinner's breath' (II.iii.110–11). Yet the play, whose Prologue aims at 'what may be digested in a play' (l. 29), and whose protagonist 'cannot fight upon ... / ... too starved a subject ...' (I.i.94–5), itself (as suited to a delayed night audience) closes on 'starvation': 'Never go home; here starve we out the night' (V.x.2).

Pandar's stages correlate the art of love with the art of cooking, *ars amatoria* with *ars coquinaria*. 'Cake' and 'wheat' are dependent on 'grinding' (I.i.14–16). So Cressid figures the amatory: disliking 'to be baked [backed] with no date in the pie [also calendar], for then the man's date is out' (I.ii.257–8). For his part, Pandar insists Troilus must tarry the 'bolting' (I.i.18–19).[4]

Next to be demonstrated is the 'leavening' (I.i.21–3), or the raising. Although Troilus has undergone these stages, Pandar points to contractual conditions 'in the word hereafter' (I.i.24–5). His terms with gestures mimic also 'the kneading, the making of the cake, the heating of the oven' (including the arousal), and the 'baking' (cf. backing).[5] Pandar closes with a warning on prevention against burning: Troilus must stay the 'cooling' (I.i.27–8), foreshadowing Cressid's inconstancy. Pandar advises it is better to tarry than to burn.

Yet 'You men', Cressid admonishes, 'will never tarry' (IV.ii.16). Audience restiveness is also suggested in that gender reproach, as well as in 'what some men do, / While some men leave to do!' (III.iii.172–3). Compare the taunt, as to an indecisive audience, 'Good night and welcome, both at once, to those / That go or tarry' (V.i.75–6).

In sum, Pandar and Cressid, in the opening two scenes, counsel the arts of love: Pandar in the first scene tutors a young man, as Cressid in the second instructs women (I.ii.289–96), in practice through the book of experience. Pandar counsels Troilus in patience; while to women, Cressid advises strategic withholding.[6]

Act I scene i

Trojan 'sport'

His Highness's Port and Sport

Gesta Grayorum

The *Gesta Grayorum*, in its account of the Gray's Inn revels, records 'Dancing and Revelling ... and after such *Sports*, a Comedy of Errors ... was played ...'. Its 'Sports intended were especially for the gracing of the *Templarians* ...' (*Gesta*, p. 31). So Troilus sorties to the 'sport ... out of town' (I.i.115). Like its presumed festive occasion, the Prologue (l. 30) invites the audience to 'do' according to its pleasures. The Inns of Court revels-produced *Comedy of Errors*, eschewing precedence at its close, bids, 'now let's go hand in hand, not one before another' (*CE*, V.i.426). So Troilus closes his opening scene with the invitation: 'Come, go we then together' (I.i.117–18).[7]

'Sport' is twice noted by the Trojan friends: as Aeneas asks about 'good sport', Troilus invites him 'to the sport abroad' (I.i.117; cf. Hector, IV.v.239). Departing for the *ludicrum Troiae*, or sport of Troy, the Trojans in their opening scene lead into the play's own festive 'sport'.

Act I scene iii

'High and mighty'

Nestor's deference to his monarch, with 'due observance' of his *'godlike seat'* (I.iii.31), echoes that to another monarch of an Inns of Court revel, the *Prince d'Amour* (1597–98): there, the participants *'with one consent* ... have lifted to the *seat of Government* this Prince, for his lineaments and presence Prince-like ...' (p. 8). The *Prince d'Amour* revel's *'with one consent'* recurs in *Troilus'* 'That all *with one consent* ...' (III.iii.176; italics added).

Ulysses salutes his king as 'most mighty for thy place and sway' (I.iii.60). Yet Aeneas, against his own description, fails to identify in the King's 'godlike seat' (I.iii.31) that 'high and mighty Agamemnon' (I.iii.232). The King's station, apparently all too identifiable, recalls the misruling King (or Prince) of Christmas.[8] That 'high and mighty' ruler brings to mind *Gesta*: 'this your glorious Inthronization ...' (p. 16); and *Prince*: 'lifted to the seat of Government this Prince ...' (p. 8); 'this our Monarch ... most worthily enthronized, and most rightly entituled, *The high and mighty Prince* ...' (p. 9).

Act III scene ii

Love-casuistry: Court of Love trial

> ... our endeavour ... so desired and the performance so loathed ...
>
> V.x.38–9

Comparable to this work's love debate (III.ii)[9] are gender debates in the Inns of Court-produced *Comedy of Errors* and *Twelfth Night*. In *Comedy of Errors* (e.g. II.ii.110–46) are heard female complaints (cf. *TC*, III.ii.83–8) against male performance; in *Twelfth Night*, male versus female attitudes become an issue. While Orsino there praises women above men in constancy (*TN*, II.iv.32–5), Cressid here charges men (III.ii.83–8) with inconstancy in performance – 'They say all lovers swear more performance than they are able' (III.ii.83–4). (Cf. Cupid in Marston's law-revels echoic *Fawn*, V.i, 'that young men are proud in appetite and weak in performance'.)[10]

As III.i displays a Helen–Paris Court of Love, III.ii enacts its Cressid–Troilus Court of Love. The Court of Love includes a trial or arraignment, recurrent in Inns of Court revels, and suited to a law-student audience. While the Grecian council scene (I.iii) appears rhetorically deliberative, and the Trojan council scene (II.ii) is logically (or illogically) polemic, III.ii includes a Court-of-Love *cum* legal ritual. (From such a contest, the Trojan War itself derives, following Paris' 'Judgmental' offence to two slighted goddesses.) Such Courts of Love (mock-hearings) recur in the *Prince*'s revel (1597–98).[11]

Pandar advises 'deeds' as (legalistically, in terms of performance) 'words pay no debts' (III.ii.54). Recalling III.ii's words–deeds motif, Troilus (in V.iii) tears up Cressid's words as he blames her deeds. (In the play's last seven scenes, Troilus never refers to her again.) Among Pandar's 'debts' is the intimate *debitum* of marriage (II.ii.175–6: cf. Chaucer's 'marriage debt'). As her uncle predicts of Cressid, 'she'll bereave you [Troilus] o'th'deeds', as well as your words, 'if she call your activity in question' (III.ii.55–6) – if she summon up your acts for account.

While Cressid alleges men can do more, but refuse, Troilus responds that men desire to do more, but are incapable. (Cf. *Gesta*, p. 72: 'My Desire was greater than the Ability of my Body'.) At its middle (III.ii.80–97; cf. III.i.51–2), as in its epilogue, the play focuses on promise versus performance – performance not only erotic, but also votive, legal–contractual, and theatrical.

Here, Troilus' opposition to judgment solely by the outcome or 'event' (II.ii120) seems contradicted by his 'allow us as we prove' (III.ii.90). By ironic foreshadowing, should the lovers prove false, Pandarus' 'reputation', like his 'honour', would be questioned. Those present as witnesses swear that, 'to the world's end', 'all constant men will be Troiluses, all false women Cressids, and all brokers-between Pandars'! (III.ii.200–3).

As the lovers exit to their consummation, Pandar holds the door and wishes Cupid's blessings on other inexperienced 'maidens here' (III.ii.209). He expounds the marital relation in legalese terms of 'fee-farm' (III.ii.49–50), 'debts ...' (III.ii.54), 'in witness ... the parties interchangeably' (III.ii.57). Pandar's legal–commercial diction recurs also in 'close [come to terms] sooner' (III.ii.48), as well as in 'a bargain made. Seal it, seal it. I'll be the witness' (III.ii.196–7).

Pandar, who acts for others, complains ultimately of breach of contract by law of agency.[12] He is 'attorney' or 'agent' (also as Pandar, solicitor), who as scapegoat ultimately 'dies' for (or, on account of) the 'performance'. Agents in law are authorized to act for another, while the actor is the dramatist's mediating 'agent'. Pandar is also the agent as agent: His 'poor agent despised!' (V.x.36) is thus multiply self-reflexive.

By Pandar, love is labelled as business (cf. 'bargain', III.ii.196) to be 'closed' at night: 'An 'twere dark', assures Pandar, 'you'ld close sooner' (III.ii.48).

Act V scene viii

Hector's slaying

Les Violences de la Fête

Y.-M. Bercé, *Fête et Révolte* ...

Thy Chase had a Beast in View

Dryden, 'Secular Masque', l. 87

Accompanying festive *ludicra* are *seria* and variety, while revels festivities have traditionally been linked to a culminating violence. So here, Hector, spokesman (in II.ii) of restraining law, is himself ultimate victim of the violent Achilles. As Achilles' eruption probes the limits of licence, Hector's and Achilles' confrontation (as of law versus natural force, *nomos* versus *physis*)[13] acts out a conflict of the play's values. Revenging his love-and-pleasure deprivation, Achilles thus counterposes Hector's own legally-restraining opposition to 'pleasure and revenge' (II.ii.171).

From the start, Hector is empathically distanced from the audience: the audience first hears of Hector as 'coped' by Ajax, forcing him, with 'disdain and shame', to 'fasting and waking' (I.ii.33–5) – capitulating to the superior power of Ajakes. Hector 'today was moved' (I.ii.5); 'Hector was stirring early' (I.ii.50). The intestinal motif is rehearsed in Hector's own first speech, with its self-comparison: 'There is no lady of more softer bowels...' (II.ii.11). Introduced unheroically,[14] Hector as heroic warrior is compromised not only by his initial Ajax-defeat (I.ii.33–5), and by his ladies' 'bowels' self-comparison, but also by his aborted 'non-duel' (IV.v); by his maladroit transmittal to Menelaus of his wife's non-greetings (IV.v.180); by his inability to recognize the celebrated Achilles (IV.v.233); by his comically imperceptive demand of the unmistakably demotic Thersites: 'Art thou for Hector's match? / Art thou of blood and honour?' (V.iv.25–6); and by his espousal of mercy (V.iii.40–9) with its prompt violation in his merciless slaying of Patroclus (V.v.47), and, covetously for his 'hide', of the knight in shining armour (V.vi.31; V.viii.1–2). Hector is thus, with his brothers Troilus and Paris, distanced from the audience's empathy.

Hence, Hector's slaying 'touches us not with pity' (*KL*, V.iii.233) or 'woe or wonder' (*H*, V.ii.363). While Coriolanus' killing succeeds his brief speech, and the death of other figures (such as Hotspur, Hamlet, Othello, Lear) is preceded by their utterances, Hector perishes almost wordlessly – no dying speech allowed. Hector, introduced unheroically as 'coped' by Ajax (I.ii.33–4), is at last unheroically memorialized by Ajax (V.ix.5–6). Instead of heroic death and epitaph, Hector's is finally a two-line invidious encomium – uttered by the brutishly grudging Ajax. Audience disempathy, as suggested above, would qualify the alleged 'tragic' effect of Hector's slaying – itself anticipatable as a Homeric *scène à faire*. Hector in his slaying thus elicits less 'tragic pity' than a sense of antinomian misrule and of violent contingency culminating a festival.[15]

Act V scene x

'Painted cloths'

Revels' audience-familiarity is suggested in Pandar's comradely advice to 'set this [bathetic tale] in your painted cloths' (V.x.45). Comic presumption exhibited by 'Lord' Pandarus is, like his oxymoronically-titled name, another class joke, while his taste suggests common home furnishings. Pandar familiarly 'answers you right painted cloth' (*AYLI*, III.ii.273). Such 'painted cloths', visible on stage, in entertainments and in homes, were cheap substitutes for tapestries. Thus, in a series of encompassing frames, or *mise en abyme*, the matter of Troy is inset with the tale of Troilus and Cressida, itself inset with the bathetic fall of Pandar, in turn inset with the mini-fall of the humble-bee – a tale recommended to be set within his beholders' painted cloths. Pandar's tale within a 'painted cloth' recalls not only Arachne's weaving depiction of the gods' amours (cf. Ariachne's, V.ii.152), but also the *Iliad*'s Helen and her weaving of tales-within-the-tale. As Elizabethan hangings often contained Trojan War themes,[16] Pandar's interior-decorating advice suggests a Trojan *récit spéculaire*, a reflective play-within-a-play.

'Like a base pander hold the chamber-door' (*H5*, IV.v.14: cf. *O*, IV.ii.91–4) – door-keepers controlled entrances to theatrical and bawdy houses. Pandar's 'Brethren and sisters of the hold-door trade' (V.x.50) thus suggests the 'agent'-procurer, or theatrical entrepreneur, who has 'taken such pains to bring' pleasure-seekers 'together' (III.ii.199).

Pandar, in a final intrusion, puts himself between the play's close and the audience. As another erotic servant, Pompey, familiarly addresses his spectators: 'I am as well acquainted here as I was in our house of profession. One would think it were Mistress Overdone's own house, for here be many of her old customers' (*MM*, IV.iii.1–4). 'Here' (*TC*, V.x.51), this conflation of 'real' and enacted audience, is suggested in both *Measure for Measure* and *Troilus* by an audience-familiar 'hold-door' pander. As Pandar 'here' embraces the spectators in his mystery, so Pompey identifyingly adds, with similar pride in his mystery, 'Then have we here ... forty more, all great doers in our trade' (*MM*, IV.iii.1–4, 12–19).

Scapegoating

Revels' festivity recalls degree scapegoating. The scapegoat himself suggests an inverted king's double – a carnival king crowned at festival, when, inhibitions released, order is disordered, and hierarchies are reversed. During this limited period, the throne is occupied by the most incongruous: 'due observance of thy [dubiously] godlike seat' (I.iii.31), or (questionably) 'authentic place' (I.iii.108), is accorded to the allegedly 'most mighty for thy place and sway' (I.iii.60). If Agamemnon is mock-ruler in the public realm, Pandar is misruler in the private realm, and is duly deposed.

As ultimately ejected Carnality, Pandar recalls the scapegoat, grotesque bearer of communal ill regularly expelled: in ancient Italy, Saturnalia; in modern times, Carnival.[17] After a brief career of dominance and dissipation, Carnival is ejected. Those times of expulsion were 'preceded ... by a period of general license, during which the ordinary restraints of society are thrown aside, ... offences [e.g. as in *Troilus*, *lèse majesté*] are allowed to pass unpunished' (Frazer, *Golden Bough*, IX.225). In the play, 'sacrificial' figures are cast out: Prince Hector from the war plot, Lord Pandarus from the love plot. Pandar's end (cf. Frazer, *Golden Bough*, IX. 306–11) combines a scapegoat's ritual cursing and expulsion.

Such figures as Pandar and Falstaff are phallephoric, and in the tradition of the Aristophanic *pharmakoi*. Noted in its double sense by Rabelais, *pharmakon* (cf. remedy, drug) is also scapegoat: as the vicarious Pandar bears in the flesh the sufferings of his carnal world, he lives and 'dies' for (and through) others' carnalities. Pandar is paradoxically both healer and scapegoat, insofar as what he temporarily 'heals', concupiscence, is beyond cure.

'Baudie compagnon'

Pandar, as end of carnality, farewell to flesh, has affinities with Rabelais' soon-to-die 'baudie campagnon', Quaresmeprenant (oncoming Lent, the days preceding Ash Wednesday). Like Quaresmeprenant, Pandar's 'act', with his existence, is 'slave to limit' (III.ii.82). Seasonally, where once his 'endeavour' had been 'so desired', his 'performance' is now 'so loathed' (V.x.38–9). As Falstaff is from temporarily enacted 'Kingship' deposed (*1H4*, II.iv.435), Pandar is by his princely companion cast down. *Troilus*, ultimately, is time's carnival: the defeat of flesh by temporality. Such is desire viewed in the aftermath of appetite's 'fulfilling bolts' (Prologue, l. 18).

If Pandar suggests licensed Carnival, 'Mistress Thersites!' (II.i.35), a scold against pleasure, anticipates restrictive Lent. Like Malvolio, Thersites (Detraction) is recalcitrant to playfulness; as anti-festive 'agelast', the spirit of holiday eludes him. Judgmental spectre at the banquet of sense, Thersites implicitly flatters the 'fair beholders' (Prologue, l. 26) by combining in one unfair figure anti-festive traits to be disavowed: these include hostility to communal enjoyment, and disempathy with pleasure.

Like his 'marriage' sponsorship (III.ii), Pandar's own 'baptism' in rejection (V.x.33–4) suggests a parodic ritual; at birth, marriage or coronation, the infant, the female spouse or the monarch assumes a name. Henceforth, forever 'pander' (V.x.34) is Pandarus' *nom de bouc émissaire*, or scapegoat name: he has, like Calchas and his daughter, 'Incurred a traitor's [trader's] name' (III.iii.6). So the injudicious trading Pandar had praised the traitorous Antenor as 'one o' th' soundest judgments in Troy whosoever' (I.ii.191–2). Cressid's exchange for Antenor (traitor–trader, Troy's betrayer) helps mark her (Troilus' betrayer – 'traitor' was also love-betrayer) as, like her father, a traitor (trader) – a slur projected upon the audience by the mock-insulting Pandar: 'O traitors [Q, F] and bawds ... Good traders in the flesh ...' (V.x.37, 45). To his own initial identity-question, 'what Pandar [is]'? (I.i.101), Troilus thus ultimately responds: 'Broker-lackey!' (V.x.33). Paradoxically, the *senex-puer* (Curtius, *European Literature*, pp. 98–101) Pandar is dismissingly 'baptized' by the 'skilless as unpractised infancy' Troilus (I.i.12). Recalling young Hal's rejection of the old Falstaff, 'the rude son should strike his [surrogate] father dead' (I.iii.111). So the lover condemns his mentor ('Thyself upon thyself!', II.iii.26) to be 'his name': forever – Pandar.

Pandar makes less his 'grace' in contrast to the advice to Falstaff: 'Make less thy body ... and more thy grace' (*2H4*, V.v.52). If Pandarus or Carnality (*homo animalis*) is, like Falstaff, the Old Man (*vetus homo*) to be cast off, Troilus dismisses concupiscence, not through repentance, but through disappointment. While Lord John Falstaff is cast-out 'tutor and the feeder of a prince's "riots"' (*2H4*, V.v.62), 'Lord' Pandar (or Don Carnal), incarnating Carnival, is one with whose name 'ignomy' is to live forever (V.x.33–4). The 'honour and lordship' he asserts as 'my titles' (III.i.16–17) are, by degradation, no longer his. Following Pandar's mortal premonitions (V.iii.101–7), he signals a ritual departure and (V.x.55) a disease-incubated return.[18]

Gulled goose to 'galled' goose

Lo, here a parfit resoun of a goos!

Chaucer, *The Parliament of Fowles*

Unruly audience-response, anticipatable at such festivities, is recurrent in revels' tradition, including *Gesta Grayorum* and its recorded disorder at performance. In his epilogue, Pandar takes arms against a potential sea of hisses.

Regarding 'goose',[19] fools get such sores – fools *are* such sores – fools hiss – the name of the sore ('goose') is also a symbol of hissing, and of one who hisses. Pandar's concluding verse thus by admonitory application 'proves' an unruly hissing spectator a galled goose. Pandar postpones his will-making, lest some diseased fool of a spectator should respond by hissing. The play moves from adders (II.ii.172), vipers (III.i.134), and serpents' hisses (V.i.88), to geese (V.x.53).

The work, moreover, travels from 'Armed' Prologue to the epilogue's 'arméd tail' (V.x.43). As, at midpoint, Pandar recites a song of erotic 'death' and revival (III.ii.124), at his close he offers a song of erotic subsidence. He thus comments in burlesque-miniature terms on the outcome: the bee's fatal loss of 'sting' (suggesting male subdual) 'subdued in arméd tail' (V.x.42, 43). Having 'lost his honey and his sting', Pandar's diminutive mock-hero and his 'Sweet honey and sweet notes together fail' (V.x.44).

Revels ritual: 'Some two months hence'

Like the Carnival figures of popular rituals, Pandar foreshadows his demise (V.iii.103), and promises 'Some two months hence ... here' – presumably, an appropriate place, before that audience – to make his will (V.x.51).[20]

From Christmastide to 'Some two months hence' approximates Candlemas, and preparation for Lent. Pandar's promise anticipates the testament and death of Carnival. Academic misrule ceremonies ended at the start of Lent, with a mock-funeral procession: the Lord of Misrule was carried out on a bier, symbolizing the demise and burial of the Carnival Lord.

Inverting Cressid's Henrysonian 'poetically-just' punishment by disease,[21] the play's *audience* is to inherit Pandar's bequest of diseases. So, in Rabelais' *Gargantua and Pantagruel*, along with the 'Author's Prologue', folly-as-speaker mock-insults his audience as 'my very esteemed and poxy friends'. Pandar's farewell to his 'diseased' spectators thus recalls Rabelais' salutation to his readers: 'vous, Verolez très précieux'.[22] As Pandar addresses 'Brethren ... of the hold-door trade',[23] similarly uncomplimentary is Pandar's salute to 'sisters of the hold-door trade' (V.x.50). Pandar's epilogic audience-address seems a little more than kin and less than kind. Embracing his listeners as fellow flesh-traders, Pandar's 'Brethren and sisters of the hold-door trade' (V.x.50) thus proffers revels' mock-insult to a familiar and festive audience.

Arrival of night[24]

Masks and Reuels to defeate the night

Thomas Dekker, Satiromastix

Pandar's spectators' 'eyes, half out' (V.x.47) and Aeneas' 'Never go home: here starve we out the night' (V.x.2) suggest a nocturnal witnessing vigil – as at a revel. Cf. the night-emphases (V.i.71–7): 'good night' mentioned five times, with the culminating 'Good night and welcome, both at once, to those / That go or tarry', capped by Agamemnon's 'Good night', As night, 'stickler-like' (V.viii.18), separates the combatants, its hour is at length to release the spectators.

A convention of revels entertainments, both in England and on the continent, is the arrival of night (cf. V.x.47). On the Duchess' lover remaining overnight, she assures him, 'you are a Lord of Misrule', to which he responds, 'True, for my reign is only in the night' (John Webster, *Duchess of Malfi* (1614), III.ii). So Richard Carew's *Survey of Cornwall* (1602 sig. S4 v) remarks his neighbours and kin spending 'a great part of the night in Christmas rule'. An account (*Gesta*, p. 32) of the Gray's Inn 1594–95 revels notes: 'So that Night was begun, and continued to the end, in nothing but Confusion and Errors: whereupon, it was ever afterwards called, *The Night of Errors* ...'.

To summarize, the play reflects numerous revels conventions: for example, food and 'sport' allusions, a mock-ruler, a Court of Love, the arrival-of-night topos, fleshly references, carnival and scapegoating, misrule-violence, unruly audience-response, mock-testament, and mock audience-insult. Such conventional festive elements, among others, connect *Troilus and Cressida* with an Elizabethan revels tradition.

Notes

1.   On revels, see Martin Butler, 'Entertaining the Palatine Prince: Plays on Foreign Affairs 1635–1637', *English Literary Renaissance*, 13 (1983), 319–344. He notes, p. 327, the Middle Temple Christmas revels' strong tradition of festive controversy, involving costly burlesque and parodies of authority within a mock-court.
       Cf. Inns of Court law-student revels and the French law clerks' Basoche, including mock-courts and legal bawdry. See Howard G. Harvey, *The Theatre of the Basoche* (Cambridge, Massachusetts, 1941). See also Jody Enders, *Rhetoric and the Origins of Medieval Drama* (Ithaca, NY, 1992), pp. 129–61.
2.   Prologue, ll. 28–9; cf. *Digest* of Justinian, and 'play' as 'plea' – see Appendix II.
3.   See *OED*, bait, sb. 1 †6 1662: Thomas Fuller, *The History of the Worthies of England*, ed. P.A. Nuttall (1840), II.507: 'He rather took a bait than made a meal at the inns of court, whilst he studied the laws therein'. Further food

references include post-repast 'orts ... / ... fragments, scraps, the bits and greasy relics' (V.ii.158–9). Foods in the play comprise cheese (II.iii.41), nuts (II.i.101) and fruit (II.iii.119), conventionally postprandial, as well as culinary preparations: fry (V.ii.59–60); lard (V.i.56; enlard, II.iii.193); broil (I.iii.378); brew (IV.iv.7); boil (I.iii.349); baste, seam (II.iii.183); sauced (F I.ii.23); seethe (III.i.41); stew (III.i.42).

Cressid's reference to 'minced' in the context of 'pie' (I.ii.257, 258) recalls minced pie as a Christmastide food – appropriate to Christmastide revels. See, in Jonson's *Masque of Christmas*, the character of Minced Pie, a cook's wife. Other characters include Misrule, an offspring of Christmas, Cf. *Christmas Messe* (1619; in David L. Russell, ed., *Stuart Academic Drama*, New York, 1987, pp. 166–80), comprising Mincepy among other Christmas characters. See P.C., *The Exaltation of Christmas Pye* (1659). Gordon Huelin, 'Christmas in the City', *Guildhall Studies in London History*, 3 (1978), 165. Cf. 'alimentary metaphors' (Curtius, *European Literature*, pp. 134–5). J.R. Fryar, 'Some Social Customs of the Old English Christmas', *Ecclesiastical Review*, 39 (1908) 601–17, on porridge (I.ii.243, an older name of pudding), as food common at Christmas.

4.   Cf. 'bolts', 'bolting', Prologue, l. 18; I.i.19, 21, and legal sifting. See bolt, Appendix II. Cf. winnowing (I.iii.28; III.ii.166; 'chaff and bran', I.ii.242). On traditional chaff and winnowing imagery, cf. M. O'R. Boyle, 'Thomas Aquinas' Repudiation of his *Opera Omnia*', *New Literary History*, 29 (1997), 383–99.

5.   On backing, see Beryl Rowland, 'A Cake-Making Image in *Troilus and Cressida*', *Shakespeare Quarterly*, 21 (1970), 191–4.

6.   In Shakespeare, outside this play, Cressid is mentioned in *MV*, *H5*, *TN*, *AWEW*. Troilus is named in *RL*, *TS*, *MV*, *MAAN*, *AYLI*, *TN*. Pandar is mentioned in *MWW*, *MAAN*, *TN*. Only one Shakespearean play, the Middle Temple-produced *Twelfth Night*, names all three of *Troilus*' major characters: Feste (who also cites the Inns of Court 'Gorboduc', IV.ii.14) declares, 'I would play Lord Pandarus of Phrygia, sir, to bring a Cressida to this Troilus ...' (*TN*, III.i.51–2). *TN* and *TC* both suggest a similar audience.

7.   Cf. *Gesta*'s masque of Amity (3 January 1594/95), with its four pairs of legendary friends entering arm in arm, thus avoiding 'emulation of precedencie'. See Marie Axton, *The Queen's Two Bodies* (1977), p. 83.

8.   The indecorous King Agamemnon in his 'godlike seat' recalls 'the medieval Feast of Fools' deposition of the mighty from their seat, and exaltation temporarily of the lowest. This deposition was sung at the 'Magnificat': '*Deposuit potentes de sede: et exaltavit humiles*'. While this was being sung, the precentor's *baculus* was transferred to the *dominus* who was to become revels' lord. Chambers, *Medieval Stage*, I.278.

9.   See Schlumbohm, *Jocus und Amor*.

10. In the Middle Templar Marston's *Fawn* – a play with Inns of Court revels affinities – punishments are imposed for transgressions of Cupid's laws. Such penalties respond to complaints: for example that love is abused and basely bought and sold; that affection is feigned. On the *Fawn* in relation to Inns of Court revels, see Finkelpearl, 'Christmas Revels'. Cf. *Troilus* and motifs of the Court of Love, woman's inconstancy, ship of fools, and similar patterns in *The Fawn*'s 'solemn foolery'. Cf. Finkelpearl, 'Marston's *Histrio-Mastix*', pp. 223–34; reply by James F. Bednarz, 'Marston's Subversion of Shakespeare and Jonson: *Histriomastix* and the War of the Theaters', *Medieval and Renaissance Drama in England*, 6 (1993), 103–27.

11. See W.A. Neilson, *The Origins and Sources of the Court of Love* (Boston, Massachusetts, 1899). Finkelpearl, *John Marston*, pp. 45–61. See Jonson, *Cynthia's Revels*, V.vii and V.ix–xi. On the Court of Love and Marston, cf. Marston, *Fawn*, pp. 22–4, 28–32. See in that play (IV.iv.255–62) the 'Court of love ... in the name of Dan Cupid'. Cf. Joel Kaplan, 'John Marston's *Fawn*: A Saturnalian Satire', *Studies in English Literature*, 9 (1969), 335–50. In Marston's *Fawn* (IV.i), a gravamen is abuse of courtship in securing, through flattery, a woman's agreement to a form of marriage. Other love-derelictions in previous revels include slander; braggadocio; or possessing more than one mistress.

12. See A.R. Braunmuller, '"Second Means": Agent and Accessory in Elizabethan Drama', *Elizabethan Theatre*, 11 (1990), 177–203.

13. *Nomos* versus *physis*; cf. F. Heinimann, *Nomos und Physis* (Basle, 1945); M. Pohlenz, 'Nomos und Physis', *Hermes*, 81 (1953), 418–30.

14. 'Hector' had also a sense as bully, swaggerer or prostitute's protector. (Cf. Williams, *Dictionary*, s.v.).

15. Such festive violence has been studied by Natalie Z. Davis in *Society and Culture*, pp. 152–87, 315–26. See also Emmanuel Le Roy Ladurie, *Carnival in Romans* (New York, 1979), regarding a 1580 revels, pp. 218–63; Y.-M. Bercé, *Fête et Révolte des mentalités du XVIe et XVIIe siècles* (Paris, 1976). See *Gesta Grayorum*'s account of festive disorder: D.S. Bland, '"Night of Errors" at Gray's Inn, 1594', *Notes and Queries*, n.s. 13 (1966), 127–8. See also David Underdown, *Revel, Riot, and Rebellion: Popular Politics and Culture in England, 1603–1660* (Oxford, 1985); René Girard, *La Violence et le sacré* (Paris, 1972); Robert C. Davis, *The War of the Fists. Popular Culture and Public Violence in late Renaissance Venice* (Oxford, 1994). Peter Burke, *Popular Culture in Early Modern Europe* (1978), pp. 157–8; Michael Bristol, *Carnival and Theater* (New York, 1989); François Laroque, *Shakespeare's Festive World* (Cambridge, 1991); on misrule and riot, linked to festivity, cf. Jonson, *Time Vindicated to Himself and to His Honour*, ll. 253–7; and *Bartholomew Fair*, V.i. On festive-abusive language or billingsgate see Mikhail Bakhtin, *Rabelais and his World* (Cambridge, Massachusetts, 1965).

16. On Trojan iconography, cf. John Doebler, 'When Troy Fell: Shakespeare's Iconography of Sorrow and Survival', *Comparative Drama*, 19 (1965–66), 321–31. See Jill L. Levenson, 'Shakespeare's *Troilus and Cressida* and the Monumental Tradition in Tapestries and Literature', *Renaissance Drama*, n.s. 7 (1976), 43–84. D.C. Allen, 'Some Observations on *The Rape of Lucrece*', *Shakespeare Survey*, 15 (1966), especially pp. 189–98.

17. Cf. Frazer, *Golden Bough*, IX.225–6, 306, 312, Part 6, 'Scapegoat', p. 278. René Girard, *The Scapegoat* (Baltimore, Maryland, 1986); C.G. Stridbeck, 'Combat Between Carnival and Lent', *Journal of the Warburg and Courtauld Institutes*, 19 (1956), 98–106. Cf. Sandra Billington, *Mock Kings in Medieval Society and Renaissance Drama* (Oxford, 1991).

18. Dedicated to the masters of the bench of Lincoln's Inn, William Prynne's *Histriomastix* (1633) condemns unruly revels associated with Inns of Court celebrations. Panders were said professionally to frequent the theatres. Indeed, panders and actors were linked, as in Prynne's view that many players were common panders.
     Panders were featured in an annual medieval rite of folly, the *festum fatuorum*: priests and clerks danced in the choir in the costumes of panders. Cf. a letter of 1445 by the Dean of the Faculty of Theology, University of

Paris, to the bishops and chapters of France, on clerks dressed in the vestments of panders, *lenonum*, Chambers, *Medieval Stage*, I. 293–4.

Pandar's distinction between 'lordship' and 'grace' ('Grace! not so, friend: honour and lordship are my titles', III.i.16–17), recalls a reference by a Middle Templar diarist, about the time of the play. Cf. Manningham, *Diary*, January 1602, fol. 88b: 'Lord is a name sometyme of place and sometyme of grace'.

Regarding Pandar's 'Why should our endeavour be so desired and the performance so loathed?' (V.x.38–9), his epilogic complaint on audience mis-response recalls an academic revels' conclusion: that of the *Christmas Prince*, 1608 (St John's College, Oxford; Malone Society reprint, 1922, p. 288). This revel's end complains, like Pandar, of disappointing audience response to a 'performance' (V.x.39).

In a revels-produced comedy is the precautionary 'let no quarrel nor no brawl to come / Taint the condition of this present hour' (*TN*, V.i.356–7). Recording revels' disorders, cf. C.E. McGee and J.C. Meagher, 'Preliminary Checklist of Tudor and Stuart Entertainment': 1485–1558, *Research Opportunities in Renaissance Drama*, 25 (1982), 31–114; and 1558–1603, 24 (1981), 51–155. Cf. Puck's 'now to scape the serpent's tongue' (*MND*, V.i.433). Hissing, implies Pandar, signifies one has been 'galled' – a galled goose hisses. The 'galled goose' (V.x.53) is both diseased and a disease, the carrier as his own symptom. 'Thyself upon thyself!' (II.iii.26).

19.   Cf. 'goose' or 'botch in the ... yard; a winchester goose'. See Cotgrave, *Dictionarie*, s.v. *clapoir*, Cf. other references, s.v. Winchester, in Sugden, *Dictionary*.

20.   'The last will and testament of Christmas' is read in Thomas Middleton's *Inner Temple Masque* (1619). There is a mock-dethronement 'some two months' after the usual Christmas festivities, in the *Christmas Prince*'s *Ira Fortunae* (9 February 1608). A mock-dethronement occurs in *Philomathes* (also an entertainment within *Christmas Prince*, 1608), St John's College, Oxford, 'some two months' after the usual Christmastide festivities. At the end of *Philomathes* is an appeal to a revels Lord to make his will: '... you must die ... therefore while you have your good witts about you, *Fac quid vobis*, Make your will that wee may know amongst so many well deserving men, that doe lay Claime to this your Castell, to whome as rightfull heire itt shall lawfully descend ...'. Then 'To make an end of this nightes sporte, all departed merry and very well pleased ...'.

Pandar is to experience 'the powd'ring-tub of infamy' (*H5*, II.i.75). Cf. the 'two months hence' till when Pandar will 'sweat and seek about for eases' (V.x.51, 54), and Francis Beaumont and John Fletcher, *Knight of the Burning Pestle* (1607), III.i: 'This beast caught us, and put us in a Tub, / Where we this two months sweat ...'. Not only does Pandarus promise to bequeath the viewers his afflictions, but they are also ignominiously to be made a Pandar's heir. The pander's heirs, notes Juvenal's *Satire III* (Loeb ed. p. 43), remarking the breakdown of degree, 'born in any brothel, take their seats'.

Pandar is to return to 'make' (including publish) his will. Cf. Giles Jacob, *A New Law-Dictionary* (Dublin, 1773), s.v. Publication: '... Publication of a *Will*, which is a solemnity requisite to the Making thereof, by declaring it to be last Will of the testator, in the Presence of such a number of witnesses ...'. For the 'making' of a will, an audience of law students 'here' (V.x.51: 'my will shall here be made') would be appropriate witnesses. Witnesses recur at mid-play, as in Pandar's 'I'll be the witness' (III.ii.107); and climactically in V.ii, Troilus and others witnessing his love-betrayal as 'Love's Martyr'.

'The testament', notes C.R. Baskervill (*The Elizabethan Jig* (Chicago, 1929), p. 47, 'was a favorite form of legal parody'. Cf. E.C. Perrow, 'The Last Will and Testament as a Form of Literature', *Transactions of the Wisconsin Academy of Sciences*, 17, part 1 (1914), 692–753. See W.N. King, *The European Ancestry of Villon's Satirical Testament* (Syracuse University Monographs, l, New York, 1941). See Edward Wilson, *The 'Testament of the Buck* and the Sociology of the Text', *Review of English Studies*, 45 (1994), 157–84, listing burlesque testaments in English and Scots, to c. 1565. See also Ulrich Bach, *Das Testament als literarische Form*, Düsseldorfer Hochschulreihe 3 (Düsseldorf, 1977); Bach, *Kommentierte Bibliographie englische literarischer Testamente vom 14. bis zum 20. Jahrhundert.* Anglistische Forschungen 163 (Heidelberg, 1982). Julia Boffey, 'Lydgate, Henryson, and the Literary Testament', *Modern Language Quarterly*, 53 (1992), 41–56.

See also C.L. Barber, *Shakespeare's Festive Comedy* (Princeton, New Jersey, 1972), pp. 43–5. Udall's *Rafe Roister Doister*. Nashe's *Summer's Last Will and Testament*. Donne's 'The Will'. Thomas Middleton, *A Chaste Maid in Cheapside* (V.i). See in Middleton and William Rowley's *Inner Temple Masque, or Masque of Heroes* (1618/19), the will of Kersmas in legal form: here recalling Pandar's diseases and mock-will, is the death of December or the Old Year: 'toward his end / Full of diseases'.

21.   *Testament of Cresseid*, II.316–18, 376–7, 438–51.
22.   Rabelais, *Gargantua and Pantagruel*, Prologue, 1 (*Oeuvres*).

Revels' affinities with the fleshly trade are recurrently noted. Cf. the Gray's Inn revels, 1594–5, where the Lord of Misrule bears titles of familiar London places of resort. See Joseph Lenz, 'Base Trade: Theater as Prostitution', *ELH*, 60 (1993), 833–55.

23.   Cf. the Inns of Court's Thomas Lodge (1584), *An Alarum against Usurers* (1584), *Complete Works*, Hunterian Club, 1883, I.3: 'the brothell house brotherhoode'.

Pandar's address to 'sisters of the hold-door trade' (V.x.50) includes a 'sisterly' euphemism. This euphemism recurs in a letter from Dudley Carleton to John Chamberlain during the Christmas celebrations on 15 January 1605: 'The Temples have both of them done somwhat since Twelftide but nothing memorable, save that it was observed on Friday last at night the greatest part of the femal audience was the sisterhoode of Blackfriars'. Chambers, *Elizabethan Stage*, IV.139–40, citing *S.P.D. Jac. I*, xii.13. Cf. 'sisters' in a similar context: Nashe, *Pierce Penniless* (*Works*, I. 217): 'our unclean sisters in Shoreditch and Westminster'. On 'sisters' as euphemism, cf. also Butler, 'A Pimp' (*Characters*, p. 235): 'a Solicitor of Love, a Whore's Broker [cf. V.x.33] ... Agent [cf. V.x.36] for the Flesh [cf. V.x.45] ... maintaining constant Correspondence ... with all *Lay-Sisters* ...'.

24.   On the approach of night as a revels-epilogue topos, cf. a school-revels summary: John Mason [of Cambridge], *Princeps Rhetoricus* (1648), Epilogue, p. 20. Cf. Marston, *Mountebank's Masque* (*Works*, ed. A.H. Bullen, 1867, III.441).

8. Law

This chapter examines the play's legal reflections, of interest and comprehensible to law students, and suited to their revels tradition.[1]

Act I scene i

'Infancy'

Initially, Troilus avows himself as 'skilless as unpractised infancy' (I.i.12). Cassandra addresses 'Soft infancy, that nothing canst but cry' (II.ii.105).[2] The term 'infancy' (legally, not of full age), indicated, if addressed to an Inns of Court audience, young law student. Thus, F.L[enton], *Characterismi* (1631, sig. F4) notes, 'A yong Innes a Court gentleman. Is an Infant ...'. So also Nashe (*Works*, III.213) refers to 'an infant squib of the Innes of Court'.

Pandar and Troilus (himself a knight-*enfant*) are summoned up in other comments by L[enton], *Characterismi* (sigs F4–F5v): The Inns of Court 'Infant, newly crept from the Cradle of learning, to the Court of liberty ...' is left to 'foule vice ... which layes siege to his tender Walls ...'. Like Troilus, 'He is a youth very apt to bee wrought upon at his first entrance', and like Pandarus, 'there are Fishers of purpose for such young fry'.

Both Trojan brothers, Troilus and Hector, are introduced in self-avowed terms of unheroic immaturity. Troilus, as noted above, confesses himself 'skilless as unpractised infancy' (I.i.12); so Hector claims, compared to himself, 'There is no lady [also, boy actor] of more softer bowels' (II.ii.11).

Act II scene i

'No man is beaten voluntary'

To Thersites' claim, 'I serve here voluntary', Achilles (recalling the railer's beating) adjudicates: 'Your last service was sufferance, 'twas not voluntary' (II.i.95–6). To this verdict, Achilles appends an Aristotelian dictum: 'No man is beaten voluntary' (II.i.96; *Nicomachean Ethics*, 1136 b 14). This is also a traditional legal maxim, that no man suffers injury voluntarily – that is, no injury can be claimed by one who consents.[3]

Arbitrator in the quarrel of Thersites versus Ajax, Achilles foreshadows other such judgmental verdicts: Hector on Troilus and Paris, versus Hector (II.ii); and Diomedes on Paris versus Menelaus concerning the right to Helen (IV.i). The choice of arbitrator is ironical: the war-withdrawn Achilles here on an issue of force; and the love-opportunist Diomedes on the cuckolder Paris versus the cuckold Menelaus. Transcending judicial arbitration, 'that old common arbitrator, Time, / Will one day end it' (IV.v.225–6).[4]

Playing on the ambiguous 'voluntary' (II.i.96), Achilles notes Thersites as 'under an impress' – not only under duress, but also an impressed soldier. With a tactlessness in the play that is recurrent (e.g. at IV.i.8–11), Achilles reminds Thersites of the latter's own pummelling. Ajax was free to beat you, Achilles implies, and you were forced to take it. Achilles' legalistic adjudication rules that 'voluntary' applies to him who does the beating, not to the victim who suffers it – the latter's experience is legally termed 'sufferance' (II.i.95–7).[5]

Act II scene ii

'Nature craves'

Legalistically, Hector observes, 'To persist / In doing wrong extenuates not wrong, / But makes it much more heavy' (II.ii.186–8). (This assertion contradicts Paris' peculiar claim to 'persist' in retaining Helen in order to 'have the soil of her fair rape / Wiped off in honourable keeping her', II.ii.148–9.) Hector's dictum ironically foreshadows his own persistent commitment to his vow – his own fatal 'persistive constancy' (I.iii.21).

Further, Hector's claim regarding Helen of matrimonial right is undercut by his 'Nature craves' (II.ii.173) – ambiguously, Hector's *law* of nature, or law of *nature*? Hector's 'law of nature' *is* 'corrupted through affection'

(II.ii.176–7) – for example Paris' affection for Helen, transgressing matrimonial right. (Both Hector and Ulysses subvert the law of nature they assert.)

Hector's defence of natural law is related to an *argumentum e consensu omnium*, an argument from the consensus of all, with roots in presophistic as well as sophistic, Platonic and Aristotelian notions of the correctness of common judgment. Hector's assertion of moral 'law / Of nature and of nations' (II.ii.184–5) is related to the consensus of nations. 'Nature craves' the return of what is owed, but determination of the owner seems also a question of who currently possesses, an issue said to comprise points of the law (cf. Liebs, B1, D62, J61, J93, J94, M35, O10, P78, U31).

Question of ownership is related to the legalistic injunction to 'deliver her possession up' (II.ii.152) – that 'All dues be rendered to their owners' (II.ii.174). Hector's defence of the 'nearer debt' of marriage seems subverted in Helen's reported claim to her 'husband' Paris (I.ii.164–5), and disregard (cf. IV.v.180) for her lawful spouse, Menelaus. Indeed, what 'Nature craves' may be, rather than natural law, merely the appetitive 'natural' craving of the moment. Having passed through naturally craving Greeks, Cressid (V.ii) is about to yield to what Diomedes' 'nature craves'.[6] Pursuing natural impulse, Troilus inverts law's reason to a dismissal of 'reason'. Supporting folly Troilus, for example, rejects reason's lack of 'Manhood and honour' (II.ii.47). Such 'reason' is repudiated as an impediment to valour: 'reason and respect / Make livers pale and lustihood deject' (II.ii.49–50).[7]

Hector's legalistic assertion (II.ii.173–4),[8] and his 'What nearer debt in all humanity / Than wife is to the husband?' (II.ii.175–6), suggest the wife as a debt owed to the husband (cf. Chaucer's 'marriage debt'). The *nearer* [closer or more intimate] debt', rather than that between wife Helen and husband Menelaus, is, however, now that between Helen and Paris. Insofar as Hector will (at II.ii's end) fight to keep Paris' Helen, he will side with the *ami*, Paris, against the *mari*, Menelaus – despite the latter's 'nearer [legal] debt'.

Regarding Helen, from an initial cost-benefit argument, Hector shifts to principles of value estimation, thence to natural law, and wife's debt to husband. Hector's 'What nearer debt in all humanity / Than wife is to the husband?' (II.ii.175–6)[9] seems in the next act implicitly answered: abducted spouse to common-law adulterer. For his part, Troilus here champions not only Helen, but implicitly also his brother Paris' *franchise*, or erotic liberty and adulterous freedom.[10]

'Laws of nature and of nations'[11]

Trojan discussion of natural law takes place paradoxically within a war instigated by appetitive craving and transgression of natural law. Following Hector's argument comes the proof. If Helen, Hector superfluously recalls, is the Spartan king's wife, 'As [again, redundantly] it is known she is, these moral laws / Of nature and of nations' should prevail (II.ii.183–5).

Act III scene ii

Oath-dialectic

Recurrently, oaths and their violation are of legal concern.[12] Pandar is by predilection the transient negation of the absolute oath. His is a promise of mutable relativity (of what 'nature craves'), implicit even at the moment of 'betrothal', thus a wry commentary on its hopes.

An oath provides a guarantee against freedom – that freedom the oath-bound priestess Cassandra paradoxically claims ('vows to every purpose must not hold', V.iii.24): oaths in III.ii are sworn within a contradictory determined context. Personages at this point seem already, ironically, what they swear they are not to be. Pandar, bidding the lovers kiss, legalistically instructs them, 'Seal it, seal it. I'll be the witness' (III.ii.196–7). Ultimately (V.x.51), he promises to make his own will 'here', in this place, before the spectators' own 'witness'.

Traditionally, each betrothed partner is vulnerable to the other through mutual trust: As in the *Book of Common Prayer*, betrothal includes 'I plight thee my trouth'. If 'plight' implies place at risk, 'trouth' includes truth and faith pledged, through trust in the other's faithful truth.

Against Troilus' and Paris' defence of Helen's abduction, legal maxims could be cited. Hector, for instance, warns that a bad cause relates to a bad outcome: 'bad success in a bad cause' (II.ii.117). Compare the legal maxim, Liebs E54, 'ex iniuria jus non oritur' (justice or law may not arise out of injury): Paris' injurious abduction of Helen cannot legally be a basis for arguing her retention. More generally applicable to Helen's rape is legally 'ex turpi causa non oritur actio' – no right of action arises from a disgraceful or immoral consideration.[13]

'The forme of solemnization of matrimonie'

A Pimp ... joins Man and Woman together in the unholy State of Incontinence. His Life is a perpetual Wedding, and he is curst as often as a Matchmaker.
                                             Samuel Butler (1612–80), *Characters*

My Clarke a Pimpe, a Pander was my Priest.
                                             Thomas Cranley, *Amanda* (1635)

Though Vico defines marriage as 'a chaste carnal union consummated under fear of some divinity',[14] in III.ii 'marriage' is not under authority of the divine – but of Pandar. The 'bond of matrimony' is here the impulse of panderly mediation. Paradoxically, Pandar, symbol of love-transience, presides over a relation sworn to last forever: here the marriage of true minds admits the mocking impediment of a Pandar. As sponsor of the 'marriage', Pandar, by his role as Cressid's 'guardian' interposes his 'authority'. (Later, she will call Diomedes her 'guardian': V.ii.8, 48.) When Pandarus offers his word for Cressid (III.ii.108), it is manifestly the word of a pander – to an audience of gentlemen-lawyers, such assurances of his word by 'Lord' Pandarus could have seemed risible.

The carnal Pandar's presumption of a traditionally sacramental role suggests his coupling of others also as an act of *dis*ordination. The union he sponsors lacks the coherence of 'Our inward souls / Married in league, coupled and link'd together / With all religious strength of sacred vows' (*KJ*, III.i.226–8).[15] Pandar's closing bed-offering anticipates Lear's Fool: in both *Lear* (I.v.51–2) and *Troilus* (III.ii.209–10), vice-types' concluding couplets advising inexperienced 'maidens'. Pandar's end-of-scene audience-address ('And Cupid grant all tongue-tied maidens here / Bed, chamber, pandar, to provide this gear!' III.ii.209–10) similarly suggests an anti-edificatory message. Pandar's mid-play 'here' (III.ii.197) and his end-play 'here' (V.x.46, 51) point to his immediate audience and its occasion.

Audience legal-awareness is implied in Pandar's erotic legalism: 'I will show you a chamber with a bed; which bed, because it shall not speak of your pretty encounters, press it to death' (III.ii.206–8). Pressing to death – 'peine forte et dure' – of condemned prisoners was a penalty for 'standing mute' – to speak might endanger their heirs' estate.[16]

Act III, scene iii

Kinship bonds: 'one touch of nature'

Though Ulysses through defence of 'degree' and 'authentic place' (I.iii.108) asserts social distinctions, here he levellingly affirms, in contrast, the 'one touch of nature' that 'makes the whole world kin' (III.iii.175).[17]

Upon the presumed kinship by nature of mankind is founded a premise of natural law. As it binds all beings, natural law brings to mind the community of creatures. 'Nature' (comprising sexuality; concupiscence) is how the whole world is produced, and in being so produced, forms natural kinship. Kinship bonds are examined here in their love, war and social disintegrations, and parodied ultimately in Pandar's insinuating audience-kinship (V.x.50). By 'law of kynde' Cressid is appetitively disposed, as she prepares to supplant Troilus after the appetite 'of Cressid's kind' (*H5*,

II.i.76). Kinship considerations emerge also on a low animal-level (V.vii.18–19), as well as on an illegitimacy-level subversive of degree (V.vii.19–20). Cuckolders should not fight with cuckolds; they depend on each other – an ironic vision of what correlates society. 'One touch of nature' here does 'make the whole world kin' (III.iii.175) – interrelatedly, bastards, panders, cuckold, and cuckold-makers – kindred 'traders [traitors] in the flesh' (V.x.45). Although Hector spares Ajax as kin (IV.v.119–35), and spares Achilles through chivalric kinship (V.vi.14), Hector is himself fatally not spared by the unchivalric and less-than-kind Achilles (V.viii).

In 'one touch of nature makes the whole world kin, / That all with one consent praise new-born gawds' (III.iii.175–6), Ulysses offers a choice of legalistic clichés: line-end stopped – by which all men are, by one touch of nature, kin; and run-on, by which all men kindredly 'praise new-born gawds'. If stopped at line end, Ulysses provides the commonplace that nature (or natural erotic desire, or natural obsolescence) affects mankind – or that men share a common nature. If run on, the line suggests qualifyingly that this common nature entails love of novelties. As Ulysses' degree principle is, following its declaration, subverted, so, here subverted, is a foundation of law itself.

With such notions are other legalistic commonplaces scanned in the play, including 'kind', 'degree' and 'consanguinity',[18] recalling Hector's 'law / Of nature' (II.ii.176–7). Ulysses' (III.iii.17) 'One *touch* of nature makes the whole world *kin*' foreshadows Cressid's claim to 'know no *touch* of consanguinity / No *kin* … so near me / As the sweet Troilus' (IV.iv.97–9). If Ulysses' 'one touch of nature' speech intimates a mock-evocation of natural law, Pandar's obsessive concern for kindred suggests parodic law of nature.

Exemplifying human love of novelties are Diomedes' allure as Cressid's novel 'gawd', and Hector's fatally gleaming, coveted Grecian armour (V.vi). The service is greater than the gawd as is the sacrificial war for the 'gawd' Helen. Such discrepancy Troilus and Hector discover, in the 'fair without, foul within' of their glitter-provoked enticements.

Ulysses' 'touch of nature' (III.iii.175) remarks on 'changeful potency' (IV.iv.97), and on the deteriorating effect of time upon 'vigour of bone' or 'desert in service' (III.iii.172). Thus, in sequence, Ulysses' lines comment both upon time's disabling effects, and upon the ceaseless quest for novelty. Pandar (like Dame Nature or Dame Kinde) is the arouser and purveyor of 'kind', of yearning for 'new-born gawds' (II.iii.176). Ulysses on change anticipates Cressid's enticement by 'new-born gawds', as the 'whole world' (III.iii.175, 176) appetitively seeks change and gratification in novelty.

For her part, Cressid's legalistic diction seems unusual utterance by a young girl separating from her lover. Further, her reference to 'consanguinity' (IV.ii.97) anticipates Hector on degrees of kin- or blood-relations (IV.v.120–35): 'The obligation of our blood' forbids 'A gory emulation' (IV.v.122–23) – contrasting with the Grecian 'bloodless emulation' (I.iii.134).

Pandar as concupiscent impulse himself suggests 'one touch of nature [that] makes the whole world kin' (III.iii.175). Further, his concern for kin has a heavy irony: 'I will not', he assures Troilus, 'dispraise your [ravingly mad] sister Cassandra's wit' (I.i.48–9). Pandar's family pride has a double edge: 'Our kindred ... are burs ... they'll stick where they are thrown' (III.ii.108–11).

In sum, Ulysses' 'one touch of nature' suggests the human-kinship bond: of niece, uncle, lover, new lover, adulterer, cuckold and complaisant adulteress. Indeed, love of 'kynde', as opposed to love 'celestial', preoccupies both Chaucer's poem and Shakespeare's play, along with the 'wrecched worldes appetites' (Chaucer, *Troilus and Criseyde*, V.1851).

'Parties interchangeably'[19]

Pandar's phrase, 'parties interchangeably' (III.ii.57), used legally in preparation of marriage contracts, suggests also dramatic interchanges. (Cf. Pandar's wish that 'my heart were in her body', I.ii.78–9.) In addition, such comminglings 'interchangeably' anticipate part-'commixtions' (IV.v.124; cf. I.ii.19–30). Hector refuses further to combat Ajax (IV.v.119), since he cannot be sure which portion of the mongrel-warrior's body (II.i.13; V.iv.12) is Greek or which is Trojan. Battle would be between relatives, one of whom, to avoid, in his opponent, his *own* bloodshed, remains ludicrously 'half ... at home' (IV.v.84). Since Grecian Ajax is, by blood, already half-exchanged for Trojan, Hector breaks off the combat-exchange. In refusing to fight Ajax for fear of shedding his own blood, Hector suggests a choice of Solomon; in shedding blood, the dangerous dilemma of Shylock.

Act IV scene i

Judgment of Paris: Diomedes

Paris' tactless imprudence in soliciting the rival Greek love-opportunist's judgment on rights to Paris' own abducted Grecian beloved does not itself show judgment, and is injudiciously upside-down. For Paris is himself legendary judge-arbiter of women – indeed, of goddesses,[20] and Diomedes is hardly impartial in his judgment of women. (Diomedes insults both Trojan brothers, Paris here, and Troilus in IV.iv.) The play comprises a Judgment *of*, and *on*, Paris – within a war from whose 'Judgment' (by the 'event') it derives. Paris' own war-instigating 'Judgment' is recalled in the judgment of

Hector *on* Paris (II.ii.113–88) and of Diomedes *on* Paris (IV.i.56–68).

As Paris poses an indelicate query regarding his royal beloved, he asks it of an enemy from whose land he has stolen a married queen. He asks it, moreover, of one who is, like himself, an opportunist in love. In his love-demand, Paris' Helen-debate topic suggests an exercise *in utramque partem*, argument on both sides. Diomedes, like his love-opportunist analogue Edmund, would 'study deserving' (*KL*, I.i.31). Such disputes as to who deserves Helen more – husband or lover (with the ironies in 'deserves') – provided academic issues of controversies, or questions. Such debates were succeeded (cf. II.ii.163–93) by judgments attempting to clarify opinions.

Act V scene iii

Oaths and words

> Which *Swearing*, or OATH, is a Forme of Speech, added to a Promise; by which he that promiseth, signifieth, that unless he performe, he renounceth the mercy of his God, or calleth for vengeance on himself.
>
> Thomas Hobbes, *Leviathan* (1651)[21]

As III.i and III.ii inspect the 'after' and 'before' of connubiality, V.ii and V.iii ('preposterously') examine the 'after' and 'before' of oath-transgression. (As in V.ii Cressid betrays her oath to Troilus – following Helen and her marital-vow violation – so in V.iii Cassandra and Andromache plead vainly with Hector to betray *his* oath.) V.iii is split into Oaths and Words. As this scene unfolds, oaths become words, and words become air.

Hector's fatally kept oath in war parallels Troilus' faithfully kept vow in love. (Both brothers are surprised by betrayal and a failure of reciprocity: Hector in war, Troilus in love.) V.iii comprises not only the Trojan women's supplications to Hector, but also Hector's merciful response (V.iii.40–2) to his own suppliant captives. The Hector–Troilus 'mercy' exchange anticipates Hector's next-scene mercy to Thersites (V.iv.25–9), and, ironically, Hector's merciless slaying of the Greek-in-shining-armour.[22] Paradoxically, while Hector does not (cf. V.iii) yield to his pleading kindred, he yields to the supplicating foe (V.iii.37–43). His 'mercy' is thus self-destructively misplaced. In contrast to Hector's merciful response to an enemy (V.iii.40–6) is Achilles' merciless response to Hector (V.viii).[23]

Act V scene iii's ironical juxtapositions include 'charity' in the vow-dissuasion debate of Andromache and Hector, followed directly by the 'ruthlessness' debate of Hector and Troilus (V.iii.40–9). This scene debating the validity of vows comes full circle in the vow-betrayed Troilus' tearing of Cressid's letter to him (V.iii.108). Hence, V.iii, which starts with Troilus' appeal to Hector to discard vows or words, ends with Troilus' discarding Cressid's words. In this same scene in which Hector defends words, Troilus proclaims (cf. Pandar's 'Words pay no debts', III.ii.54) the wind-to-wind bankruptcy of words.[24]

Oaths and 'charity'

> But for a kingdom any oath may be broken
> *3 Henry VI*

Recalling Elizabethan controversies over oaths, V.iii's vow debate brings to mind not only the required church-read Homilies (cf. the 'VII Official Homilie against Swearing and Perjury'), but also in the Church of England's central Thirty-Nine Articles, the final article, on oaths. Indeed, Cassandra, like Andromache, recalls this Article 39: 'as we confess that *vain and rash swearing* is forbidden ... so we judge ... that a man may swear when the Magistrate requireth, *in a case of ... charity, so it be done ... in justice ...*'.[25] Recalling this last of the Thirty-Nine Articles, Andromache considers the swearing circumstances in relation to a worthy purpose. Yet, where that Article allows oaths in a 'case of ... *charity*', Hector's wife approves not only oath-transgression, but even robbing 'in the behalf of *charity*' (V.iii.22).[26]

Andromache's and Cassandra's pleas to Hector to break his oath (V.iii.19–25) parallel Cressid's plea to Diomedes to break hers: 'I prithee, do not hold me to mine oath' (V.ii.27). Recurrently, Cressid is forsworn: to Troilus with Diomedes, and then to Diomedes while recalling Troilus and seemingly evading her vow even to the Greek.

By vow-casuistry, commitments are subverted, as in the Trojan War, itself instigated by breach of a marital vow. Loyal wife and sanctified priestess, Andromache and Cassandra pragmatize the sacred, arguing the legitimacy of oath-breaking according to circumstances. Their *dissuasio* of Hector from battle in V.iii complements Ulysses' *suasio* (III.iii) of Achilles to battle. V.iii, which opens with women's exhorting Hector to violate his vows, ends with Troilus' rejection of a woman who breaks hers (V.iii.108–12).

Purpose-changers

> hence shall we see
> If power change purpose: what our seemers be
> *Measure for Measure*

Violation of oaths through 'that ... purpose-changer ... / That broker ... / That daily break-vow ...' is denounced by Faulconbridge. Condemning 'This bawd, this broker, this all-changing word [commodity]', he also indicts the purpose-changer's 'all-changing' vow

(*KJ*, II.i.567–9, 582). Like Faulconbridge's deprecated 'purpose-changer', opposed to oath-constancy, is paradoxically the oath-bound priestess Cassandra, who changingly argues, 'But vows to every purpose must not hold' (V.iii.24).

Ironically, in V.iii Hector is himself confronted with objections similar to those he raised in II.ii against Troilus. Hector now (as Troilus then) refuses to judge his actions by fear of 'bad success' (II.ii.117). Fearing 'bad success', warning against her husband's intent, Andromache pleads, 'Do not count it holy / To hurt by being just' (V.iii.19–20): an action may claim to be just, yet have hurtful consequences. Vows maintained with such harmful results – vows judged by consequences – are not to be considered 'holy'.

Act V scene iii thus poses a dialectic of oaths: faithful commitment regardless of consequences, versus vow-abrogation in view of such commitment's possible consequences. (In that regard, it recalls II.ii's antithesis of absolute versus utilitarian notions of the justness of an action. There Troilus argued against evaluation of 'the justness of each act' only by its 'event', while Hector warned against eventual 'bad success in a bad cause', II.ii.117–20.) In V.iii Hector seems to reverse himself, favouring full commitment to an oath over fear of 'bad success in a bad cause'.

In V.iii, Hector himself ironically takes on Troilus' recklessness, which he had in II.ii opposed, and rejects his own previous restraining counsel. Whereas in II.ii Hector credits Cassandra's dire prophecies and chides Troilus with them, in V.iii Hector fatally rejects his mad sister's prescience – while Troilus repeats his previous Cassandra-dismissal.

As Andromache implies that vows are to be evaluated also by their proposed ends (V.iii.24–5), she holds purposes or ends so important that they allow unlawful means (V.iii.21–2).

Regarded traditionally, Andromache's claim (V.iii.23) seems upside down: Rather than the purpose (as she claims) making strong the vow, the vow as sacred (sworn by the gods) makes its 'purpose' strong. Then she inverts another principle: 'But vows to every purpose must not hold' (V.iii.24). Yet vows are themselves sworn (cf. *KJ*, II.i.567–9) to withstand vicissitudes of purpose. While Cassandra here implicitly undermines her own sacred vows as priestess, Hector's wife implicitly subverts her own marital vows. She implies it is as lawful *not* to adhere to vows, if adherence has ill effects. She would, moreover, be willing to perform 'violent thefts / And rob in the behalf of charity' (V.iii.21–2) – the end, 'charity,' could justify the means, 'violent thefts'. Like Angelo, Andromache would casuistically recommend a 'charity in sin' to save a relative's life.

Ironically, Hector himself shortly (V.vi–viii) by 'violent thefts' (V.iii.21) uncharitably 'robs' Patroclus' and the Grecian knight's lives. He slays the latter covetously for his shining armour (V.vi.31; V.viii.2), mercilessly, and hardly 'in the behalf of charity' (V.iii.22). As charity is a virtue the love-betrayed Troilus has cast out (V.iii.44–58), both brothers confirm Ulysses on 'charity' and love as 'subject all / To envious and calumniating Time' (III.iii.173–4). Debating vows, V.iii also disputes mercy, a traditional knightly virtue. As Hector defends mercy, and promptly violates it (V.vi.27–31), analogous inconsistency occurs in Ulysses' contradictions on degree; and in Hector, on law and justice. 'Prince of chivalry' (I.ii.230), Troilus would (in V.iii) violate chivalric behaviour – including 'magnanimous deeds' (II.ii.200) – that he had previously avowed.

In sum, two circumstantial arguments are thus in V.iii launched against Hector's vow-absolutism: Andromache's ends–means, and Cassandra's vow-casuistry. Where Hector's wife argues that good purposes or ends justify bad means (V.iii.21), his prophetess-sister implies that vows may be violable when their swearing is 'hot and peevish' (V.iii.10). (Hector's wife thus emphasizes the vow's end; his sister recalls circumstances of the vow's beginning.) As V.iii's vow-debate implies a commentary on Helen's and Cressid's vow-violations, all four of the play's 'woman's answer[s]' (I.i.108) – Cressid's, Helen's, Cassandra's, Andromache's – concern oath-abrogation.

In response to his male lover's slaying, Achilles, re-entering battle, transgresses 'An oath [of war-abstention] that I have sworn' to a female lover (V.i.41) – in process of such violation, killing her (Polyxena's) brother, Hector. Whereas Achilles breaks his oath to a woman, Hector defends his oath against womanly appeals to break it. The vow-keeper Hector is, in consequence, slain by the vow-violator Achilles.

Against Hector, spokesman (in II.ii) of law, the furious Achilles celebrates in blood the bounds of licence. Restraint and law, the sacrificial victim Hector had himself proclaimed (II.ii.180–2). If 'pity is the virtue of the law' (*TA*, III.v.18), Hector 'stands for' law (II.ii) and, Troilus claims, 'pity' (V.iii). Yet Achilles (becomes, in V.viii, Sansloy or Ate) is beyond law and pity. As a character in Marston's *Fawn* declares, "tis against the nature of love not to be violent' (Act III, l. 270), Achilles' love-deprived violence recalls the inverted violence against nature.[27] Violating the law of kind, or natural law, as well as the law of chivalry, Achilles recalls those who take 'the mends in' their 'own hands' (I.i.70) – who, not having a law, are a 'law unto themselves' (cf. Romans II, 14–15).

To summarize, this chapter has examined the play's legal reflections (including oaths and their violation). Such allusions, of interest and comprehensible to a legal audience, would have been suited to a law-students' revel.

Notes

1.   For law students, manuals were available: for example, Fraunce, *Lawiers Logike* (1588); John Doddridge, *The English Lawyer* (1631); Fulbecke, of

Gray's Inn, *Direction*. Fulbecke's law manual for Inns of Court students was known to Shakespeare, as argued by Guy Butler, 'William Fulbecke: A New Shakespeare Source'?, *Notes and Queries*, n.s. 33 (1986), 363–5.

Cf. also John A. Alford et al., *Literature and Law in the Middle Ages: A Bibliography of Scholarship* (New York, 1984); R.J. Schoeck, 'Recent Scholarship in the History of Law', *Renaissance Quarterly*, 20, (1967), 279–91.

2.   Cf. Cassandra's address to 'Soft infancy' (II.ii.105) and Francis Beaumont's 'Grammar Lecture' at the Inns of Court: 'A young [law] student [also 'infant'] is a soft imytating peece ...' Eccles, *Grammar Lecture*, p. 405.

3.   Aristotle's 'no one suffers injustice voluntarily' (*iniustum patitur nullus volens*, *Nicomachean Ethics*, V. 9; 1136 b 6; cf. V. 11, 1138 a 12). Cf. Aristotle, *Rhetoric*, I.13. 1373, 27–30: to be wronged, one must suffer such wrong against his will. Cf. *Nicomachean Ethics*, V 9.4 and 5, V.9.1–8. 1136 a 10–1138 b 14. Cf. paraphrase in Thomas Aquinas, *Sent. Eth.*, V, 14.

Cf. also 'Volenti non fit injuria': Liebs, *Rechtsregeln*, V 36, citing Justinian, *Digest* 47, 10, 1 par. 5. Cf. also Liebs N106; N182; S3; S5. Cf. Herbert Broom, *A Selection of Legal Maxims* (1969), pp. 181–191, *Volenti non fit injuria*, an elaborate commentary on the maxim. See *Digest*, IV.771, 772. The maxim, 'Injuria non fit volenti', is indexed in C.P. Richter, *Expositionis ...* (Jena, 1654), sig. Cc3.

Cf. the *Liber Sextus* of Pope Boniface VIII, Rule 27. See *Enchiridion titulorum Iuris* (Louvain, 1554), p. 234, on Boniface VIII, 'De Regulis Iuris'. Sexti. Scienti et consentienti, non fit iniuria neque dolus'. (No injury or fraud is committed against one who knows and consents.) This legal maxim stems ultimately from Justinian, *Digest*, lex 145: 'nemo videtur fraudare eos qui sciunt et consentiunt'. (Cf. Liebs, S 3: 'Sciens non fraudatur'. Cf. Liebs, S 5.) That rule contracted became the well-known 'volenti non iniuria' – or, as in Achilles, 'No man is beaten voluntary' (II.i.96).

Suggesting such maxims' disparity between law and ethics, see Agrippa's *Of the Vanitie*, p. 334: '... injurie is not donne to him that is willinge. It is leefull for them that trafficke to deceive one an other. The thinge is so much worthy as it maye be solde for ...'.

So Hobbes (*Elements*, I.xvi.5) observes, 'forasmuch as both the buyer and the seller are made judges of the value, and are thereby both satisfied: there can be no injury done on either side'. Cf. Hobbes, *Elementorum Philosophiae Sectio Tertia De Cive, entitled in the first edition Philosophicall Rudiments*, ed. Howard Warrender (Oxford, 1983), III.vii: 'It is an old saying, *Volenti non fit iniuria* (the willing man receives no injury)'. Cf. Hobbes, *Leviathan*, ed. Richard Tuck (Cambridge, England, 1991), p. 104: 'Whatsoever is done to a man, conformable to his own Will signified to the doer, is no injury to him'. ['Nothing done to a man, by his own consent can be Injury.'] (Cf. Hobbes III, 137.)

4.   Adapting a proverb widely applied to the law is Pandar's 'time must friend or end' (I.ii.77–8), recalling Tilley, *Proverbs*, M 63, 'As a man is friended, so the law is ended': that is, the law is partial, depending on one's friends.

5.   In addition, 'voluntary' and 'privileged', among other meanings, comprised those military who could afford service in the army without pay, and were thus less subject to legal restraint. Cf. Marston's *Pigmalion*, ll. 17–20. See Jonson's *Poetaster*, V.iii. 590, on the 'voluntary gent.', or the gentleman volunteer (cf. *OED*, s.v. 'voluntary' 7b). On the 'voluntary' as opposed to Inns of Court men, cf. the Middle Templar Sharpham's *Cupid's Whirligig*, p. 18;

Mistress Correction, an old bawd, boasts of her custom: 'I have ... Knights ... and Antients, voluntary Gentlemen ... I entertain no Mutton eating Innes-a court men'.

'Privileged' (II.iii.57), Achilles' label for Thersites, recalls Achilles' earlier response to Thersites' claim to 'serve here voluntary' (II.i.94); that is, not pressed into service. 'Privileged' suggests also legal–parliamentary use: as in 'decline the whole question' (II.iii.52); 'move the question' (II.iii.81).

On Aristotle and the voluntary, cf. Appendix III. See also Odd Langholm, 'Economic Freedom in Scholastic Thought', *History of Political Economy*, 14 (1982), 260–83. See *Lyttleton: His Treatise of Tenures*, ed. T.E. Tomlins (New York, 1970), pp. 93–4, on estate by sufferance. Achilles' response, 'your last service was sufferance, 'twas not voluntary' (II.i.95–6), discriminates two legal terms: that which is passively endured or given consent; and that which is willingly chosen. On a distinction between sufferance and will, see *A Readable Edition of Coke upon Littleton*, ed. Thomas Coventry (1830), section 57b: 'Tenant at sufferance ... distinguished from tenant at will'.

6.   The wilful 'craves', in the context of 'law', recalls Shylock's 'I crave the law' (*MV*, IV.i.206). Hector's 'Nature craves / All dues be rendered to their owners' (II.ii.173–4) is a legal proverb. Cf. M.C. Wahl, 'Das parömiologische Sprachgut bei Shakespeare', *Shakespeare Jahrbuch*, 23 (1888), 45n. Hector's restraining law against 'hot passion of distempered blood' (II.ii.169) contrasts with 'Young blood doth not obey an old decree' (*LLL*, IV.iii.213); and 'The brain may devise laws for the blood, but a hot temper leaps o'er a cold decree' (*MV*, I.ii.18–19).

     Analogously, Hector recalls a traditional antithesis between legal constraint and folly: cf. the Chief Justice versus Falstaff; and law versus Erasmus' Stultitia and Rabelais' Panurge. See Falstaff's critique of the 'rusty curb of old father antic the law' (*1H4*, I.ii.61) – the law inverted (by a vice) and applied to an 'antic'. (Cf. *2H4*, IV.iv.62; *MM*, I.iii.20.)

7.   On folly versus degree, cf. Heather Arden, 'The Theme of Social Hierarchy in the *Sottie*', *Fool's Play* (Cambridge, England, 1980), pp. 138–57, 196–206.

8.   Hector's view on law's restraining power is emphasized in Rainolde's *Foundacion*, fol. xxxiii v, citing Demosthenes: law is 'a restraint to with holde and kepe backe the wilfull, rashe, and beastilie life of man'. Yet the lawful Hector's attempt to check appetite in II.ii is contradicted later in the play, as in Hector's own appetitive drive: 'Dexterity so obeying appetite / That what he will he does, and does so much / That proof is called impossibility' (V.v.27–9). Pursuing the Greek knight in sumptuous armour, Hector exhibits not mercy, but (like his brothers Paris and Troilus) appetitive desire: 'I like thy armour well ... I'll be master of it ... / I'll hunt thee for thy hide' (V.vi.28–31).

9.   On the 'nearer debt of wife to husband' (II.ii.174–6), cf. the 'marriage debt' conjugal duty to be performed (1 Corinthians 7.3). See Chaucer's 'marriage debt': Hornsby, *Chaucer and the law*, pp. 100–103. Legally, the nearer debt of wife to husband is construed in the maxim, 'Uxor non est sui juris sed sub potestate viri' (A wife is not in her own right, but is under the power of her husband). See Elizabeth Makowski, 'The Conjugal Debt and Medieval Canon Law', *Journal of Medieval History*, 3 (1977), 99–114. On wife and debt, see W. N[oy], *A Treatise of the Principall Grounds and Maximes* (1641), pp. 12–14.

     Cf. John Trayner, *Latin Maxims and Phrases* (Edinburgh, 1894), on the right-to-Helen dispute. Trayner offers other legal maxims, evoking the contest over the right to the abducted Helen: for example 'ex dolo non oritur actio' (a right of action does not arise out of fraud); 'ex maleficio non oritur contractus' (no contract arises from crime); 'ex pacto illicito non oritur actio' (no right of action arises from an illegal agreement).

10. To control *franchise*, marriage (invoked by Hector, II.ii.175–8) was said to have been instituted. Cf. *Franchise* in the medieval *Roman de la Rose*, countered by Danger or Dominion who opposes liberty. *Franchise* (shaking off Danger or control) leads to social upheavals and wars.

11. 'The law of Nature', notes Giles Jacob (revised by T.E. Tomlins), *A New Law-Dictionary* (Dublin, 1773), s.v. law, 'is that which God at man's creation infused into him, for his preservation and direction'. See Lausberg, *Handbook*, pp. 73–4. See A.P. D'Entrêves, *Natural Law* (1951); Frederick Pollock, 'The History of the Law of Nature', 'Laws of Nature and Laws of Man', in *Jurisprudence and Legal Essays*, ed. A.L. Goodhart (1961), pp. 124–68; Otto Gierke, *Natural Law and the Theory of Society, 1500 to 1800* (Boston, Massachusetts, 1960); Bernard McCabe, 'Francis Bacon and the Natural Law Tradition', *Natural Law Forum*, 9 (1964), 111–21, 66, J 182. On law of nature cf. Liebs, *Rechtsregeln*.

Tracing pre-Renaissance origins of law of nature versus law of nations, see M.H. Keen, *The Laws of War in the Late Middle Ages* (1965), pp. 9–19. *Ibid.*, pp. 11, 14: 'Medieval lawyers tried to follow Roman lawyers' concept of *jus gentium* ... Based on natural reason, it was an extension to human affairs of natural law or *jus naturale*'. R.S. White, *Natural Law in English Renaissance Literature* (Cambridge, England, 1996). Norbert Bobbio, *Thomas Hobbes and the Natural Law Tradition* (Chicago, 1993). On early use of the two laws, of nature and of nations, see Joan D. Tooke, *Just War in Aquinas and Grotius* (1965), pp. 73–81. On 'moral laws / Of nature and of nations' (II.ii.184–5), see Alberico Gentili, *De Jure belli libri tres* (1598) – not the first to formulate such a legal combination, as Campbell (*Comicall Satyre*, p. 192) supposes.

That combination of the two laws appears earlier (cf. Keen, cited above), in Cicero, as well as in other Roman jurists. Virtually identified are law of nature and of nations in the *Institutes*, II, I, 11, p. 10. Cf. Agrippa, *Of the Vanitie*, pp. 334–5; Robert Crompton, *A Declaration of the ende of Traytors* (1587), sig. E.ii: 'as we are bound by ye lawes ... of nature and by the lawes of this land ...'; see Fulbecke, *Direction*, fol. 60 v; Donald R. Kelley, 'Clio and the Lawyers: Forms of Historical Consciousness in Medieval Jurisprudence', *Medievalia et Humanistica*, n.s. 5 (1974), 41–5.

Law and the Trojan War are traditionally linked: Helen's conflict, indeed, is regarded as having instigated law. Cf. the medieval *Roman de la Rose*, ll. 13923–35, where La Vieille counsels the reading of Horace (*Satires*, I.iii.107–8): 'nam fuit ante Helenam cunnus taeterrima belli / causa'. Law becomes a recognized Trojan contribution and concern: the Trojan Hector in II.ii 'stands for' law, though his brothers (Troilus, Paris, and later Hector himself, II.ii.end) subvert it. Hector's relation to law suggests him, among the Nine Worthies, as one of the champions of pagan law. Cf. Horst Schroeder, *Der Topos der Nine Worthies in Literatur und bildender Kunst* (Göttingen, Germany, 1971).

Hector's proclaimed 'law in each well-ordered nation' (II.ii.180) recalls, founded upon a basis of Roman law, a common stock of legal principles. This is termed, almost in Hector's words, by Thomas Ridley (*A View of Civile and Ecclesiastical Law*, 1607, sig. [Bl v]), 'the common law of all well governed Nations'.

Hector's 'fear of bad success in a bad cause' (II.ii.117) recalls conventional censure of lawyers for supporting a 'bad cause'. Cf. Thomas Scott, *Vox Dei*

(1624), pp. 42–7; Scott, *The Projector* (1623), pp. 23–4; Edward Gee, *Two Sermons* (1620), Thomas Scott, pp. 24–5; John Squire, *A Sermon Preached at Hartford Assizes* (1618); J. Davies, *Le Primer Report des Cases* (Dublin, 1615), sigs *6–*10; *The Exact Law-Giver* (1658), pp. 9–10.

As Pandar in direct address employs legalisms (III.ii.207–8), so Troilus presumes in the audience a legal awareness: 'no perfection in reversion shall have a praise in present' (III.ii.91–2). No 'perfection' which may by reversion return to its original grantor can now be considered. Cf. III.iii.148–50.

On reversion, see *A Readable Edition of Coke upon Littleton*, ed. Thomas Coventry (1830), sections 18, 19. Reversion comprises return of an estate to the grantor, following termination of the grant. Cf. Clarkson and Warren, *Law of Property*, pp. 72–3: 'Shakespeare usually uses the term reversion to express the idea of a hope or expectation as opposed to an interest in possession'.

12. On oaths and law, see Hornsby, *Chaucer and the Law*; Joseph Plescia, *The Oath and Perjury in Ancient Greece* (Tallahassee, Florida, 1970). On the traditional sanctity of oaths, see E.L. Wheeler, 'Sophistic Interpretations and Greek Treaties', *Greek, Roman, and Byzantine Studies*, 25 (1984), 253–74. Frances A. Shirley, *Swearing and Perjury in Shakespeare's Plays* (1979); Christopher Hill, *Society and Puritanism in Pre-Revolutionary England*, 2nd edition (New York, 1967), pp. 382–7. See Brian Cummings, 'Swearing in Public: More and Shakespeare', *English Literary Renaissance*, 27 (1997), 197–232.

Oaths and their fulfilment recall promise and performance – erotic, theatrical, legal–commercial: II.ii.106; III.i.53; III.ii.83; III.ii.85; V.i.90; V.x.38–9. Cf. Paul Zumthor, *New Literary History*, 12 (1981), 497: 'The essence of law is constituted in the performative language of the prince'.

On 'perform' and 'performance' in a legal sense (to fulfil a promise, contract, or obligation), see Luke Wilson, '*Hamlet*, Equity, Intention, Performance', *Studies in the Literary Imagination*, 24 (1991), 92–113; Luke Wilson, 'Promissory Performances', *Renaissance Drama*, n.s. 25 (1994), 59–87. Slade's Case (1597–1602), with Coke opposing Bacon, brought into further prominence legal issues of promise and performance. See A.W.B. Simpson, 'The Place of Slade's Case in the History of Contract', *Law Quarterly Review*, 74 (1958), 381–96. Cf. J.H. Baker, 'New Light on *Slade's Case*', *Cambridge Law Journal*, 29 (1971), 51–67, 213–36. See response to Baker: A.W.B. Simpson, *A History of the Common Law of Contract: The Rise of the Action of Assumpsit* (Oxford, 1975), pp. 296–7.

Legalistically, the play's promise-and-performance pattern is linked to its infidelity- and oath-dialectic. Cf. condemnation of the 'false-hearted' Diomedes: 'he will spend his mouth and promise ... but when he performs ... it is prodigious' (V.i.86–91). All promises, declared Thomas Aquinas, are by natural law binding: 'Man is obliged to man by any promise and this is an obligation of natural law'. Aquinas thus holds that promises, like oaths, are a type of self-prescribed law (*Summa Theologica*, II-II, q88, a3, ad 1), while promises are binding as a matter of fidelity (II-II, q88, a3; a3, ad 1; q110, a3, ad 5). *Coriolanus*, I.viii.1–2: 'I do hate thee / Worse than a promise-breaker'. Late scholastics claimed that infidelity was a type of injustice. (Like Diomedes, promise-breakers share a special odium in Shakespeare: Parolles, for instance, is described as 'an endless liar, an hourly promise-breaker', *AWEW*, III.vi.10). Cf. *MM*, V.i.404–5: 'Being criminal, in double violation / Of sacred chastity and of promise-breach': On relations of promise and oath, see Craig McDonald, 'The Inversion of Law in Robert

Henryson's *Fable of the Fox, the Wolf, and the Husbandman*', *Medium Aevum*, 49 (1980), 244–53. See James Gordley, *The Philosophical Origins of Modern Contract Doctrine* (Oxford, 1991).

Both buyer and seller, recurrently noted in the play, recall legal–commercial conventions; cf. IV.i.77–80. Cf. J.W. Baldwin, 'The Medieval Theories of the Just Price', *Transactions of the American Philosophical Society*, 44, Part 4 (1959), 1–92; R. de Roover, 'The Concept of the Just Price Theory and Economic Policy', *Journal of Economic History*, 18 (1958), 418.

13. Paris' argument that a good result follows from his transgressive action contradicts legal proverbs. Cf. Liebs, *Rechtsregeln*, N143: 'Non sunt facienda mala, ut eveniant bona' (You are not to do evil that good may come of it). Cf. also Dent, *Index*, E203; and Liebs, E48; E54; E56; E61; and notes 12 and 34.

Hector argues that the law of nature cannot be 'corrupted through affection', and that 'great minds (II.ii.176–8), through partial indulgence/ To their benumbed wills, may not resist law of nature's claim'. Hector here would oppose retention of another man's wife on grounds similar to Aquinas': it is transgression of an objective right or rule.

14. *New Science of Giambattista Vico*, eds T.G. Bergin et al. (Ithaca, NY, 1948), p. 151.

15. Pandar as counterfeit priest recalls the medieval *Roman de la Rose*, where Genius (see *TC*, IV.iv.50) celebrates a mass, not of the divine, but 'de toutes choses corrompables' (IV.16.282). As in Pandar's copulative imperative, Genius encourages coupling while, moreover, excommunicating celibates. His view is based on literalizing the biblical command to increase and multiply. Pandar, like Genius, inverts the order of God and reason, as the play's eponymous lover (II.ii.32, 35, 46–9), like Amans, had abandoned reason. Lacking this faculty (the *Roman de la Rose*'s Raison), Natura and Genius are devotees of concupiscence.

Pandar as one of the 'brokers-between' (III.ii.202–3), as 'broker-lackey' (V.x.37), suggests 'broker' in his intermediary role (Pandar as, equivocally, 'solicitor'), going 'between and between' (I.i.74). Cf. *OED*, s.v. broker 5 †b. On lawyer as broker, see also Peter Clark, ed., *Country Towns in Pre-Industrial England* (Leicester, England, 1981), p. 23; Clive Holmes, *Seventeenth Century Lincolnshire* (1980), pp. 47–52.

16. Cf. *Gesta*, p. 23, 'to stand mute'. Cf. *R2*, III.iv.72, 'O, I am press'd to death through want of speaking'! and *MAAN*, III.i.76; *MM*, V.i.522–3. On *peine forte et dure* see Elizabeth Hanson, 'Torture and Truth in Renaissance England', *Representations*, 34 (1994), 53–84; John H. Langbein, *Torture and the Law of Proof* (Chicago, Illinois, 1977), pp. 74–7 and notes; James Heath, *Torture and English Law* (Westport, Connecticut, 1982); H.R.T. Summerson, 'The Early Development of the Peine Forte et Dure', in E.W. Ives and A.H. Manchester, eds, *Law, Litigants and the Legal Profession* (1983), pp. 116–25. Thomas Coventry, ed., *A Readable Edition of Coke upon Littleton* (1830), *Co. Litt.* 319a: 'If the party upon his arraignment refuse to answer he shall be judged for his contempt to *peine fort et dure*, which works no attainder for the felony, or forfeiture of his lands, or corruption of blood'. See illustration of pressing-to-death punishment, *Shakespeare Survey*, 17 (1965), plate XIII. Cf. another legal punishment: '*Pandarus*. I must needs confess – *Cressida*. 'Without the rack' (I.ii.138–9). Confessions upon the rack were commanded by royal prerogative to obtain information.

17. On kinship bonds in an Inns of Court play, see Philip Dust, 'The Theme of "Kinde" in *Gorboduc*', *Salzburg Studies in English Literature*, 12 (1973),

43–81. 'Kind' and its variants (e.g. kindliness, unkind, unkindly) recur in that play, remarks I.B. Cauthen, Jr (ed., Thomas Sackville and Thomas Norton, *Gorboduc* (Lincoln, Nebraska, 1970), p. xxin.) numerous times; as do 'nature' and its variant 'unnatural'. On *Gorboduc*, see S.F. Johnson, 'The Tragic Hero in Early Elizabethan Drama', in *Studies in English Renaissance Drama, in Memory of Karl Julius Holzknecht*, eds Josephine W. Bennett et al. (New York, 1959), pp. 157–71. See also S.F. Johnson, *Early Elizabethan Tragedies of the Inns of Court* (New York, 1987). Recalling the Inns of Court play, *Gorboduc*, and its 'kind' and natural-law premise, is Ulysses' 'One touch of nature makes the whole world kin' (III.iii.176).

In addition to their 'kind' law of nature concerns are other links with *Gorboduc* – its king cited in the Inns of Court revels-produced *Twelfth Night* (IV.ii.14): both *Gorboduc* and *Troilus* are tied to the Trojan line; both involve misrule as well as advice to a ruler; and both contain materials of concern to law-student audiences.

18.   On consanguinity and inheritance, see Thomas Coventry, ed., *A Readable Edition of Coke upon Littleton* (1830), sections 12a, 12b, 20, 23a, 23b–24b. On consanguinity, see M. Hale, *Successionibus apud Anglos* (1700), chart facing sig. B, 'The Degrees of Consanguinity'. Hector–Ajax ties (cf.I.ii.33–5) are indistinguishable through mingled blood (IV.v.119–38). The 'consanguinity' that Cressid claims (like Juliet) to be subservient to her love, turns to serve mere expedience.

Cressid's legalisms extend to her query, 'Have the gods envy?' (IV.iv. 28). Cf. Svend Ranulf, *The Jealousy of the Gods and Common Law at Athens* (New York, 1974), I.63–84, on divine envy and injustice.

Hector catalogues blood relations in ludicrous particularity: 'Were thy commixtion Greek and Trojan so / That thou couldst say "... my mother's blood / Runs on the dexter cheek, and this sinister / Bounds in my father's"' (IV.v.124–9). Hector's complex genitive, 'My father's sister's son' (IV.v.120), is, in its Homeric-parodic pile-up, evocative of consanguine inheritance or kindred-mingling disorder. 'Consanguinity' (IV.ii.97) is used in Shakespeare only in *Troilus*, while a variant of this legalism appears but once in the canon, in the Inns of Court produced *Twelfth Night* (II.iii.77–8): 'Am not I *consanguineous*?' Sir Toby demands, 'Am I not of her blood?' Burlesque-sounding phrases such as 'my father's sister's son' (*TC*, IV.v.120) suggest also familiar echoes. Cf. *The Book of Common Prayer* with 'A Table of Kindred and Affinity' on relations forbidden by the Church to marry. The well-known table includes 'Father's father's wife', 'Mother's father's wife', 'Father's mother's husband', etc.

19.   For this legal phrase (III.ii.57), *OED* notes, s.v. *interchangeably*, 1. '... formerly freq. in the wording of legal compacts, citing 1547 ... The seyd partyes, enterchaungeably have putt theyr Seales'.

20.   On the Judgment of Paris in pageants, see Sydney Anglo, *Spectacle, Pageantry, and Early Tudor Policy* (Oxford, 1969), pp. 255–6. Cf. M.J. Ehrhart, *The Judgment of the Trojan Prince Paris in Medieval Literature* (Philadelphia, Pennsylvania, 1987). Karl Reinhardt, 'The Judgement of Paris' in *Homer: German Scholarship in Translation*, ed. G.M. Wright and P.V. Jones (Oxford, 1997), 170–91; Christopher Rees, 'Some Seventeenth-Century Versions of The Judgment of Paris', *Notes and Queries*, 24 [v.222], 1997, 197–200.

21.   The safety of the King himself, ... every man's estate in particular, and the state of the realm in general, doth depend upon the truth and sincerity of men's oaths ... The Lawe and civill policy of England, being chiefly founded

uppon Religion and the feare of God, doth use the religious Ceremony of an oath not onely in legall proceedings but in other transactions ... esteeming oaths not only as the best touchstone of trust in matters of controversy, but as the safest knot of Civill societie, and the firmest band to tie all men to the performance of their several duties ...

The Case of Concealment ... (1614), Ellesmere MS quoted by M.A. Judson, *The Crisis of the Constitution ... 1634–1645* (New Brunswick, New Jersey, 1949), pp. 51–2

A person who promises under oath incurs two obligations: one to the person promised; the other to God. Cf. Thomas Aquinas, *Summa Theologica*, II-II. q89, a7, ad 3.

22.   Hector's treatment of captives (V.iii.40, 42) recalls Caxton (NVS, p. 434), citing Virgil's admonition, 'Non est misericordia in bello' (no pity or mercy in war). Legally, it recalls an extensive normative system of military law, and a broad literature of medieval and Renaissance concerns with treatments of military prisoners – an issue in, for example, *1 Henry IV* and *Henry V*. See Meron, *Henry's Wars*, pp. 77–81, on recognized rules and chivalric protocols regarding law and mercy, surrender and granting of quarter. As they recall controversial issues of military law, Hector's and Troilus' conflicting views on treatment of captives would have engaged a law-student audience.

23.   Hector's 'fair play' versus Troilus' 'Foole's play' (Q, F; V.iii.43–4) prepares for Achilles' unfair play against Hector, who, in effect, exhibits 'Fooles play'. Troilus complains against Hector's mercy, that when 'the captive Grecian falls ... You bid them rise and live' (V.iii.40–2); cf. P. Karavites, *Capitulations and Greek Interstate Relations* (Göttingen, Germany, 1982), pp. 86ff., 111ff.

24.   Here, in his 'Go, wind, to wind!' (V.iii.110), as he tears up Cressid's letter, Troilus recalls a commonplace: (e.g. Tibullus, *Elegies*, III.6.q.v.49): 'Jove laughs at lovers' perjuries, and bids / The winds scatter them as nothing worth'. Troilus thus (as in *RJ*, II.ii.92–3) summons up a classical topos going back to Hesiod. Cf. Ovid, *Ars*, 5.633f: 'Iuppiter exalto perjuria ridet amantum / et iubet Aeolios irrita ferre Notos'. Further instances of this topos, 'Worte in den Wind sprechen', are given in Gerald Kölblinger, *Einige Topoi bei den lateinischen Liebesdichtern* (Vienna, 1971), pp. 3–23.

25.   Cf. 'Against Swearing and Perjury', *Certain Sermons or Homilies* (1547) (ed. R.B. Bond, Toronto, 1977), pp. 128–36; cf. p. 130: 'By lawfull othes, mutuall societie, amitie and good order is kept continually ...'; p. 132: 'how much ... [God] abhorreth breakers of honeste promises confirmed by an othe made in his name ...'. See Gilbert Burnet, *An Exposition of the Thirty-Nine Articles of the Church of England* (1700), pp. 391–6; Thomas Rogers, *The Catholic Doctrine of the Church of England: An Exposition of the Thirty-Nine Articles* (Cambridge, England, 1854), pp. 356–62; E.C.S. Gibson, ed., *The Thirty-Nine Articles* (1898), pp. 788–91.

26.   Rationalization of vow-breaking recurs; for example in *Two Gentlemen of Verona* (1593): 'Unheedful vows may heedfully be broken' (II.vi.11). 'Unheedful vows' recalls both the last of the Thirty-Nine Articles and Cassandra's exemption of unheedful votive 'rashness' or 'hot and peevish vows' (V.iii.16).

'The end being good, the means are well assigned'. Marston, *Dutch Courtesan*, IV.ii. end. Following such views, Andromache would violate a legal and general maxim: Never do evil (ill) that good may come of it. Cf. *MV*, IV.i.216; Dent, *Index*, E203. As St Paul (Romans 3.8) denounces those who say 'let us do evil, that good may come', the Apostle adds, of these, 'damnation is just'.

27.   On the *violenti* against nature, See Dante, *Inferno*, XI.28–51.

Conclusion

Our revels now are ended
Tempest, IV.i.148

Close inspection of Shakespeare's *Troilus and Cressida* confirms its divergence from the so-called 'problem play' category. When interpreted within Renaissance contexts, the work appears generally not to support the Victorian 'problem-play' limitation of 'pessimistic', 'decadent', 'dark', 'unpleasant' or 'bitter'.

What emerges at least as strongly is, among other elements, an academic classic-burlesque, or world-upside-down *sottie* or misrule piece: a 'Fooles play' (Q, F, V.iii.43). Further, in its mock-epic perspectives, this Trojan War play sustains a commonplace view (exemplified in Horace as well as in Montaigne) relating the Trojan War and folly.[1] Inverting mock-epically 'the tale of Troy divine', the piece tends to *dramma giocosa* and *erudita*. It encompasses in its *ludicra* both the *seria* and the variety in such works: in Chaucerian terms, 'Take yt in ernest or in game'.[2]

I

non minus eruditis quam festivis
Title-page to Frobenius' Erasmus, *Encomium Moriae* (1515)

Like Erasmus' *Encomium Moriae*, More's *Utopia*, the *Epistolae Obscurorum Virorum*, Rabelais, Lyly, Nashe, Shakespeare's *Love's Labour's Lost*, Harington's *Metamorphosis of Ajax*, Donne's *Catalogus Librorum Aulicorum* and *Ignatius His Conclave*, Jonson, and certain of Milton's *Prolusions*, *Troilus* comprises the tradition of learned folly. That learned-jesting tradition,[3] *festivitas* as opposed to *gravitas*, is described in the commentator Girardus Listrius' prefatory letter to the Frobenius edition of Erasmus' *Encomium Moriae* (1515):

> there are truly many things in it which cannot be understood except by the learned and attentive ... partly on account of the allusions both frequent and silently present, and partly because of the clever subtlety which cannot easily be sensed ... For there is nothing requiring more talent than to joke learnedly.[4]

Such un-'bitter' playfulness or 'solemn foolerie'[5] as pervades much of *Troilus* is suggested by its Q 1609 Epistle-writer: 'such sauored salt of witte[6] is in his Commedies, that they seeme (for their height of pleasure) to be borne in that sea that brought forth *Venus*. Amongst all there is none more witty then this'; and by the Q 1609 Epistle-writer's repeated reference to the work as comic or a 'comedy'. Its proclivity to Listrius' 'clever subtlety which cannot easily be sensed' is suggested by the Epistle-writer's 'had I time I would comment upon it ... for so much worth, as ... I know to be stuft in it. It deserves such a labour, as well as the best Commedy in *Terence* or *Plautus*'.

The Q Epistle's sales-advertising 'neuer clapper-clawd with the palmes of the vulger ... nor like this the lesse, for not being sullied, with the smoaky breath of the multitude', need not, by these terms, preclude the play's private perfomance. Such popularity deficiencies the Epistle's sales appeal turns rather to commercial advantage: it makes a virtue of necessity. Rather than conventionally arguing on the commodity's popular success it contends the work's 'unsullied' condition to be a merit. Indeed, it declares its availability for purchase to be a rarely advantageous chance: 'thanke fortune for the great scape it hath made amongst you ... you should haue prayed for them rather then beene prayd'.[7] Nor need the Epistle's insistence on the more saleable genre 'comedy' obviate the work's private-performance or revel-origin – a provenance which may account for the existence of the Epistle itself, intended to arouse interest in the virtues of a specialized commodity. Both Epistle and play thus help sustain scholars' deduction that the work was directed to a private or special audience.

II

In sum, this study in successive chapters has shown *Troilus and Cressida*, to a significant extent, to be consistent with an Elizabethan law-revels tradition. The play's parallels with that tradition (cf. 'Revels criteria', Introduction) include not only legal and burlesque elements associated with the revels, but also pervasive reflections of festive misrule. Such festive inversions comprise rhetoric and logic, themselves basic to law and forensic pleading, as well as propaedeutic to legal studies. Further, as Alexander concludes, 'Where an audience sufficiently learned to enjoy Shakespeare's deliberately cynical treatment of classical material, and sufficiently sophisticated to be addressed in the terms used by Pandarus, could be found outside the Inns of Court it is difficult to guess'.[8] Since no other hypothesis seems better able to account for such pervasive aspects and allusions, the evidence here presented confirms that the play was directed to a festive law audience.

As *Troilus*' allusions would, finally, have eluded the capacities of the Epistle's 'vulger', its bawdy familiarity, *lèse majesté*, scurrility and mock-insult would have been unsuited to the court. Its spectators, as is now believed, would rather have been such as those who attended licensed and wittily suggestive entertainments, or world-upside-down misrule revels, at London's 'Third University', the Inns of Court.[9]

Notes

1. Horace, *Epistles*, I.ii.6–8; Montaigne, Book II, ch. 12. Cf. Rainolde, *Foundacion*, sigs Gl–Giii v. Recognition of Trojan War folly is coupled with condemnation of Helen: cf. Thomas Nashe, *Red Herring*, III.184; Christopher Marlowe, *Edward II*, II.iv.11–16; *RL*, l. 1369, Joseph Swetnam, *The Araignment of lewd, idle, froward and unconstant Women* (1615), sig. D3; John Ford, 'Honor Triumphant: or the Peeres Challenge' (*Nondramatic*, pp. 43, 44–5).

2. Chaucer, *House of Fame*, II.822. On jest and earnest, see Curtius, *European Literature*, pp. 417–35. This jest-earnest doublenesss – *spoudogeloios* – appears in Homer on the gods. See L. Giangrande, *The Use of Spoudaiogeloion in Greek and Roman Literature* (The Hague, 1972). On the jest-earnest duality, see further Branham, *Unruly Eloquence*, pp. 26–8, 47–51, 56–7, 235 n.79; p. 227 on Renaissance uses of the serio-comic and *spoudogeloios*. See Caspar Dornavius, ed., *Amphitheatrum Sapientiae ... Joco-seriae* (Hanoviae, 1619).

3. On the Renaissance *facetiae* tradition, see K. Vollert, *Zur Geschichte der lateinischen Facetiensammlungen des XV und XVI Jahrhunderts* (Berlin, 1911). Cf. *Facétie et littérature facétieuse à l'époque de la Renaissance*. Actes du colloque de Goutelas ... 1977 (*Bulletin de l'Association d'Etude sur l'Humanisme, la Réforme et la Renaissance*. Special issue. 4th year, no. 7, May 1978). See also Barbara C. Bowen, 'Rabelais and the Rhetorical Joke Tradition', in R.C. La Charité, ed., *Rabelais's Incomparable Book* (Lexington, Kentucky, 1986), pp. 213–25. Guy Demerson, *Humanisme et Facétie: Quinze études sur Rabelais* (Orléans, 1994). W. David Kay, 'Erasmus' Learned Joking: The Ironic Use of Classical Wisdom in *The Praise of Folly*', *Texas Studies in Literature and Language*, 19 (1977), 248–67. Learned folly comprises in this play, as in Rabelais, legal humour or folly.

4. Gerardus Listrius, preface to Erasmus, ... *Moriae Encomium* (Oxoniae, 1608), sig. A2 v: 'Verum sunt in eo permulta, quae non nisi ab eruditis & attentis possint intellegi ... partim ob allusiones, & crebrae & tacitas, partim ob argutiam in iocando, quam non facile sentiat ... Nihil enim ingeniosus, quam eruditi iocari'. *Des. Erasmi Roterodami Opera Omnia*, ed. J. Le Clerc, 10 vols (Leiden, The Netherlands, 1703–06), IV.401. Cf. J.A. Gavin and T.M. Walsh, '*The Praise of Folly* in Context: The Commentary of Girardus Listrius', *Renaissance Quarterly*, 24 (1971), 193–209.

5. Cited in an Inns of Court revel: see John Evelyn, *Diary*, ed. E.S. De Beer (Oxford, 1955), III.307, on 'the solemn foolerie of the *Prince de la Grange* at *Lincolne Inn*'.

6. On salt (or *salus*) as component of wit, cf. Quintilian, *Institutes*, VI.3.18–19; Jonson, *Poetaster*, IV.iii.87–8; *Volpone*, Prologue, l.34. Cf. 'Panegyrick Verses' to Thomas Coryat's *Crudities* (1611; Glasgow, 1905), I.68.

7. The inserted Epistle's denials of public performance concur with Q (state 2's) title-page denial; its cancellation of Q state 1's title-page claim to public performance: 'As it was acted by the Kings Maiesties Seruants at the Globe'. See Philip Williams, Jr., 'The Second Issue of Shakespeare's *Troilus and Cressida* 1609', *Studies in Bibliography*, 2 (1949–50), 25–33. Replacement of Q state 1 title-page by Q state 2's was of a piece with the printing of the Epistle. The second leaf of the cancellans (f 2) contains the Epistle (ending on f 2v). Substituted title-page in state 2 and the Epistle, Williams shows, are consequential, and both were decided on and printed before Q copies were issued.

8.   Alexander, *Shakespeare* (1964), p. 247. Deductions regarding Marston's *Fawn* seem apropos to *Troilus*: rather than viewing Marston's play, Finkelpearl holds ('Christmas Revels', p. 209), as 'a dark, bitter comedy, suffused with ... sex loathing and disillusion, we will probably come closer to the original tone of this and some of Marston's other plays if we hear in them the spirit of the revels with their playful irreverence and "solemn foolery"'. Noting the widely-entertained Inns of Court-*Troilus* hypothesis, see G.K. Hunter, *English Drama, 1586–1642* (Oxford, 1997), p. 356.

9.   See John Hamilton Baker, *The Third University of England, the Inns of Court and the Common-Law Tradition* (Selden Society, 1990).

Appendix I *Troilus* and law-revels' language

Dictional similarities of *Troilus* with contemporary Elizabethan law revels include the following:

Troilus and *Gesta Grayorum* (1594–95)

'the glorious planet Sol' (I.iii.89); *Gesta*, p. 15, 'the glorious Planet Sol'
'buck and doe' (III.i.117); *Gesta*, p. 25, 'Bucks or Does'
'ill opinion' (V.iv.16); *Gesta*, p. 8, 'Ill Opinion'
'meddle ... farther' (I.i.14); *Gesta*, p. 19, 'meddle further'
'the desire is boundless and the act a slave to limit' (III.ii.81–2); *Gesta*, p.
    72, 'my Desire was greater than the Ability of my Body'
Achilles and Patroclus; *Gesta*, p. 36 (twice), 'Achilles and Patroclus'
Agamemnon, Achilles, and Ulysses; *Gesta*, p. 75, 'Agamemnon ... Achilles
    & Ulysses'
'juggling ... knavery' (II.iii.70–71); *Gesta*, p. 33, 'knavery and jugglery'
'due observance' (I.iii.31); *Gesta*, p. 30, 'due observation'
'instruments / Of ... war' (Prologue, ll. 4–5); *Gesta*, p. 84, 'Instrumente of
    warres'

Troilus and the *Prince d'Amour* (1597–98)

'with one consent' (III.iii.176); *Prince*, p. 8, 'with one consent'
'high and mighty' (I.iii.232); *Prince*, p. 9, 'high and mighty'
'oyez' (IV.iv.143); *Prince*, p. 47, 'o yes' ('a Cryer made o *yes*')
'consanguinity' (IV.ii.97); *Prince*, p. 47, '*consanguineo*'
'prerogative' (I.iii.107); *Prince*, p. 12, 'Prerogative'
'the ports desired' (II.ii.76); *Prince*, pp. 1, 4, '*Porto desiderato*'

In addition, see *Prince*'s injunction (p. 43) against certain words: 'that in no case he use any perfumed terms, as spirit, apprehension, resolution, accommodate, humours, complement, possessed, respective, & C.' Most of these prohibited terms recur in *Troilus*:

spirit, sprite, I.i.60; II.ii.156; III.ii.33; III.iii.106; IV.iv.135; IV.v.15, 246; V.ii.95; and spirits, Prologue, l. 20; II.ii.210, IV.v.56
apprehension (apprehend, apprehended), II.iii.114; III.ii.73; III.iii.124
resolution, II.ii.191
humours, I.ii.22
complement: cf. complimental, III.i.40
possessed (possess, possession), II.ii.152; II.iii.168; III.iii.5, 7, 89; IV.iv.112

While the Middle Temple's *Prince d'Amour* (1597–98), p. 43, condemns 'perfumed Terms', the Middle Templar John Hoskyns (c. 1600) also warns a Temple student against such 'perfumed Termes of the Tyme' (*Life*, p. 121).[1] Most of these words recur in *Troilus and Cressida*. Hoskyns' censured terms are given below; for their recurrence in *Troilus* see the *Prince* list above.

apprehensiveness
compliments (complimental)
spirit, spirits

As most of those 'mocked' terms in *Prince* and Hoskyns recur in *Troilus*, their dramatic re-emergence would seem (appropriately to a misrule occasion) to burlesque such diction. The Middle Templar Hoskyns' stylistic admonitions to the Temple student for whom they were intended thus coincide in condemning 'perfumed terms of the time' with the Middle Temple's *Prince d'Amour* revel and the latter's own reprehended 'perfumed terms'. Further, the Middle Templar Hoskyns and the Middle Temple's *Prince*, in their 'mocked' terms, also coincide with *Troilus*, which itself features such 'mocked' words. If directed to a revels audience, *Troilus* could, not surprisingly, reflect the terms and dictional burlesque of contemporary Elizabethan revels.

Note

1.   Hoskyns, *Life*, pp. 121, 264; cf. Hoskyns, *Speech and Style*, p. 7.

Appendix II *Troilus* and legal terms

It goes like law-French,
And that, they say is the court-liest language

Ben Jonson, *The Alchemist* (1612)

Fie, they [Inns of Court men] are all for French;
they speak no Latin.

Thomas Middleton, *A Chaste Maid in Cheapside* (1630)

I

In addition to the Law French *dismes* (II.ii.19, tithes),[1] other Law French terms in *Troilus* would have been comprehensible to a legal audience. This section sets out the play's terms as are listed in J.H. Baker, *Manual of Law French* (Aldershot, 1990).[2] LF = Law French.

While some of Shakespeare's works tend to be legally allusive, and some of the following words are also extra-legal, the profusion of quasi-legal, legalistic, and legal–commercial terms here suggests an audience attuned to their usage and significance.[2]

authentic (I.iii.108; III.ii.180) LF *authentik*, authentic (of an instrument), authenticated
avoid (II.ii.65) LF *avoider* ... to make void ... to avoid in pleading (by averring new matter which takes away the effect of confessed matter)
degree (e.g. I.iii.108, 125, 127) LF *degre* (L. *gradus*), rank; step; relationship, degree of consanguinity
dismes (II.ii.19) LF tenths, tithes. See John Rastell, *An Exposition of ... Termes of the Lawes* (1602), s.v., as a Law French term. Cf. John Cowell, *The Interpreter* (Cambridge, England, 1607), s.v.
fee-farm (III.ii.49–50) (L. *foeda firma*) LF tenure in fee-simple subject to a fixed rent; absolute possession; lease (cf. Clarkson and Warren, *Law of Property*, p. 15)
fee-simple (V.i.22) LF estate in absolute possession; simple, plain, mere; absolute, unconditional (cf. Clarkson, *Law of Property*, pp. 51–5)
maxim (I.ii.293) LF *maxime*

office (I.iii.88, 231; V.vi.4) LF position or employment; department of an officer, the practice side of the court ... business, task

order (I.iii.181; IV.v.70) LF *ordre*, order; form (i.e. usual procedure), rule; legal society or brotherhood (cf. I.iii.104: 'brotherhoods in cities')

play (Prologue, l. 19; 'digested in a play'; cf. this phrase's legalism, as in the *Digest* of Justinian) LF *play, ple, plee, plea*: legal action; pleading – in particular, the defendant's answer to the declaration

prove (proof, I.ii.130; I.iii.34; V.v.5, 29) LF proof; probate; witness. Cf. LF *prover*, to prove; to establish facts, by evidence; to establish or demonstrate a proposition, by reasoning or citing authority (cf. Q prover, II.iii.66)

tail (V.x.43) LF *taile*, limitation

tortive (I.iii.9) LF *tort*, wrong, injury

II

Like the Law French terms above, the following terms in *Troilus* comprise those which would be of interest to and understood by a legal audience.

addition, I.ii.20; II.iii.244; III.ii.93; IV.v.141. Cf. Cowell, s.v.: 'signifieth in our common law a title ... over and above his ... surname ...'.

admission, II.iii.164

admits, IV.iv.9

affined, I.iii.25

as *aforesaid*, II.iii.59. Cf. Jonson, *Poetaster*, V.iii.226, in a passage parodying legalisms

agent, V.x.36

allege, II.ii.168

answer, answered, answering, I.iii.15; II.i.126; III.iii.35; IV.iv.132

apply, 'Thy latest words', I.iii.32–3

approbation, I.iii.59

approve, III.ii.173

arbitrator, IV.v.225

argument, Prologue, l. 25; I.i.94; II.iii.71, 94, 95, 96; IV.v.26, 27, 29

assault, III.i.41

attaint, I.ii.25

attest, II.ii.132; V.ii.122; *attest of eyes and ears*, (or legal witness), V.ii.122

authentic author, III.ii.180 (cf. *authentik*, LF above)

authority, V.ii.144

avoid, see LF above

avouch, II.ii.84

bait, V.viii.20 (*OED*, s.v., refreshment for lawyers)

bargain made, III.ii.196

bastard, V.vii.15, 16, 17, 18, 20, 22

bequeath, V.x.55

bias, I.iii.18

blank of danger, III.iii.231

bolts, Prologue, l. 18; cf. *bolting*, I.i.19, 21. Cf. A. Chroust, 'The Beginning, Flourishing and Decline of the Inns of Court ...', *Vanderbilt Law Review*, 10 (1956), 109–11; Carl I. Hammer, Jr, 'Bolts and Chapel Moots at Lincoln's Inn in the Sixteenth Century', *Journal of the Society of Public Teachers of Law*, 11 (1970), 24–8. W.R. Prest, *The Inns of Court 1590–1640* (1972), pp. 115–36.

broker, III.ii.202–3; broker-lackey V.x.33

'*brotherhoods in cities*', I.iii.134: urban male societies or confraternities – cf. the Inns of Court

buy, sell, bought, II.i.45; II.i.69; IV.i.78, 80; IV.iv.40

call ... activity in question, III.ii.55–6

calumniate, V.ii.124. Cf. this legalism in *AWEW*, I.iii.56–7; and Jonson, *Poetaster*, 'calumnious', V.iii.247

captive, V.iii.40

cause, II.ii.117, 164, 192; V.ii.143. Cf. Vinogradoff, *Outlines*, I.23n., 'The cause is the aim or the intention inherent in the contract and therefore known or supposed to be known, by both parties'.

charge, IV.i.59

choice, I.iii.347, 348. Cf. Appendix III

cited, III.ii.180

claim, IV.v.51

close (verb, as of a contract), III.ii.48

co-act, V.ii.118

cognition, V.ii.64 (law: 'the action of taking judicial ... notice', *OED*, 3)

commission, seals a, III.iii.231

condition, Prologue, l. 25; I.ii.74; III.iii.9. Cf. *OED*, 2. *Law*. 'In a legal instrument, e.g. a will, or contract, a provision on which the legal force or effect is made to depend'. Cf. Fraunce, *Lawiers Logic*, fol. 95v; *The Exact Law-Giver* (1658), pp. 89–96.

confess, II.ii.86; III.ii.118

confess ... rack, I.ii.138–9. Cf. Ben Jonson, *Every Man in His Humour*, II.iii: 'confesse ... racke'.

confession, III.ii.153

confidence, Prologue, l. 23. Cf. *OED* 6. *Law*.

consanguinity, IV.ii.97

conscience, V.x.28

consent, III.iii.176. Cf. Agrippa, *Of the Vanitie*, ch. 91, p. 333: 'the Civil Lawe is that which men doo with a common consent'. Cf. 'All with one consent' (III.iii.176)

consigned, IV.iv.45
conspire, V.i.61
corresponsive, Prologue, l. 18
corrupted, II.ii.177 ('law / Of nature ... corrupted')
cost, II.ii.51
counterfeit, II.iii.24

damage, II.ii.3
danger, cf. *blank of danger*
date in the pie, I.ii.258
date is out, I.ii.258
debt(s), II.ii.175; III.ii.54. Cf. *debitum*'s associations with law. *Vivarium*, 7 (1969), 103: '*debitum*' had a strong juridified ring arising from its traditional associations with the notions of law, right (*ius*) and a legalistic conception of justice.
debtor, IV.v.51
deceptious, V.ii.123
decision, II.ii.173
decline the whole question, II.iii.52; *delivery*, IV.iii.1
deeds, III.ii.54, 55
deem, IV.iv.59
deliver her possession up, II.ii.152
demand, II.iii.66; III.iii.17
denied, III.iii.22; *denies*, II.ii.24; *deny*, IV.ii.49
depravation, V.ii.132
determination, II.ii.170
digested in a play (Cf. LF 'play', above), Prologue, l. 29. Cf. Jonson, *Poetaster*, I.ii.230, on 'digest' ('And give me stomach to digest this law –'), punning on Justinian's *Digest*, the codification of Roman law. Along with legal 'digested', 'plays ... pleas' (Epistle, *TC*, Q, 1609, l. 9) is a recurrent theatrical–legal pun; cf. Helge Kökeritz, *Shakespeare's Pronunciation* (1953), p. 198, and E.J. Dobson, *English Pronunciation 1500–1700* (Oxford, 1967), II. 775, 776. See Alexander Radcliffe, *The Ramble* (1682), p. 119, on the approach of a law term: 'instead of Playes we now converse with Pleas'; Waterhouse, *Fortescue*, pp. 519–20, on legal associations between *play* and *plea*, *pleadings* and *placitare*.
discharging, *discharge*, III.ii.86, IV.iv.41
discoveries, V.i.23
disdain, I.ii.34; I.iii.129; V.vi.15
dismes, see LF above
disposition, IV.i.50
due, IV.v.51
due of birth, I.iii.106
dues ... rendered to ... owners, II.ii.174

effect, V.iii.109

election, II.ii.61 (legal: cf. Fulbecke, *Direction*, sig. L4)

errour(s), V.ii.110; V.iii.111 (cf. *OED*, a legal term, 'a fault in a judgement ...')

evasion(s), II.i.68; II.ii.67; II.iii.113.

exchange, III.iii.21

execute, execution, I.iii.210; V.v.38; V.vii.6. Cf. Liebs, E 49: 'Executio est finis et fructus legis'. J 175: 'Juris effectus in executione consistit'. Cf. J 158. Cf. John Donne, sermon, 21 April 1616: 'A Law is not a Law without Execution'.

extenuates not wrong, II.ii.187

fee-farm, see LF above

fee-simple, see LF above

fees, III.iii.49

forestall, I.iii.199. Cf. R.H. Britnell, '*Forstall*, Forstalling and the Statute of Forestallers', *English Historical Review*, 102 (1897), 89–102.

forfeits, IV.v.187

forsworn, V.ii.23

gaging, V.i.40

glozed, II.ii.165. Cf. Jonson, *Poetaster*, III.v.36; IV.i.129–30

granted, grant, I.iii.211

guardian, V.ii.8, 48

hand, 'question now in hand', (II.ii.164). Cf. John Heywood, 'case now in hand', in Schoeck, 'Heywood's Case of Love', p. 298.

[heirs] hairs, I.ii.158, 164) (cf. the legalistic pun on heir/hair in *CE*, III.ii.124)

hereafter, 'there's yet in the word hereafter', I.i.24–5

illegitimate, V.vii.18

imbecillity, I.iii.114 (legal: weakness or incapacity)

indulgence, partial, II.ii.178

infancy, I.i.12; III.ii.105

inheritors, IV.i.66

inseparate, injurious 'a thing inseparate', V.ii.148

insisture, I.iii.87

instance(s), I.iii.77; V.ii.153, 155; V.x.40

instant, III.iii.153

instruments, Prologue, l. 4

interchangeably, III.ii.57 ('formerly frequent in wording of legal compacts', *OED*, s.v.)

in witness whereof, III.ii.56–7

issue, II.ii.89; II.iii.6

joint, II.ii.193.
joint and several, II.ii.193; cf. *joint and motive*, IV.v.57. Cf. Broom, p.
    366: 'Where the language of a covenant is such that the covenant may
    be construed either as joint or as several, it shall be taken, at common
    law, to be joint or several, according to the interest of the
    covenantees'.
judgement(s), I.ii192; II.iii.124; and *passim*
justice, I.iii.116–17, 118
justness, II.ii.119

law, 'law in each well-ordered nation', II.ii.180
law, 'law / Of nature', II.ii.176–7
lawful, V.iii.20
laws, 'moral laws', II.ii.184
laws, 'laws / Of nature and of nations', II.ii.184–5

matter (cf. legal *res*), II.i.8; II.iii.93
maxim, I.ii.293, see LF above
motion, III.iii.183
motive, IV.v.57. Cf. Paul Vinogradoff, *Outlines of Historical Jurisprudence*
    (Oxford, 1920), I.23n.: 'The *motive* is the impulse that prompted the
    [legal] transaction'.
move the question, II.iii.81. Cf. *question*.
mystery ... of state, III.iii.201–2

nearer debt ... wife ... husband, II.ii.175–6. Cf. Clarkson and Warren, *Law
    of Property*, pp. 44, 148, 201
negation, V.ii.127
negotiations, III.iii.24
note, II.iii.124; IV.i.45 (law: 'abstract of essential particulars relating to
    transfer of land by process of Fine, which was engrossed and placed on
    record', *OED*, sb. 2, 12)

oath(s), III.ii.41, 174; IV.v.178; V.i.41; V.ii.27
obligation, IV.v.122. Cf. H.-P. Schramm, 'Zur Geschichte des Wortes
    "obligatio" von der Antike bis Thomas von Aquin', *Archiv für
    Begriffsgeschichte*, 11 (1967), 119–47
offence, III.i.73
omission to do, III.iii.230. Cf. *Gesta*, p. 21, 'Fault ... of ... Omission'.
opinion, I.iii.336, II.ii.188, *passim*
owners, II.ii.174
oyez, IV.v.143. Cf. *Prince*, p. 47, 'an arraignment ... in the great Hall of the

Temple ... a Cryer made *o yes* ... [to] command all ... to keep silence ...'.

part, 'For my private part, / I am no more touched ...', II.ii.125–6
partial, II.ii.178
particular(s), I.ii.20, 115; I.iii.341; II.ii.9, 53; IV.v.20
parties interchangeably, III.ii.57. See, regarding this close of an indenture,
    Clarkson and Warren, *Law of Property*, p. 126n. Cf. *interchangeably*
pay no debts, III.ii.54
perfection in reversion, III.ii.91
perform(ance), *performs* III.ii.83, 85; V.i.90; V.x.30
per se, I.ii.15
pie, I.ii.258 (calendar)
pledge, V.ii.66, 78
policy, I.iii.197; IV.i.203; V.iv.9, 12, 16
possess, III.iii.89; IV.iv.112
possessed, II.iii.168; III.iii.7
possession, II.ii.152; III.iii.5
prefixed, IV.iii.1
prenominate, V.v.250
prerogative, I.iii.107
in *present*, III.ii.92
press ... to death, III.ii.208
primogenitive, I.iii.106. Combining allusions to prerogative and
    primogeniture is John Cooke, *The Vindication of the Professors and the
    Profession of the Law* (1646), sig. F4 v: 'Prerogative of primogeniture, a
    double portion belonging to the eldest sonne'
privileged, II.iii.57; IV.iv.130. Cf. R. Some, *A Godly Treatise* (1588), p. 139:
    'You are a priuiledged man: you may say what you list'
proceed, II.iii.57
proceedings, V.vii.7
process, IV.i.9
proclaimed, II.i.24
proclamation, II.i.20, 23, 30
promise, 'registered in promise', III.iii.15
proof, I.ii.130; I.iii.34; V.ii.113; V.v.5, 29. See LF above
proposition, I.iii.3
protest, II.ii.138; III.ii.174
protestation, IV.iv.66
prove, see LF above
prover (Q), III.iii.66
publish, publishing, publication, I.iii.326; V.ii.113, 119

quarrel, Prologue, l. 10; II.i.89; II.ii.123, 138; II.iii.72, 205. Cf. Jacob, *A
    New Law-Dictionary* (Dublin, 1773), s.v. *Querela*

question, IV.i.13; cf. *call ... activity in question*, III.ii.55–6; *question now in hand*, II.ii.164; move the *question*, II.iii.81; *decline the whole question*, II.iii.57

quoted, IV.v.233

rack, I.ii.139 (see *confess*)

rape, II.ii.148

ravished, Prologue, l. 9

reader (law lecturer), IV.v.61. On 'reader' as an Inns of Court term, see Paul Brand, 'English Customary Law: Education in the London Law School, 1250–1500', in Olga Weijers, ed., *Vocabulary of Teaching and Research Between Middle Ages and Renaissance* (Turnhout, Belgium, 1995), p. 213 n.

recompense, III.iii.3

record, I.iii.14

recordation, V.ii.116

recovery, II.iii.176

recreant, I.iii.287

redeeming, V.v.39 (law: freeing mortgaged property, recovering [a pledge]).

registered in promise, III.iii.15

rejoindure, IV.iv.36

remainder, II.ii.70. Cf. Clarkson and Warren, *Law of Property*, pp. 73ff.

remedy, I.iii.141; IV.iv.55

remuneration, III.iii.170. Also legal payment; cf. D.S. Bland, 'Learning Exercises and Readers at the Inns of Chancery in the Fifteenth and Sixteenth Centuries', *Law Quarterly Review*, 95 (1979)

render or receive, IV.v.36

rendered to ... owners, II.ii.174. See *dues*

report, II.iii.134 (cf. *OED* 3 c *Law*. A formal account of a case)

reproof, I.iii.33

reserve, III.ii.84

revenue, II.ii.206

reversion, III.ii.91 (law: 'the return of an estate to the donor or grantor, or his heirs, after the expiry of the grant', *OED*, 1; see Clarkson and Warren, *Law of Property*, pp. 72–5. Cf. *CE*, III.ii.123–4)

right and wrong, I.iii.116; II.ii.171

right with right wars, III.ii.172

rob, robbed, robber's, I.ii.19; IV.i.6; IV.iv.42

rogue, roguery, V.i.16; V.iv.28

rule, law, V.ii.133, 141

seal (cf. *close*, verb, above, re legal contract), III.ii.48, 196; III.iii.231; see also *commission*

sequestering, III.iii.8

several, II.ii.193. See *joint*

show ... cause, II.iii.87–8. Cf. *OED*, s.v. cause, 3b '... esp. in Eng. law, to argue against the confirmation of a ... provisionally granted ... judgement'

specialty of rule, I.iii.78

staples, Prologue, l. 17, 'massy staples' (cf. Staple Inn, Inn of Chancery preparatory to Inns of Court)

stolen, II.ii.44, 93

strike off, III.iii.29

subduements, IV.v.187

subscribe, II.iii.146; IV.v.105. Cf. Jonson, *Poetaster*, V.iii.287 and note

sue, I.ii.292

sufferance, I.i.30; II.i.95 (cf. Chapter 8, II.i)

suited (*suit*), Prologue, l. 24

surety, security, guarantee, I.iii.220; II.ii.14, 15; V.ii.61

swear, *swearing*, *sworn*, I.ii.108, 174; II.iii.31; III.ii.41, 42, 83; IV.i.24; IV.ii.52; IV.v.45; V.i.41; V.ii.26, 63, 85; V.iii.15; V.iv.9

tail, V.x.43. See LF above

taint, I.iii.373; III.iii.232

terms, I.iii.159

theft, II.ii.92

thieves, II.ii.94

torments, V.ii.44

tortive, I.iii.9 (cf. *OED*, s.v., '*Law*. Pertaining to ... a tort', citing 1544 tr. Littleton's *Tenures*; *OED* 'tort': '*Eng. Law*. The breach of a duty imposed by a law, whereby some person acquires a right of action for damages'.) See LF above

touched, touches, II.ii.126 (see *part*). Cf. 'As far as toucheth my particular' (II.ii.9) and John Heywood, 'as touchyng my parte', in Schoeck, 'Heywood's Case of Love', p. 296n.

traitor, III.iii.6; V.x.37

treason, II.ii.150

trial, I.iii.14, 336

truce, I.iii.182, 262; II.ii.75; IV.i.13. Cf. Meron, *Henry's Wars*, pp. 52–62 and *passim*

turpitude, V.ii.112

underwrite, II.iii.127

varlet(s), I.i.1; V.i.15, 16, 96; V.iv.2

vassalage, III.ii.38, 61

voluntary, II.i.94 96, 97; cf. legal maxim, 'No man is beaten voluntary' (II.i.96). See Chapter 8 and Appendix III *vow(s)*, Prologue, l. 7; I.ii.283; I.iii.270; IV.iv.37; V.i.43; V.ii.139; V.iii.16, 24

vowing, III.ii.85

warrant, II.i.86; II.ii.96

whetstone, V.ii.76. (Legally, the traditional punishment for lies and slander was standing in the pillory with a whetstone around one's neck.)

will, V.x.51. Cf. Clarkson and Warren, *Law of Property*, pp. 238–40.

witness, III.ii.57, 197; IV.i.9

wranglers, II.ii.75; cf. wrangling, legal disputing (*1H6*, II.iv.6). Cf. Ben Jonson, 'An epigram to the Counsellor that Pleaded and Carried the case,': 'the names ..., of ... wranglers ... / put / Upon the reverend Pleaders'. See citation in Baker, *Manual*, p. ix: Roger North (d. 1734), on 'wrangler' as noisy would-be lawyer: 'A man may be a wrangler, but never a lawyer, without knowledge of the authentic books of the law in their genuine language'.

wrest, III.iii.23. Cf. L. Barry, *Ram Alley*, I.i, on the law: ''tis within the power of us lawyers, / To wrest this nose of wax which way we please'.

wrong, I.iii.116 and *passim*.

Notes

1. On Shakespeare's 'dismes' and Stratford tithes, see E.K. Chambers, *William Shakespeare* (Oxford, 1980), II.118–27, 148; S. Schoenbaum, *A Documentary Life* (Oxford, 1975), pp. 192–93.

2. Cf. legal dictionaries: *inter alia*, Alexander Scot, *Vocabularium Utriumque Juris* (Lugduni, 1601); J. Rastell, *Termes of the Lawe*; *Les Termes de la Ley* (Portland, Maine, 1812); John Cowell, ... *The Interpreter* (Cambridge, England, 1607); Giles Jacob, *A New Law-Dictionary* (Dublin, 1773). Cf. D.S. Bland, 'Some Notes on the Evolution of the Legal Dictionary', *Journal of Legal History*, I (1980), 75–84. Legal and rhetorical terms tended to overlap. Cf. Schoeck, 'Heywood's Case of Love', p. 285.

Appendix III *Troilus* and Aristotle's *Nicomachean Ethics*

In *Troilus and Cressida* occurs a particular pattern of parallels with Aristotle's *Nicomachean Ethics* (=EN), regarding ethical–legal questions surrounding an action: issues of the role of the voluntary or the involuntary; of volition and choice; of choice and virtue; and of virtue and habitual action.[1]

Aristotle's *EN* was familiar to Elizabethan higher education, and was reprinted in translation in numerous editions, with commentaries, in the sixteenth century.[2]

Twice Shakespeare alludes to Aristotle by name: first, Aristotle's 'checks' recalling his ethics, in *Taming of the Shrew* (I.i.32); Cf. *TS*, I.i.18–20 on 'Virtue and that part of philosophy / ... that treats of happiness / By virtue specially to be achiev'd'; and second, in *Troilus*, on Aristotle and 'moral philosophy' (II.ii.166–7).[3]

Opening *EN* Book III, Aristotle distinguishes those actions that are 'voluntary' from those that are 'involuntary', remarking the necessity to determine their limits. Such a course, he adds, is 'useful also for legislators with a view to the assigning both of honours and of punishments' (1109 b 32–4). What Aristotle examines, in effect, is the procedure of determining culpability for an act.[4] Under what circumstances, and to what extent, is one responsible for one's action? In addition to the voluntary and the involuntary, there are such act-related dualisms as volition and choice, choice and virtue, and virtue and habitual practice. Such ethical–legal issues are appropriate to a play whose war-plot turns on an abductor's culpability for an action, and the subsequent issue of prescriptive possession – the Grecian claim to Helen against her Trojan possessors.[5]

The voluntary[6]

In *Troilus*, *EN*'s voluntary–involuntary distinctions seem exemplified. A passage (I.iii.354–6), which I have previously glossed,[7] suggests a parallel *EN* instance of the voluntary. Aristotle defines the voluntary as 'that of which the moving principle is in the agent himself' (1111 a 23–4). In *Troilus*, recalling the agent's responsibility for acts, is Nestor's explanation: 'Limbes are in his instruments, / In no lesse working, then are Swords and

183

Bowes / Directiue by the Limbes' (I.iii.354–6). These lines occur in *Troilus*, Folio (1623), and are omitted, along with other relatively specialized lines, from Quarto (1609).[8] Aristotle, *EN*: 'because the movement of the limbs that are the instruments of action has its origins in the agent himself, and where this is so it is in his power either to act or not' (1110 a 14–18).[9] Where *EN* has 'limbs ... are the instruments', F *Troilus* has 'Limbes are in his instruments'.

Limbs are instruments of the agent's responsibility, as are the swords and bows employed by those limbs. Such a passage in *Troilus* on the responsibility and voluntariness of acts could have been recognizable to an academic, especially legally instructed, audience, and, as rehearsed by the ancient Nestor, drawn reminiscent response.

The involuntary

If Nestor (I.iii.354–6) had been voice of the voluntary, the combat-withdrawn Achilles is arbitrator of the involuntary. Responding to Thersites' 'I serve here voluntary' Achilles legally discriminates: 'Your last service was sufferance, 'twas not voluntary. No man is beaten voluntary. Ajax was here the voluntary, and you as under an impress' (II.i.95–7). Mocking Thersites' 'service', including being beaten, Achilles argues this could not be 'voluntary'. His 'no man is beaten voluntary' echoes Aristotle's own familiar terms: the Philosopher denies that a man can be wronged or injured voluntarily. In John Case's commentary on *Ethics*, *Speculum ... Moralium* (Oxford, 1585), p. 231, is the assurance, 'No one voluntarily suffers injury ... no one voluntarily and maliciously harms himself: therefore no one willingly suffers injury'.[10]

In such instances as those above, *Troilus* (II.i.94–7) recalls basic legal procedure, including determination of the degree of responsibility for an action. What is the minimum requirement of the law before a person can be held accountable? 'Those things ... are thought involuntary', says Aristotle, 'which take place under compulsion ... and that is compulsory of which the moving principle is outside, being a principle in which nothing is contributed by the person who acts or is acted upon ...' (1109 b 35–1110 a 3). Since Thersites is, Achilles' verdict adjudicates, under duress or subject to force, his role is not voluntary. Legally, the involuntary may not be subject to punishment, in conditions where the defendant is compelled to do something by external force. In contrast to the involuntary and vulnerable compelled victim Thersites, Ajax, pounding the railer, was 'here the voluntary' (II.i.96–7).

Choice

Legally, responsibility for an act implied that it be both voluntary and a matter of deliberate choice (*prohairesis*; cf. *electio*).[11] 'The origin of action ...', notes Aristotle, 'is choice and that of choice is desire and reasoning ...'. Further, 'choice cannot exist either without thought and intellect or without a moral state' (1139 a 32–4). As it 'involves reason and thought' (1112 a 15–16), choice is, moreover, a deliberative act of soul. Including both desire and thought, an act of choice works to 'elect' by 'merit' (Cf. I.iii.349): 'excellence [virtue] makes the aim right' (1144 a 8).

In sum, observes Aristotle, 'choice is either desiderative thought or intellectual desire, and such an *origin* of action is *a man*' (1139 b 4–5).[12] In his upside-down summary, doting Nestor garblingly inverts this: Choice, he echoes Aristotle, is an 'act of soul' and of virtue which 'Makes merit her election' (I.iii.349). Yet, instead of, as in Aristotle above, choice's action being in '*origin* ... a man', in Nestor choice's *result* is 'a man':

> ... choice, being mutual act of all our souls,
> Makes merit her election, and doth boil,
> As 'twere from forth us all, a man distilled
> Out of our virtues ...
>
>   I.iii.348–51

If the ancient Nestor inverts choice, youthful Troilus inverts 'election'. Possessing a sense akin to 'choice', 'election' is also applied to spousal choice. When Troilus, as defending advocate of the abductor Paris, announces, 'I take today a wife, and my election / Is led on in the conduct of my will' (II.ii.61–2), he does not only invert the relation of 'election' and 'will'. Defending Paris' retention of Helen, Troilus in his put-case inadvertently reminds his audience of Paris' extra-marital adventure, and the abductor's continued violation of the marriage vow. (When Troilus adds, arguing for Helen's retention, 'how may I avoid, / Although my will distaste what it elected, / The wife I chose' (II.ii.65–7), his argument ignores the demand on the wilful Paris to return someone *else's* chosen wife.)

Rather than, as with Troilus, submitting election to will, Aristotelian commentators insisted on the distinctive superiority of election (or discriminating, rational choice) to will. As Case's *EN* commentary, *Speculum ... Moralium*, p. 93, demands, 'Quid electio? & an sit voluntas ...'? he insists, along with others, that 'Electio non est voluntas'. If Troilus' 'election is led on' by his will, which is 'enkindled by mine eyes and ears – / Two traded pilots 'twixt the dangerous shores / Of will and judgement' (II.ii.64–5), he lacks the reasoned deliberation Aristotelians attributed to 'election'. So Case (p. 93) discriminates 'electio' from passions, reflecting on 'beasts who are not governed by election and counsel'. Troilus (II.ii.38–50) dismisses reason, as Hector qualifies the 'way of truth'

(II.ii.188–9). Hence, contrary to law, Troilus suggests an inversion of an Aristotelian rule, of law as proceeding from practical wisdom and intellect.

Virtue

As law is concerned with choice, and 'excellence [virtue] makes the aim right' (1144 a 8), virtue is also of ethical–legal concern. Virtue is acquired through practice and habituation (1103 a 14–18), which laws establish.[13] Aristotle notes, 'The law bids us practise every excellence [virtue]' (1130 b 24). 'Legislators make the citizens good by forming habits in them, and this is the wish of every legislator' (1103b 2–4). Indeed, Aristotle insists that virtue is not merely internal, but formed through habitual communication. 'Complete excellence in its fullest sense', he notes, *EN*, '... is the actual exercise of complete excellence. It is complete because he who possesses it can exercise his excellence *towards others* too and not merely by himself ...' (1129 b 30–3; italics added).

Communication to others helps form one's virtues or parts. 'By doing the acts that we do in our *transactions with other men* we become just or unjust ...' (1103 b 13–14; italics added). This emphasis on the interpersonal communicative role of virtue is attributed to Aristotle in Henry Peacham's *Thalia's Banquet furnished with an hundred and odde dishes of newly devised Epigrammes* (1620, sig. [A8]): 'Saith *Aristotle*, Vertue ought to be / Communicative of her selfe and free ...'.

As the Trojans, notes Hector, 'Have glozed' (II.ii.165), the Greeks, too, 'glose'. They elaborate Aristotle's view in evocation of a familiar mode of academic–legal instruction, the textual gloss: 'I do not strain at the position', pronounces Ulysses:

> It is familiar – but at the author's drift;
> Who in his circumstance expressly proves
> That no man is the lord of anything,
> Though in and of him there be much consisting,
> Till he communicate his parts to others.
>   III.iii.113–17

Carrying the virtuous parts still further, Ulysses, 'in his circumstance', observes: 'Nor doth he of himself know them for aught / Till he behold them forméd in th'applause / Where they're extended ...' (III.iii.118–20). Ulysses here rehearses, among other topoi, familiar Aristotelian tags:

> ... that man, how dearly ever parted,
> How much in having, or without or in,
> Cannot make boast to have that which he hath,
> Nor feels not what he owes, but by reflection;
> As when his virtues, shining upon others,
> Heat them and they retort that heat again
> To the first giver.
>   III.iii.96–102

Elaborating Aristotle's virtues (or 'parts') as emerging through comunication, Ulysses stresses not merely 'having' by oneself, but also communicating one's 'parts' to others (III.iii.117). In his device to re-enlist Achilles, Ulysses thus confirms Peacham's reminder above that 'Vertue ought to be / Communicative of her selfe', as 'Saith *Aristotle*'.[14]

This appendix has suggested that a particular cluster of *EN* parallels may be reflected in *Troilus*. Appropriate to an academic law-audience, such parallels concern basic ethical–legal questions surrounding an act:[15] whether the act be voluntary or involuntary; whether it involve volition and choice; its relation of choice to virtue; and the relation of virtue to habitual or communicated action.

Notes

1.   'Ethical–legal' applies especially to *EN*'s Books III (voluntary and involuntary; culpability), and V (justice). Citing Book III, chs 1 to 3, cf. H.D. Lee, 'The Legal Background of Two Passages in the *Nicomachean Ethics*', *Classical Quarterly*, 31 (1937), 140. Lee cites these chapters as reflecting basic legal theory – many of the *EN* references in this Appendix are to those Book III chapters.

    See W. von Leyden, 'Aristotle and the Concept of Law,' *Philosophy*, 42 (1967), 1–19; Max Hamburger, *Morals and Law: The Growth of Aristotle's Legal Theory* (New Haven, Connecticut, 1951). Cf. A.R.W. Harrison, 'Aristotle's *Nicomachean Ethics*, Book V, and the Law of Athens', *Journal of Hellenic Studies*, 77 (1957), 42–7. See W.F.R. Hardie, *Aristotle's Ethical Theory* (Oxford, 1980), including chapters of relevance to my treatment of voluntary and involuntary, choice, and virtue (pp. 152–81; see also chapter on Justice, pp. 182–211); and S. Sauve Meyer, *Aristotle on Moral Responsibility* (Oxford, 1993). Richard Bodéüs, *The Political Dimensions of Aristotle's 'Ethics'* (Albany, New York, 1993). Francis Sparshott, *Taking Life Seriously: A Study of the Argument of the Nicomachean Ethics* (Toronto, 1994). For a basic commentary on *EN* see R.A. Gauthier and J.Y. Jolif, *Aristote: l'Ethique à Nicomaque* (Louvain, Belgium, 1970).

    EN citations are from Jonathan Barnes, ed., Aristotle, *Complete Works*, vol 2; and J.A.K. Thomson, trans., *The Ethics of Aristotle* (Harmondsworth, England, 1986). A previous version of this Appendix appeared in the *Journal of the History of Ideas*, April 1997. Alleged parallels between *EN* and *Troilus* are collected in Kenneth Palmer, ed., *Troilus and Cressida*, Arden Shakespeare (1982), pp. 311–20 (many of Palmer's 'parallels' are, however, wide or commonplace, and not convincing).

    On *EN*'s Renaissance influence see Eugenio Garin, 'La fortuna dell'Etica Aristotelica nel Quattrocento', in *La cultura filosofica del rinascimento italiano* (2nd edition, Florence, 1979), pp. 60–71; P.R. Pogliano, 'L'Etica a Nicomaco nel Cinquecento francese', *Studi francesi*, no. 63 (1977), 394–406; Edilia Traverso, 'Montaigne e l'Ethica Nicomachea', *Montaigne e Aristotele* (Firenze, 1974), pp. 97–120. See C.B. Schmitt, 'Aristotle's Ethics in the Sixteenth Century: Some Considerations', *Aristotle and Renaissance Universities* (1984), pp. 87–112. See Schmitt, 'Auctoritates, Repertorium, Dicta, Sententiae, Flores, Thesaurus, and Axiomata: Latin. Aristotelian Florilegia in the Renaissance', in *Aristoteles Werk und Wirkung*, Zweiter Band, ed. Jürgen Wiesner (Berlin,

1987), pp. 515–37. See, on methods of Renaissance Aristotelian commentaries, Jill Kraye, 'Renaissance Commentaries on the *Nicomachean Ethics*', in Olga Weijers, ed., *Vocabulary of Teaching and Research Between Middle Ages and Renaissance* (Turnhout, Belgium, 1995), pp. 96–117. Shakespeare may indirectly have echoed *EN* views already reflected in a major source of his play; see J.E. Grennen, 'Aristotelian Ideas in Chaucer's *Troilus*: A Preliminary Study', *Medievalia et Humanistica*, n.s., no. 14 (1986), 125–38.

2.   See F.E. Cranz, *A Bibliography of Aristotle Editions, 1501–1600*, revised edition by C.B. Schmitt (Baden-Baden, Germany, 1984). *EN* was mainly available in Latin (except for the 1547 abridged English version from the Italian, *The Ethiques of Aristotle*), and translations into this and other non-English vernaculars. This circumstance would have provided little impediment to a Latin-familiar academic audience. Cf. James McConica, 'Humanism and Aristotle in Tudor Oxford', *English Historical Review*, 94 (1979), 291–317; McConica, *The History of the University of Oxford*, vol. 3 (Oxford, 1986), p. 711, on the 'new [Renaissance] international Latin and neo-Aristotelian culture that now dominated the university's higher faculties'.

      See C.B. Schmitt, *John Case and Aristotelianism in Renaissance England* (Montreal, 1983); *A Critical Survey and Bibliography of Studies on Renaissance Aristotelianism, 1958–1969* (Padua, Italy, 1971); Schmitt, *Aristotle and the Renaissance* (Cambridge, Massachusetts, 1983), pp. 34, 45, and bibliography, on a range of aids to Aristotelian study; and C.B. Schmitt, ed., *Studies in Renaissance Philosophy and Science* (1981), chs V and VI.

      Cf. emphasis on Aristotle at an academic revel (Christmas revels, 1607–08, St John's College, Oxford), *The Christmas Prince*, eds F.S. Boas and W.W. Greg (Malone Society Reprint, 1922, p. 287): 'The Creation of white knights of the order of *Aristotles* well, which should bee sworne to defend *Aristotle* against all authors'.

3.   Among the play's other legal echoes of Aristotle, cf. 'right and wrong, / Between whose endless jar justice resides' (I.iii.116–17 and *EN* VI I.1129 a Iff.) on the just act as intermediate between extremes. See justice as related to the mean (1106 b 21–4; 1133 b 29–1134 a 16). Max Salomon, *Der Begriff der Gerechtigkeit bei Aristoteles* (Leiden, The Netherlands, 1937; New York, 1979).

4.   On legal implications of an act, cf. Cicero, *De Inventione*, Book I.viii, concerning the nature of the act.

5.   Cf., on the relative merits of the voluntary and involuntary, Plato, *Lesser Hippias*, 27, 11–76. See also F.A. Siegler, 'Voluntary and Involuntary', *Monist*, 52 (1968), 268–87. See in W.F.R. Hardie, *Aristotle's Ethical Theory* (Oxford, 1980), ch. 8, 'The Distinction between the Voluntary and the Involuntary'.

6.   D.J. Furley, 'Aristotle on the Voluntary', in Jonathan Barnes et al., eds, *Articles on Aristotle, vol. 2: Ethics and Politics* (New York, 1977), pp. 47–60. A.R. Dyer, 'Aristotle's Categories of Voluntary Torts, *Nicomachean Ethics* 1135 b 8–25', *Classical Review*, 25 (1965), 250–2. Cf. Arthur Kenny, *Aristotle's Theory of the Will* (New Haven, Connecticut, 1979), pp. 69–80; W.F.R. Hardie, 'Willing and Acting', *Philosophical Quarterly*, 21 (1971), 193–206.

7.   Elton, 'Textual Transmission and Genre of Shakespeare's *Troilus*', in *Literatur als Kritik des Lebens. Festschrift zum 65. Geburtstag von Ludwig Borinski*, eds Rudolf Haas et al. (Heidelberg, 1975), p. 75.

8.   Echoing: 'the agent acts voluntarily'. On Q 1609 *Troilus*' omissions in relation to a presumed popularized redaction of a special private-performance text, see Elton, 'Textual Transmission'.

9.   Trans. J.A.K. Thomson, *The Ethics of Aristotle* (Harmondsworth, England, 1986), pp. 111–12. In *EN*'s Latin translation by Antonio Riccobono, *Aristotelis Ethicorum ad Nicomachum* (Frankfurt, 1596, sig. [G6 v]): 'sponte autem agit, etenim principium movendi partes, quae sunt tanquam instrumenta in talibus actionibus in ipso est. at, quorum in ipso principium est, ab ipso etiam pendet ea agere, & non agere'.

10. 'Nemo sponte iniuriam patitur ... nemo seipsum sponte & malitiose laedit: ergo nemo volens iniuriam patitur'. Cf. 1136 a 15–16; 1195 b 5–9.

11. See on *prohairesis* and *boulesis*, as well as choice and virtue, G.E.M. Anscombe, 'Thought and Action in Aristotle' in *Articles on Aristotle, vol. 2: Ethics and Politics*, eds Jonathan Barnes et al. (New York, 1977), pp. 61–71. On *prohairesis* and choice, cf. W.F.R. Hardie, *Aristotle's Ethical Theory* (Oxford, 1980), ch. 9, pp. 160–81. Cf. A.E. Mele, 'Choice and Virtue in the *Nicomachean Ethics*', *Journal of the History of Philosophy*, 19 (1981), 405–24.

12. 'Quemobrem aut appetendi vim habens mens est preelectio, aut appetitio mentis agitatione utens, & tale principium est homo' (Latin translation by Antonio Riccobono (Frankfurt, 1596, sig. [P6])).

13. Cf. *EN* II, 1, 4, on virtue as acquired by habituation, *ethismos*. On ethical habituation, see W.F.R. Hardie, *Aristotle's Ethical Theory* (Oxford, 1980), pp. 104–5; cf. chs 6, 7, 10, 11. See also Hardie, 'Aristotle's Doctrine that Virtue is a Mean', in *Articles on Aristotle, vol. 2: Ethics and Politics*, eds Jonathan Barnes, et al. (New York, 1977); R. Sorabji, 'Aristotle on the role of intellect in virtue', *Proc. of the Aristotelian Society*, 74 (1973), 107–29. Cf. Aquinas who, like Aristotle, holds virtue an acquired disposition to choose correctly (*habitus electivus*: in III Eth. 382). See Aristide Tessitore, *Reading Aristotle's 'Ethics': Virtue, Rhetoric, and Political Philosophy* (Albany, NY, 1996). On choice and moral virtue, cf. D.J. Allan, 'Aristotle's Account of the Origin of Moral Principles', in Barnes *et al.*, *Articles on Aristotle, vol. 2*, pp. 72–8. See W.W. Fortenbaugh, 'Aristotle's Conception of Moral Virtue and Its Perceptive Role', *Transactions and Proceedings of the American Philological Association*, 95 (1964), 77–87. Cf. Nancy Sherman, *The Fabric of Character: Aristotle's Theory of Virtue* (Oxford, 1989); T.H. Irwin, 'Aristotle on Reason, Desire, and Virtue', *Journal of Philosophy*, 72 (1975), 567–78.

14. Cf. Ulysses' 'strange fellow' who 'Writes me' (III.iii.95–6) on the necessity of 'virtues' going forth to 'others', a commonplace repeated by Achilles, and then again by Ulysses, noting the need to 'communicate' one's 'parts' to others (III.iii.95–123). (NVS, pp. 411–415, ignores Aristotle in favour of Plato, on the 'strange fellow').

15. Such questions are not merely incidental, but occupy a significant portion of Renaissance *EN* commentaries; for example Samuel Heilandus, *Aristotelis Ethicorum ad Nicomachum* (London, 1581); John Case, *Speculum quaestionum Moralium* (Frankfurt, 1589); Theophilus Golius, *Epitome doctrinae moralis* (Cambridge, England, 1634); Edward Brerewood, *Tractatus ethici* (Oxford, 1640).

References

(This list includes references more frequently cited. Place of book-publication is London unless otherwise stated.)

Agrippa, Henry Cornelius, *Of the Vanitie and Uncertaintie of Artes and Sciences* (1530), ed. C.M. Dunn (Northridge, California, 1974).

Alexander, Peter, 'Troilus and Cressida 1609', *The Library*, 9 (1928–9), 267–286.

Allen, Don Cameron, *Image and Meaning* (Baltimore, Maryland, 1968).

———— *Mysteriously Meant* (Baltimore, Maryland, 1970).

Anglo, Sydney, *Spectacle, Pageantry, and Early Tudor Policy* (Oxford, 1969).

Aquinas, Thomas, *The 'Summa Theologiae'*, 22 vols. (1913–42).

Aristotle, *Complete Works*, ed. Jonathan Barnes (Princeton, New Jersey, 1984–85), 2 vols.

———— *Nicomachean Ethics*, trans. as *The Ethics of Aristotle*, J.A.K. Thomson (Harmondsworth, England 1986).

Axton, Marie, *The Queen's Two Bodies: Drama and the Elizabethan Succession* (1977).

Bacon, Francis, *Essayes*, ed. Michael Kiernan (Cambridge, Massachusetts, 1985).

Baker, John Hamilton, *Manual of Law French* 2nd edn (Aldershot, England, 1990).

Baldwin, T.W., *William Shakspere's Small Latine and Lesse Greeke*, 2 vols. (Urbana, Illinois, 1944).

Beaumont, Francis, and John Fletcher, *Works*, 10 vols. (Cambridge, England, 1905–12).

Blundeville, Thomas, *The Arte of Logicke* (1619).

Boas, F.S., *Shakespere and his Predecessors* (1896; New York, 1969).

Bradley, A.C., 'Shakespeare the Man', *Oxford Lectures on Poetry* (1904).

Bradshaw, Graham, *Shakespeare's Scepticism* (Ithaca, New York, 1987).

Branham, R.B., *Unruly Eloquence: Lucian and the Comedy of Traditions* (Cambridge, Massachusetts, 1989).

Broom, Herbert, *A Selection of Legal Maxims*, (Philadelphia, Penn., 1969).

Butler, Samuel, (1612–80), *Characters*, ed. C.W. Daves (Cleveland, Ohio, 1970).

Campbell, Oscar James, *Comicall Satyre and Shakespeare's 'Troilus and Cressida'* (San Marino, California, 1938).

Carew, Thomas, *Poems*, ed. Rhodes Dunlap (Oxford, 1964).

Chambers, E.K., *Elizabethan Stage*, 4 vols (Oxford, 1967).
———— *Mediaeval Stage* (Oxford, 1967), 2 vols.
———— *William Shakespeare: A Study of Facts and Problems* (Oxford, 1930), 2 vols.
Chaucer, Geoffrey, *Poetical Works*, ed. F.N. Robinson (Boston, Massachusetts, 1953).
Christmas Prince (1608), ed. F.S. Boas and W.W. Greg, Malone Soc. (Oxford, 1927).
Cicero, *De Inventione*, ed. Loeb (Cambridge, Massachusetts, 1949).
Clarkson, Paul S. and C.T. Warren, *The Law of Property in Shakespeare and the Elizabethan Drama* (Baltimore, Maryland, 1942).
Coke, Edward, *A readable edition of Coke upon Littleton*, ed. Thomas Coventry (1830).
Cotgrave, Randle, *A Dictionarie of the French and English Tongues* (1611) (Columbia, South Carolina, 1950).
Cowell, John, ... *The Interpreter* (Cambridge, England, 1607).
Curtius, E.R., *European Literature and the Latin Middle Ages* (New York, 1963).
Davis, Natalie Z., *Society and Culture in Early Modern France* (Stanford, California, 1975).
Dekker, Thomas, *Satiromastix* in *Dramatic Works*, ed. Fredson Bowers (Cambridge, England), vol. 1 (Cambridge, England, 1953).
Dent, R.W., *Proverbial Language in English Drama, Exclusive of Shakespeare, 1495–1616* (Berkeley, California, 1984).
———— *Shakespeare's Proverbial Language: an Index* (Berkeley, California, 1981).
Doddridge, John, *The English Lawyer* (1631).
Donne, John, *The Complete English Poems*, ed. A.J. Smith (Harmondsworth, 1971).
———— *Paradoxes and Problems*, ed. Helen Peters (Oxford, 1980).
Dugdale, W., *Origines Juridiciales* (1680).
Eccles, Mark, 'Francis Beaumont's *Grammar Lecture*', *Review of English Studies*, n.s. 16 (1940), 402–14.
Elton, W.R. *'King Lear' and the Gods* (San Marino, California, 1966; revised edition, Lexington, Kentucky, 1988).
———— 'Shakespeare's Portrait of Ajax in *Troilus and Cressida*', *PMLA*, 63 (1948), 744–8.
———— 'Shakespeare's Ulysses and the Problem of Value', *Shakespeare Studies*, 2 (1968), 95–111.
———— 'Textual Transmission and Genre of Shakespeare's *Troilus*', in *Literatur als Kritik des Lebens: Festschrift ... Ludwig Borinski*, ed. Rudolf Haas, H.J. Müllenbrock, and Claus Uhlig (Heidelberg, 1975).
Erasmus, *Des. Erasmi Rotterdami, Opera Omnia*, ed. J. Le Clerc (Leiden 1703–6).

Finkelpearl, Philip J., *John Marston of the Middle Temple* (Cambridge, Massachusetts, 1969).

———— 'John Marston's *Histrio-mastix* as an Inns of Court Play: A Hypothesis', *Huntington Library Quarterly*, 29 (1966), 223–34.

———— 'The Use of the Middle Temple's Christmas Revels in Marston's *The Fawne*', *Studies in Philology*, 64 (1967), 199–209.

Ford, John, eds. L.E. Stock et al., *Nondramatic Works of John Ford* (Binghamton, N.Y., 1991).

Fortescue, John, *De Laudibus Legum Anglie*, ed. S.B. Chrimes (Cambridge, England, 1942).

Fraunce, Abraham, *The Arcadian Rhetorike* (1588).

———— *The Lawiers Logicke* (1588) (Menston, England, 1969).

Frazer, James George, *The Golden Bough*, 12 vols. (1911–15).

Fulbecke, William, *A Direction or Preparative to the Study of the Law* (1600), (Aldershot, England, 1987).

Gilby, Thomas, *Barbara Celarent: a description of scholastic dialectic* (1949)

Giuliani, Alessandro, 'The Influence of Rhetoric on the Law of Evidence and Pleading', *Juridical Review*, 7 (1962), 216–51.

Gorboduc, by Thomas Norton and Thomas Sackville, in *Three Tudor Tragedies*, ed. William Tydeman (1992).

Hall, Joseph, *Works* (1625).

Harington, John, *A New Discourse of a Stale Subiect, called the Metamorphosis of Aiax*, ed. Elizabeth S. Donno (1962).

Henryson, Robert, *The Testament of Cresseid*, ed. Denton Fox (1968).

Hobbes, Thomas, *The English Works*, ed. William Molesworth, 11 vols (1839–45).

Homer, *Chapman's Homer, The Iliad; the Odyssey ...* ed. Allardyce Nicoll, 2 vols. (New York, 1955).

Horace, *Horace on Poetry*, ed. C.O. Brink, 3 vols. (Cambridge, England, 1985).

———— *Satires and Epistles*, ed. Edward P. Morris (Norman, Oklahoma, 1968).

Hornsby, Joseph A., *Chaucer and the Law* (Norman, Oklahoma, 1988).

Hoskyns, John, *Directions for Speech and Style*, ed. H.H. Hudson (Princeton, New Jersey, 1935).

———— *The Life, Letters and Writings of John Hoskyns*, ed. L.B. Osborn (New Haven, Connecticut, 1937).

Hotson, Leslie, *Shakespeare's Sonnets Dated* (New York, 1949).

———— *The First Night of 'Twelfth Night'* (1954).

———— *Mr. W.H.* (New York, 1964).

Ives, E.W., 'The Law and the Lawyers', *Shakespeare Survey*, 17 (1965), 73–86.

Jacob, Giles, *A New Law-Dictionary* (Dublin, 1773).

Jonson, Ben, *Works*, ed. C.H. Herford and P. Simpson (Oxford, 1925–52), 11 vols. *Poetaster*, ed. Tom Cain (Manchester, England, 1995).

Justinian, *Digest*, eds. Theodor Mommsen et al. (Philadelphia, Pennsylvania, 1985).

Kyd, Thomas, *Spanish Tragedy*, ed. Philip Edwards (Cambridge, Massachusetts, 1959).

Langholm, Odd, 'Economic Freedom in Scholastic Thought', *History of Political Economy*, 14 (1982), 260–296.

────── *The Legacy of Scholasticism in Economic Thought* (Cambridge, England, 1998).

Lausberg, Heinrich, *Handbook of Literary Rhetoric*, ed. David E. Orton and R. Dean Anderson (Leiden, 1998).

Lenton, Francis, *Characterismi* (1631).

────── *The Yong Gallants Whirligigg* (1629).

Liebs, Detlev, *Lateinische Rechtsregeln und Rechts-Sprichwörter*, 6th ed. (Munich, 1998).

Lily, William, *An Introduction of Grammar, 1567*, ed. V.J. Flynn (New York, 1945).

Maclean, Ian, *Interpretation and Meaning in the Renaissance: The Case of Law* (Cambridge, England, 1982).

Manningham, John, *The Diary of John Manningham of the Middle Temple*, ed. R.P. Sorlien (Hanover, New Hampshire, 1976).

Marlowe, Christopher, *Complete Works*, ed. Fredson Bowers, 2nd edn (Cambridge, England, 1981).

Marston, John, *The Plays of John Marston*, ed. H.H. Wood, 3 vols. (Edinburgh, 1934–39).

────── *Parasitaster or the Fawn*, ed. D.A. Blostein (Manchester, England, 1978).

Mason, John, [of Cambridge], *Princeps Rhetoricus* (1648).

Meron, Theodor, *Henry's Wars and Shakespeare's Laws* (Oxford, 1993).

Milton, John, *The Works*, 18 vols. in 21 (New York, 1931–38).

Montaigne, M.E. de, *Essays. John Florio's Translation*, ed. J.I.M. Stewart, 2 vols (1931).

Nashe, Thomas, *Works*, ed. R.B. McKerrow, 5 vols (Oxford, 1958).

Pope, Alexander (attrib.), *The Art of Sinking in Poetry* (1727), ed. E.L. Steeves (New York, 1952).

Prest, W.R., *The Inns of court under Queen Elizabeth I and the Early Stuarts, 1590–1640* (1972).

Puttenham, George, *The Arte of English Poesie*, eds. G.D. Willcock, et al. (Cambridge, England, 1970).

Rabelais, François, *Oeuvres*, trans. Thomas Urquhart and P.A. Motteux, 2 vols (New York, 1931).

Rainolde, Richard, *The Foundacion of Rhetorike* (1563), ed. F.R. Johnson (New York, 1945).

Rastell, John, *An exposition of certaine difficult and obscure words, and termes of the lawes of this realme* (1615).

Rhetorica ad Herennium, trans. Harry Caplan (Loeb, 1964).

Rich, Barnabe, *Opinion Diefied*, (1613).

Richardson, Alexander, *The Logicians School-master* (1629).

Roman de la Rose, Guillaume de Lorris and Jean de Meun, trans. Charles Dahlberg (Princeton, New Jersey, 1971).

Schlumbohm, Christa, *Jocus und Amor: Liebesdiskussionen vom mittelalterlichen 'joc parti' bis zu den preziösen 'questions d'amour'* (Hamburg, 1974).

Schoeck, R.J., 'Heywood's Case of Love: A Legal Reading of John Heywood's *The Play of Love*', *Studia Neophilologica*, 39 (1967), 284–301.

Seneca, L.A., *Moral Essays*, trans. John W. Basore (1928–35).

Sharpham, Edward, *Cupid's Whirligig* (1607), ed. A. Nicoll, 1926.

———— *Works*, ed. C.G. Petter (New York, 1986).

Spenser, Edmund, *Poetical Works*, ed. J.C. Smith and E. de Selincourt (1953).

Stanford, W.B., *The Ulysses Theme*, 2nd edn (New York, 1964).

Sugden, E.H., *A Topographical Dictionary of the Works of Shakespeare and his Fellow Dramatists* (Hildesheim, Germany, 1961).

Tilley, M.P., *A Dictionary of Proverbs in England in the Sixteenth and Seventeenth Centuries* (Ann Arbor, Michigan, 1950).

Trimpi, Wesley, *Muses of One Mind* (Princeton, New Jersey, 1983).

Vinogradoff, Paul, *Outlines of Historical Jurisprudence*, 2 vols (Oxford, 1920).

Waterhouse, Edward, *Fortescutus Illustratus, or commentary on that nervous treatise, De Laudibus Legum Angliae* (1663).

Webster, John, *Complete Works*, ed. F.L. Lucas, 4 vols (1919).

Williams, Gordon, ed., *A Dictionary of Sexual Language and Imagery in Shakespeare and Stuart Literature*, 3 vols (1994).

Williams, Philip, Jr., 'The "Second Issue" of Shakespeare's *Troilus and Cressida* 1609', *Studies in Bibliography: Papers of the Bibliographical Society of the University of Virginia*, 2 (1948–49), 25–33.

Wilson, Thomas, *The Art of Rhetorike* (1560), ed. Peter E. Medine (University Park, Maryland, 1994).

———— *The Rule of Reason* (1580), ed. R.G. Sprague (Northridge, California, 1972).

Index

The index covers the introduction, the chapters and conclusion, but not the notes, appendices or references.